Illicit Trade and the Global Economy

CESifo Seminar Series
edited by Hans-Werner Sinn

See http://mitpress.mit.edu for a complete list of titles in this series.

Illicit Trade and the Global Economy

edited by Cláudia Costa Storti and Paul De Grauwe

 Seminar Series

The MIT Press
Cambridge, Massachusetts
London, England

For information about special quantity discounts, please email special_sales@mitpress .mit.edu

This book was set in Palatino by Toppan Best-set Premedia Limited. Printed and bound in the United States of America.

Library of Congress Cataloging-in-Publication Data

Illicit trade and the global economy / edited by Cláudia Costa Storti and Paul De Grauwe.
    p. cm.— (CESifo seminar series)
Includes bibliographical references and index.
ISBN 978-0-262-01655-1 (hardcover : alk. paper) 1. Organized crime. 2. International trade. 3. Globalization. I. Storti, Cláudia Costa. II. Grauwe, Paul de.
HV6441.I45 2012
364.1'336–dc23

2011020770

10 9 8 7 6 5 4 3 2 1

Contents

Series Foreword

This book is part of the CESifo Seminar Series. The series aims to cover topical policy issues in economics from a largely European perspective. The books in this series are the products of the papers and intensive debates that took place during the seminars hosted by CESifo, an international research network of renowned economists organized jointly by the Center for Economic Studies at Ludwig-Maximilians University, Munich, and the Ifo Institute for Economic Research. All publications in this series have been carefully selected and refereed by members of the CESifo research network.

Contributors

Helge Berger   Free University Berlin, Germany, and CESifo, Munich, Germany

Jonathan Caulkins   H. John Heinz School of Public Policy and Management, Carnegie-Mellon University

Vittorio Daniele   University Magna Graecia of Catanzaro, Catanzaro, Italy

Paul De Grauwe   University of Leuven, Leuven, Belgium, and CESifo, Munich, Germany

Mohammad Reza Farzanegan   Dresden University of Technology, Dresden, Germany, and ZEW Mannheim, Germany

Rachel Kenehan   The Matrix Knowledge Group, London, UK

Axel Klein   Kent Institute of Medicine and Health Sciences, Canterbury, UK

Ugo Marani   University Federico II of Naples, Italy

Kevin Marsh   The Matrix Knowledge Group, London, UK

Daniel Mejía   Department of Economics, Universidad de los Andes, Bogota, Colombia

Volker Nitsch   Technische Universität Darmstadt, Germany, and CESifo, Munich, Germany

Pascual Restrepo   Department of Economics, Universidad de los Andes, Bogota, Colombia

Peter Reuter School of Public Policy and Department of Criminology, University of Maryland

Friedrich Schneider Department of Economics, Johannes Kepler University, Linz, Austria

Cláudia Costa Storti European Monitoring Centre for Drugs and Drug Addiction (EMCDDA), Lisbon, Portugal

Laura Wilson The Matrix Knowledge Group, London, UK

1 Introduction

Cláudia Costa Storti and Paul De Grauwe

International trade has expanded massively in the postwar period. This expansion accelerated after 1980 when China opened it borders, and later toward the end of the 1980s when other major countries (India, Russia, and eastern Europe) followed suit. This opening up of borders has led to an explosion of legal international trade in goods and services and in the movements of capital and labor. In the wake of this expansion of legal international trade, illicit international trade has expanded at growth rates that most probably are of the same order of magnitude.

The expansion of illicit trade raises many issues, some of which are analyzed in great detail in this book. One of these issues arises from a paradox inherent in illicit activities. This is that the very fact that an economic activity is made illegal raises both the riskiness and the profitability of this activity. The increased risk arises from the risk of incarceration, the risk related to the absence of legal enforcement of contracts, and the risk of violence. A higher risk of an activity, however, can lead to a higher return (profitability) needed to compensate for this risk.

We illustrate this relation between risk and return in figure 1.1. It represents a simple model with perfect competition. The demand and supply curves are given by D and S, respectively. We assume that the supply curve represents the aggregate of production and distribution costs. Thus each point on the supply curve represents the minimum price the joint activity of producing and distribution has to fetch. The equilibrium is obtained in point E.

Let us now assume that the government makes the production and the distribution of the good in question illegal. This has the effect of raising the minimum price suppliers have to obtain to make the joint activity of production and distribution worthwhile. This increased minimum price must cover the increased risks associated with the

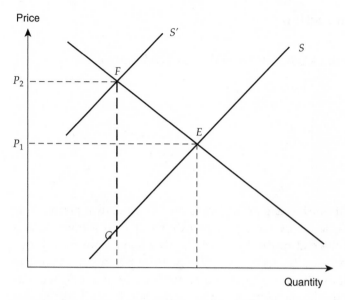

Figure 1.1
Demand and supply, perfect competition

production and distribution of the illicit commodity. We show this by the displacement of the supply curve from S to S''. The new equilibrium is obtained in point F. The market price is now P_2. This is the price paid by the consumer. The vertical distance FG can be interpreted as a risk premium obtained by the producers and distributors to compensate them for the increased risk.

The location of point F will be determined by the intensity of the law enforcement. The tighter is the latter the more this point moves upward along the demand curve, creating a larger risk premium. Thus we obtain the paradox that the tighter is law enforcement the more profitable the illicit production and distribution becomes.

This leads to a second paradox first noted by Gary Becker. In illicit markets characterized by a low price elasticity of demand (which results from the addictive nature of the drug), the resources used up in the production and the distribution of the illicit commodity increases by the very fact that it is made illegal. We show this in figure 1.2. The point E corresponds to the equilibrium obtained in the absence of legal restrictions on the production and the distribution. Point F is the equilibrium obtained when the commodity is made illicit. The shaded rectangles represent the amount spent by consumers. We observe that this

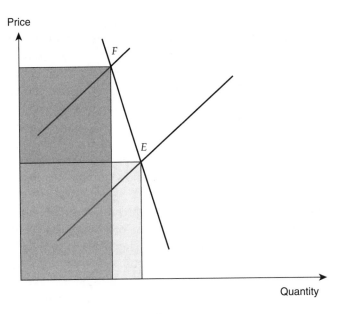

Figure 1.2
Gary Becker's paradox

amount is larger when the commodity is illicit. Since the amounts spent by the consumer must be equal to the total revenue obtained by the producers and distributors, it follows that that more resources are channeled to the latter.

This surprisingly simple model helps to explain many puzzling phenomena observed in the production and distribution of illicit commodities (e.g., drugs). One is that the more repressive the law enforcement system is, the more resources the suppliers of illicit commodities will be willing to put in these illicit activities, leading to an "arms' race" between law enforcers and the suppliers of the illicit commodities. There can be little doubt that the expansion of international trade has intensified this arms' race, leading to significant economic, social, and political problems in many countries affected by these activities. The chapters in this book aim at analyzing these different problems.

This book contains the papers presented at the CESifo workshop on "Globalization and Illicit Trade" organized in Venice on July 14–15, 2008. Chapter 2 by Peter Reuter and Jonathan Caulkins sets the tone of the workshop and focuses on illicit drugs. Reuter and Caulkins start by discussing the specificities of illegal drug markets as compared to legal markets. They discuss the role of different kinds of risks (law enforcement, crime, and violence), and build a bridge between risks and the drug price formation mechanism. In addition Reuter and Caulkins identify several intriguing puzzles that need further economic analysis. One is the great variability of the purity of illicit drugs both in time and in space. The most intriguing aspect of this purity puzzle is the sometimes observed negative correlation between purity and price. A second puzzle is that despite large increases in law enforcement efforts, which should have led to an increase in the street price of illicit drugs, we observe the opposite: the street price of drugs has declined significantly since the 1980s. Reuter and Caulkins formulate several hypotheses to explain this puzzle.

Friedrich Schneider has done important research on measuring the size of the underground ("black") economy. In chapter 3 he surveys the different estimates of the size of money laundering and the problems associated with measuring these. According to his own estimates (based on a MIMIC estimation procedure for the years 1995 to 2006 for 20 highly developed OECD countries), he finds that the volume of laundered money was 273 billion USD in the year 1995 for these 20 OECD countries (for 1.33 percent of total GDP of these 20 countries) and increased to 603 billion USD in 2006 (or 1.74 percent of the GDP of these countries). Although it remains hazardous to estimate such numbers, he does suggest that money laundering from the turnover of organized crime is quite important.

In chapter 4, Helge Berger and Volker Nitsch explore official trade data to identify patterns of smuggling in international trade. They analyze the extent to which the recorded export value in the source country deviates from the reported import value in the destination country. Analyzing four-digit product level data for the world's five largest importers for the period from 2002 to 2006, they find that the reporting gaps are highly correlated with the level of corruption in both partner countries. They interpret this as confirming the hypothesis that trade gaps partly represent smuggling activities.

In chapter 5, Mohammad Farzanegan analyzes smuggling in one country, Iran. The main results suggest that the penalty for smuggling reduces smuggling, while the tariff burden increases the incentives for illegal trade. He also finds that smuggling has a negative effect on real governmental revenues. He estimates the size of smuggling to be about 13 percent of total trade in Iran.

In chapter 6, Cláudia Costa Storti and Paul De Grauwe present a model that incorporates important aspects of globalization in a model of the cocaine and heroin markets. They trace the different channels through which globalization has affected these markets and identify several effects of globalization: the efficiency effect, the risk premium effect, and the market structure effect (competition). They formulate the hypothesis that the strong decline in the street price of these illicit drugs (as also noted by Peter Reuter and Caulkins, chapter 2) has been made possible by globalization working through these different mechanisms.

Kevin Marsh, Laura Wilson, and Rachel Kenehan, pursue this subject of globalization in chapter 7. They analyze interviews with convicted drug traffickers to determine whether there is evidence for any of these mechanisms in the UK markets for drugs. Evidence is identified to support the existence of some, but not all, of these globalization mechanisms. However, the limitations of the study mean that is difficult to assess the extent to which these observations are representative of the UK drug market as a whole.

In chapter 8, Axel Klein contributes to the exploration of the analysis of both the "drug trade" and "globalization." He presents a case study of the spread of khat, a psychoactive stimulant plant that is a class 1 drug in the United States but is imported legally as a vegetable in the United Kingdom. Drawing on first-hand research findings in the khat production/distribution field, he warns of the danger of a vast but ineffective drug control industry that imposes steeply rising social costs.

In chapter 9, Vittorio Daniele and Ugo Marani deal with a different topic: organized crime in Italy. Specifically, they examine the impact of crime on foreign direct investment (FDI) inflows in 103 Italian provinces. The results show how the correlation between organized crime and FDI is both negative and significant. Furthermore such a correlation between crime and FDI seems to be valid only for certain crimes, traditionally related to the presence of organized crime of the *mafia* type. The authors conclude that these results are consistent with the hypothesis that (certain) crimes may be perceived as a signal of a socio-institutional environment unfavorable for FDI.

In chapter 10, Daniel Mejía and Pascual Restrepo develop a simple model of the war against illegal drugs in producer and consumer countries. Their analysis shows how the equilibrium quantity of illegal drugs as well as the price depend on key parameters of the model, such as the price elasticity of demand and the effectiveness of the resources allocated to enforcement and to prevention policies. Mejía and Restrepo study the trade-off faced by the state of the drug consumer country between prevention policies (aimed at reducing de demand for illegal drugs) and enforcement policies (aimed at reducing the production and trafficking of illegal drugs) and show how the optimal allocation of resources between these two alternative uses depends also on the key parameters of the model. A calibration exercise allows the author to estimate the marginal cost to the United States of decreasing the consumption of cocaine by one kilogram using prevention or enforcement policies.

As can be seen from the summaries of the chapters, the nexus between illicit trade and globalization has many dimensions. No book can pretend to analyze all these dimensions. Nevertheless, we believe that this book sheds light on some important features of the interaction between illicit trade and globalization.

2 Purity, Price, and Production: Are Drug Markets Different?

Peter Reuter and Jonathan P. Caulkins

2.1 Introduction

Markets for drugs, prostitution and other prohibited goods and services are just that—markets. The first duty of economists is to show that the tools of conventional economics are applicable for the illegal markets as well. That is easily enough done with respect to demand. Many studies have shown that demand for illicit drugs is downward sloping and has a price elasticity not so different from that for other dependence creating substances (Grossman 2004). The erroneous belief that drug addicts cannot cut their consumption was once very widely held, so this is no small achievement. Less has been done on the supply side; for instance, there are almost no empirical studies of supply elasticity. Nevertheless, it is clear that drug selling operations can be analyzed as business activities (e.g., Reuter et al. 1990), and insights obtained from applying economic reasoning to those businesses' finances (Levitt and Venkatesh 2000); for a review, see Caulkins and Nicosia (2010).

There is, though, a second task that is not so frequently tackled, namely analyzing the distinctive features of illegal drug markets. What are the consequences for the operation of a market of the conversion of the state from an institution aimed at facilitating, or at least not hindering, markets to one that is actively hostile to those markets? How does that affect efficiency, structure, conduct, and behavior? How much does the conventional economic framework need to be adapted?

Some differences are obvious and readily explained. For example, retail drug transactions are usually made in round dollar figures ($10, $20), whereas legal prices usually end in nines ($9.99 or $19.99). Standardized purchase prices, which have been observed in many countries and over four decades (Wendel and Curtis 2000), arise because drug sales are often clandestine and hurried to reduce enforcement risks; even the act of making change is a luxury that persons seeking to avoid detection cannot afford.

Other empirical regularities are more consequential and more difficult to explain. This chapter contributes to the second task, understanding drug markets' distinctive characteristics, by considering a variety of observations, that are, at face value, counterintuitive to an economist: We start with four categories:

1. Purity. Heroin regularly travels in large shipments that are substantially impure, even though that increases the risks and costs of smuggling per pure gram of heroin.
2. (Purity-adjusted) price. Within individual markets there is a strong negative correlation between average purity and purity-adjusted price, even though the principal driver of purity-adjusted price is enforcement risk; higher enforcement risk should increase the incentives for more compact (i.e., higher purity) cocaine or heroin.
3. Price response to government intervention. The massive increase in enforcement intensity against sellers in the United States has been accompanied by a large and continued decline in the price of both cocaine and heroin.
4. Production. Production of cocaine and heroin is highly concentrated in a small number of countries that represent only a small portion of the arable land suitable for growing those crops.

In section 2.2 we begin with a discussion of the markets for illegal drugs, and specifically the identifying characteristics of the markets that lead to policy interventions. We then set out a simple conceptual framework that has been used to explain equilibrium in markets for illegal drugs, emphasizing those features that differ from the model for legal commodities. In section 2.3, we list a set of empirical oddities that the standard market model seems to handle poorly. In section 2.4, we offer some conjectures that might help account for the puzzles. Finally, in section 2.5, we offer some observations about research on drug markets.

2.2 Motivation

The markets for illegal drugs constitute an important criminal, economic, and social phenomenon in the United States and around the globe. Collectively these markets were estimated to generate 60 billion

USD in US retail sales in 2000 (and twice that in 1990) (ONDCP 2001). Globally the figure may be 150 billion USD.[1] Drug markets matter both because they generate large criminal earnings and harms as a consequence of their operation (e.g., diverting youth from education, creating disorder and crime around marketplaces) and also because they provide dangerous substances whose use generates violent crime, at least when the drug is a stimulant. According to surveys of arrestees in the United States about half of all arrestees have recently used drugs other than marijuana (National Institute of Justice 2003; Office of National Drug Control Policy 2009); the figures for England and Wales and for Australia are not much lower (e.g., Bennett and Sibbitt 2000). In other historical periods illegal gambling and bootlegging of prohibited alcohol have been large and troubling markets in the United States, but the available evidence suggests that illegal drugs are much the largest illegal market now in the United States and probably in a number of other Western countries.

Moreover governments make a large investment of both money and authority in suppressing drug markets. Drug control is probably a 40 billion USD annual effort in the United States (Walsh 2004). Reuter and Stevens (2007) estimate UK government expenditures of about 6 billion USD in 2005, on a per capita basis that is surprisingly close to the US figure though methodological and institutional differences are such that not too much should be made of that. In all countries for which budget estimates have been made, most of the money goes to law enforcement; even in the harm-reduction oriented Netherlands that turns out to be the case (Rigter 2006).

On any given day in 2005, approximately 500,000 persons were incarcerated in jails and prisons in the United States because of violations of drug prohibitions; the vast majority were involved in drug distribution, although not infrequently in minor roles (Caulkins and Chandler 2006). Of course, the United States stands out for its incarceration rates generally, so one hardly expects to find similar figures for drug incarceration for any other nation, but again, in Britain there has been a sharp increase in drug incarcerations both relatively and absolutely. The number receiving prison sentences for drug offenses rose by nearly 150 percent between 1993 and 1999, before slightly declining over the next five years; the increases for drugs were much higher than for all other offenses taken together (De Silva 2005a, b). Beyond being important in its own right, this effort competes with more traditional crime fighting efforts for criminal justice resources (Kuziemko and Levitt 2004; Rasmussen and Benson 1994).

The price and conditions under which drugs are sold have important criminal consequences. If heroin were to cost $1 a dose rather than $25, the effects on society would be very different because there might be many more users and certainly much less crime (MacCoun and Reuter 2001). Not only would the lower prices reduce the needs of dependent users to commit crimes to fund their purchases, but it would also reduce the incentives of sellers to compete violently or to resolve conflicts about transactions through violence. Current prices of illegal drugs are many times higher than would be the corresponding price in legal markets (Moore 1990; Kilmer et al. 2010). High prices are not simply an automatic consequence of illegality; for example, illegal bookmakers charge roughly the same for their services as do their legal counterparts (Strumpf 2003).

Similarly it is important to understand the distribution of earnings in the drug trades: Drug markets would generate much smaller problems if the unskilled manager of a heroin distribution gang earned what the manager of a McDonalds earns. Instead, many senior drug dealers earn as much as a successful lawyer, without the necessity of law school; some, mostly in producer and transshipment countries, earn large fortunes. Any good account of drug markets should explain the very uneven distribution of earnings in the trade.

Finally, it is important to understand how drug markets respond to various kinds of interventions. For example, how will an increased risk of incarceration or more restrictive access to specific inputs (e.g., precursor chemicals for methamphetamines) affect prices, the size of the market, and the distribution of returns across groups of participants?

2.3   Risks and Prices

Caulkins and MacCoun (2003, p. 436) give a good summary of the Reuter and Kleiman (1986) "risks and prices" model of price determination in markets for illegal drugs that has been used in many studies since, particularly studies associated with the RAND Corporation (e.g., Rydell and Everingham 1994).

• People sell drugs primarily to make money, not for pathological or ideological reasons.
• There are few barriers to entry because (1) few specialized skills and little capital are needed to be a drug supplier and (2) the domestic

distribution "industry" is fragmented, so it is not generally in the interest of individual incumbent supplier organizations to take costly action to prevent others from entering the market.[2]

• Hence people enter the drug distribution business until the returns from doing so are bid down to a level comparable to that derived from other activities, that is, to the opportunity cost of being a dealer.

• The economic return from dealing is the monetary, or accounting profit minus the dollar value of nonmonetary risks and costs incurred.

• Conventional costs of production are too small to explain or drive prices.

The risks and prices model identifies two separate sources of risks for participants, the government (arrest, incarceration, seizure of assets and drugs) and other participants (injury or robbery of drugs or money). The conventional market model deals only with the first. In many Western countries the risk of being incarcerated (on an annual basis) is substantial enough that it is plausible that compensation for those risks is a substantial cost.[3]

Violence seems to us a neglected and critical factor in explaining many aspects of drug markets. In a set of calculations using data from 1988, when drug market violence in the United States was probably near its peak, Caulkins and Reuter (1998) estimated that compensation for physical risks (serious injury or death) accounted for about 40 percent of total costs of delivering cocaine to final users.

For many final market countries outside the United States the second set of risks may be moderate. However, violence is not unknown there and can be much greater in certain source and transshipment countries. The enormous increase in drug-related homicides in Mexico, now perhaps close to 30,000 for the period October 2006 to October 2010, is a vivid reminder of how violent such a market can be. Recent data from interviews with incarcerated drug dealers in British prisons (Matrix Knowledge Group 2007) suggest that few have experienced actual violence in the course of their drug-dealing careers; nonetheless, many had carried guns and perceived violence as potentially important in the business. In this respect their careers parallel those of most police officers, who never draw the gun they always carry.[4] Even countries with low homicide rates, such as Australia and Canada, have seen outbreaks of drug-related violence, often involving biker gangs.

Risks and prices have been extended to dynamic versions (Caulkins and Reuter 2010), though the stories there are more complex. In any of these versions the risk and prices model is very classical in its assumptions about rationality of the actors.

2.4   Some Puzzles

2.4.1   Purity Puzzles

Purity is the central driver of product quality for most illegal drugs. In legal markets product quality is a minor strategic choice, representing judgments of producers about consumer preferences; frequently a variety of qualities exist in the marketplace, and usually quality information is transmitted accurately and credibly to the purchaser who makes an informed choice.[5] This holds even for the dilutable legal intoxicant alcohol; the alcohol content of beer and whiskey differ, but the alcohol content of different cans of the same beer are essentially identical. The government may even regulate purity ("proof") as, for example, in the many nations where 60 percent alcohol content is the legal maximum.

That is not the case for illegal drugs. Although they are natural products, subject only to simple refining, these drugs are "experience goods." Cocaine and heroin labs do not adhere to rigorous quality control standards, and the drugs are further diluted as they move through the distribution system. At the time of purchase the retail customer can assess only imperfectly the quantity being purchased and has even less information about its chemical composition, including its purity and hence its psychoactive effect. Imperfect knowledge of quantity stems simply from the drug's extreme potency and hence the tiny quantities involved in retail transactions.

Not only is purity not known at the time of purchase, it also may not even be determined accurately after consumption. Some adulterants mimic the drug's physical effects (e.g., numbing), and the user may have only a general notion of how much of the drug he or she actually consumed, since there is variability in response to the drug, depending on, *inter alia*, health status, concomitant use of other intoxicants, time since last ingestion, and "set and setting" or expectation and context (Zinberg 1984). The user will make an assessment of the quality of the experience, but without certainty. Consumers are thus vulnerable to strategic manipulation by sellers,[6] who can reduce purity by adding diluents and/or adulterants.

These observations characterize retail transactions. At wholesale levels transactions are more likely to take place in protected settings, so there is more opportunity, and more incentive (because of the high dollar value of the transaction), to conduct systematic testing of purity. However, it is apparently not difficult to sell bundles of varying purity. Colorimetric assays are readily available, but accurate testing would require a mass spectrometer, the purchase of which is not only expensive but also would create substantial risk of disclosure. Testing often appears to be no more sophisticated than having a "taster" snort some to see if the experience is good; that is likely to only detect rip-offs, that is bundles of very low purity.[7]

Galenianos, Pacula, and Persico (2009) present a model that attempts to explain how a market establishes positive equilibrium purity in face of such uncertainty. That is an important advance in the literature but still leaves us without a theory of what determines purity levels. A particular conundrum is why the purity of international wholesale heroin shipments is so low.

The risk of seizure and apprehension is a decreasing function of purity of the drug; the purer the drug, the smaller the volume and the easier to conceal. Prohibition may affect purity (more correctly, potency) in a more fundamental way; it is often claimed that the shift in Pakistan and Thailand from opium to heroin is a function of the Western-inspired implementation of effective prohibition, which makes the more compact and concealable heroin preferred over traditional opium.

The role of purity is particularly important for large shipments. It is substantially easier to conceal 2 kilograms of heroin than 4 kilograms, obviously for "body packers" who swallow the drugs in condoms. Higher purity can lower costs in more subtle ways as well. For example bribes are paid on a raw kilogram basis, not purity adjusted. The corrupt airport official will charge $5,000 per kilogram, regardless of whether the kilogram is 50 or 90 percent pure, if only because the official has no method of testing for purity. Small plane pilots also charge on a weight basis, not value or purity.

How then can one account for the data from Turkey on the purity of large seizures shown in figure 2.1. Not only does the average never rise much above 50 percent even for seizures of over 10 kilograms (with a value of 100,000 USD at that point in the distribution chain), but fewer than 10 percent of the seizures had a purity of 70 percent. The seizures certainly are not a random sample of shipments, and higher purity shipments have a lower risk of seizure. However, many seizures are related to investigations of individuals rather than generated by border inspections of cargo, so that bias may be slight.

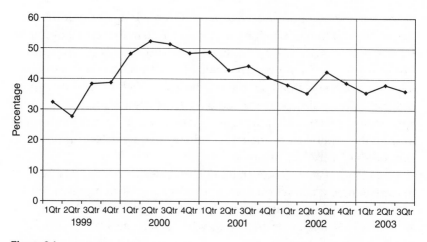

Figure 2.1
Purity of heroin seizures in Turkey, 1999 to 2003

Purity data from final market countries in Europe reinforce the puzzle. Figure 2.2 shows the purity of heroin seizures in Germany in 2002. Even for seizures greater than 100 grams, worth many thousands of dollars, the majority are of low purity. Indeed only 41 percent are more than 20 percent pure. We have observed similarly low purity in other European nations.

There are purity puzzles not only vertically, up and down the distribution chain, but also horizontally, between cities that occupy parallel positions in the distribution chain. In particular, why should there be such great variation across markets in their average purity at any one time. Figure 2.3, from Caulkins et al. (2004), shows that not only has purity varied for a given city over time but that there are persistent differences across cities. Perhaps not surprisingly, New York (as the largest single heroin market) has consistently the highest purity. That Chicago is often the lowest purity city is surprising, given that it is the second largest of these cities and one with a very active heroin market.

There are also large differences reported across countries. In 2001 the German police report an average of 18.5 percent versus a UK average of 54 percent. These differences persist over time. It is puzzling that the markets equilibrate at such different levels and points to the need for a theory of purity determination. As UCLA Professor Mark Kleiman has oft noted, low expected purity exposes the user to greater risk of fatal overdose; if a user expects 50 percent purity, at most he might be

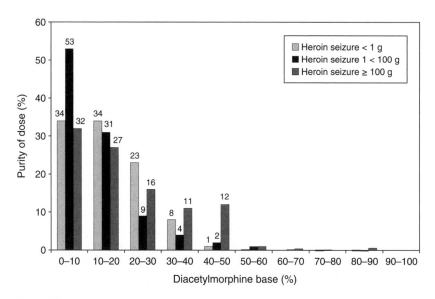

Figure 2.2
Purity of heroin seizures in Germany, by size, 2002

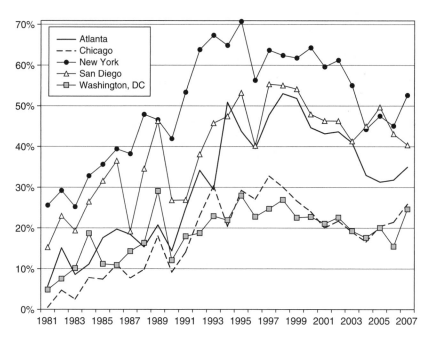

Figure 2.3
Heroin purity in five US cities, 1981 to 2003

exposed to twice the anticipated dose. With 20 percent, the actual dose could be five times as high.

2.4.2   The Negative Relationship between Purity and Price per Pure Gram

Average purity and purity adjusted price in a market have a reliable and strong negative correlation. Figure 2.4, taken from Caulkins et al. (2004), on methamphetamine (retail transactions of less than 10 grams bulk, estimated at 2.5 grams) is chosen from the many available instances because it includes many reversals in prices and is not, as with cocaine or heroin, a tale of almost uniformly declining price.

The puzzle here is more subtle. Initially it seems not a puzzle at all but a mathematical tautology. Purity-adjusted prices and purity could be inversely related because shrinking the denominator of a ratio, while holding the numerator constant, makes the ratio larger. However, the inverse relationship exists not just observation to observation, because of random noise, but in expectation across hundreds of observations in each time period. And if one wanted to reduce the pure quantity

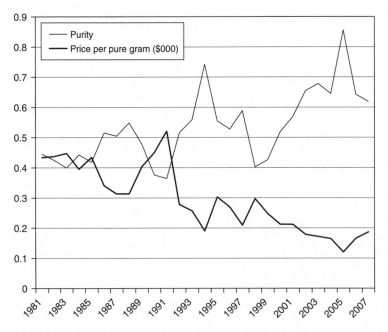

Figure 2.4
US methamphetamine price and purity

contained in a $100 bag, why not reduce the weight of drugs in the bag rather than the purity?

The negative relationship can also exist across substances. In the United States heroin typically triggers the toughest sanctions, so it is not surprising that it is more expensive, per pure gram, than cocaine, but it is surprising that it is diluted more extensively. As drug selling becomes riskier, either because of longer sentences or higher risk of apprehension, a simple maximization model would predict not only a higher price per pure gram (shift in supply curve) but also a rise in purity. That latter change reduces the risk associated with a given quantity of the drug: the higher the purity, the lower the quantity of white powder to deliver a given amount of the desired ingredient.

The puzzle is deepened by sentencing practices. In theory one could justify a sentencing structure that worked in terms of the pure drug content, since the harm caused is not a function of the gross weight of white powder but by the amount of active ingredient. However, we know of no jurisdiction that follows that procedure; all work in terms of the gross weight of what is sold. Hence there is heightened advantage in selling purer drugs.

2.4.3   Price Puzzles

When monitoring drug market prices, one needs to adjust for purity. Purity-adjusted prices can explain very well variation in use-related indicators, such as ambulance call-outs, even when "raw" prices, not adjusted for purity do not (e.g., Moore et al. 2005). A consequence of the buyer's uncertainty about purity is that measurement of purity-adjusted drug prices (either by police or researchers) becomes technically difficult, but the methods for dealing with this are by now well established (Caulkins 2007).

The best-known price puzzle concerns US price and enforcement trends. Between 1980 and 2005 there was a massive increase in drug-related incarceration in the United States, aimed at making drugs more expensive and harder to get. The purity-adjusted prices of cocaine and heroin, the principal drugs targeted, fell steadily and substantially throughout this period, while availability has remained high.

Figure 2.5 provides the most basic series, showing that cocaine and heroin prices fell by about 80 percent from 1980 to 2000 during which time drug-related incarcerations rose tenfold.

Economic theory predicts that what should drive prices is not the level but rather than intensity of punishment, meaning the punishment

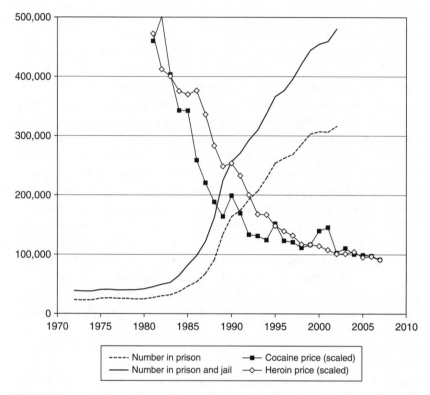

Figure 2.5
Drug prices and total drug-related incarceration, 1980 to 2005

per metric ton sold or per seller. We briefly summarize the basis for the claim that drug imprisonments rose not just in absolute numbers but in terms of the risks of incarceration for cocaine and heroin.

Converting drug incarcerations to a rate for cocaine and heroin markets requires considerable judgment with respect to both the numerator (number of cocaine and heroin dealers incarcerated) and denominator (number of active dealers). The available data on incarcerations is not drug specific. However, Sevigny and Caulkins (2004) use self-report data from a large 1997 survey of federal and state prison inmates to show that over 60 percent are serving time for cocaine or crack offenses; heroin, marijuana, and methamphetamine each account for about 10 percent of drug prisoners. There are no analyses available for the 1980s, so we rely on the impressions of observers that the share for cocaine has risen and that for heroin may have fallen somewhat.

The total drug incarcerations figure probably overstates the rise for heroin and understates that for cocaine, but we are sure in both cases that the totals have risen substantially.

For the denominator, the number of dealers, we rely on indicators from other studies, such as estimates of the population of frequent users. For the period 1988 to 2000, series are available for cocaine and heroin (ONDCP 2001). Both show substantial declines—nearly 50 percent for cocaine and 30 percent for heroin. These series have been subject to a number of revisions, but in no version of the data have they shown substantial increases. Earlier research efforts suggest that cocaine demand increased during the period 1980 to 1988, but for the post-1988 period, during which the incarceration rose most rapidly, we are confident that the number of regular cocaine consumers did not increase. For heroin 1980 to 1988, data are sparse but there is no evidence of an increase in the user population.

In theory it is possible that the number of dealers per user increased, so that a constant user population supported a larger number of dealers. There is no evidence of such a trend, and in any event such a change would have had to be extraordinarily large to change the conclusion that the risk of incarceration for a cocaine dealer or a heroin dealer rose.

The simplest explanations of declining prices are declining demand or increasing production efficiency. Although the prior discussion suggests that for cocaine, consumption has ebbed somewhat since 1988, demand was likely increasing in the early to mid-1980s, the period of fastest price declines (Caulkins et al. 2004). There has not been comparable analysis of heroin demand (as opposed to indicators of quantity consumed), but conventional wisdom would be of stable demand in the 1980s and flat demand during the 1990s. While it cannot be dismissed completely, sharply declining demand is not a very plausible explanation for the fall in prices.

Costa Storti and De Grauwe (2008) suggest that globalization may explain the decline in drug prices that has occurred in many Western countries. They identify three different mechanisms: a shift to more competitive market structures, a flow of low cost labor that reduces the risk premium, and greater efficiency in international trade generally. These may indeed be important factors in shifting the supply curve, but their analysis does not directly confront the paradox of tougher enforcement and lower prices.

Various other explanations have been offered, some of which are reviewed in Caulkins and MacCoun (2003). A more recent one by Caulkins, Reuter, and Taylor (2006) offered a model that took account of the role of violence in the formation of prices. Tougher enforcement that focused on more violent individuals would reduce the costs to the marginal supplier, defined by his willingness to incur physical risks. The result was that more enforcement would lower prices. None of these models are convincing as identifying all the factors that might be involved.

2.4.4 A Production Puzzle

Francisco Thoumi (2003) has articulated a central issue for understanding global drug markets. Production of cocaine and heroin is concentrated in a very small number of countries, even though many nations can, and have, produced these drugs. Only three nations produce cocaine for the illegal market: Bolivia, Colombia, and Peru. Yet commercial production has been located in Java (under Dutch colonial control), Formosa (Japanese control), and Bengal (British control). There is no doubt that coca can be grown in Venezuela and Ecuador. There may well be many other countries that can produce it as well.

Opium is a slightly more complicated story (Paoli, Greenfield, and Reuter, 2009). It has historically been grown in many nations, such as Iran, Macedonia, and Uzbekistan. Seven countries currently produce for the licit market, subject to regulation by the International Control Board; they include Australia and France, as well as the long-term producer, India. Yet illegal production is found in few countries and has been concentrated in two countries for most of the modern era of mass illegal heroin markets. Afghanistan and Burma have accounted for over 85 percent of global production since systematic measurement began in the mid-1980s. Since the late 1990s Afghanistan has come to dominate the global market; in the *2008 World Drug Report* Afghanistan accounted for 93 percent of global production.

Thoumi's account for why nations become active in the production of illegal drugs emphasizes the role of a weak state and tolerance for criminal activities, rather than conventional economic factors, such as factor endowment or prices. That is helpful but still leaves a large question. There are many weak states with tolerance for organized criminal activities; why do only a few end up dominating the market? One simple model emphasizes the declining marginal costs associated with corruption; having been paid to allow the growth of one hundred hectares, an authority may as cheaply protect one thousand hectares. The emphasis is on economies of scope.

2.5   Participant Characteristics, Market Outcomes, and Policy

The preceding section amply demonstrates that there is much we do not understand about drug markets. Some such ignorance can be chalked up to poor data. However, the more interesting observation is that quite a few empirical regularities shine through the fog of imperfect data, which are puzzlingly inconsistent with deductive conjectures based on standard models for how one might expect these markets to operate.

One possibility is that each little oddity has its own idiosyncratic explanation, but Occam's razor suggests looking instead for a unified explanation. We tentatively propose as a candidate conjecture that the extreme physical and enforcement risks in these markets not only drive up prices but also create strong sorting or selection effects. The resulting population of people engaged in supplying drugs is thus highly unrepresentative of the population as a whole. So general economic theories designed to apply to markets populated by typical people may sometimes fail to explain successfully puzzling aspects of drug market behavior.

We hasten to add two caveats. First, we are not, at present, going to invoke moral selection arguments. It is not implausible, on its face, that a conscience that makes it easy to break one set of laws (those against drug distribution) may also reduce the personal psychosocial cost of breaking other laws (e.g., against assault) whose violation can be a common correlate of illegal market activity. But we set aside such ideas for the moment. Second, we would not expect this principle to apply to parts of the industry that are not subject to great legal or moral sanction, such as sharing marijuana with friends or growing drug crops in regions where that is commonplace behavior. Rather, it would pertain primarily to international drug trafficking and domestic distribution of substances subject to stringent enforcement.

Our conjecture departs substantially from the economic literature on drug markets, which pays little systematic attention to the characteristics of participants, in particular dealers. In some respects this reflects admirable egalitarianism. Ethnic and racial minorities are disproportionately represented in official statistics on drug distribution, but this is studied only as a consequence of racism or other social forces, not as a cause of distinctive market behavior. However, in other respects it may also reflect a troubling lack of inquisitiveness. Males are even more disproportionately represented among those arrested for drug distribution, and whether biological or sociological, there are systematic differences in male versus female conflict resolution tactics, notably with respect to proclivity for resorting to violence, which is one of the most salient and troubling characteristics of drug markets.

Gender, of course, is easily observed and regularly tracked, so we are far from the first to make that connection. But gender may merely be a correlate of other, less easily observed individual attributes on which drug markets select and sort, such as tolerance for risk, optimism bias, and impulsivity. And perhaps a market populated by people who are strongly atypical on such dimensions that affect preferences and decision-making might operate in ways that are materially different than classical models would predict.

Behavioral economics studies how typical people may depart from classical economic models. In a related way we are contemplating what might happen if a market's distinctive institutional characteristics selected on certain attributes often addressed in that literature (e.g., optimism bias), producing a highly atypical subset of people to populate those markets, and also how that selection could feedback to further accentuate the market's distinctive institutions in a reinforcing cycle.

It is beyond the scope of this chapter to connect this conjecture to all of the puzzles above. Instead, we content ourselves with demonstrating the principle with respect to some familiar and uncontroversial characteristics of drug markets, and then close by suggesting how it may matter in a normative sense for how these markets respond to policy interventions.

2.5.1 Some Consequences of Participant Characteristics for Market Behavior

The following examples are written from a good knowledge of US markets and a working knowledge about those in western Europe and Australia and much less about transshipment countries such as Mexico and Tajikistan. The focus will be on cocaine and heroin, about which more is known; we suspect similar observations may hold for methamphetamine but presumably not for drugs such as Ecstasy and marijuana, whose markets are quite different.

Drug markets attract individuals with distinctive tastes and skills, both because of a strict prohibition regime and the characteristics of the drugs. The institutions that form around illegal markets, including the supplier enterprises and the relations among the suppliers, both reflect and interact with these distinctive participant characteristics.

For example, consider the fact that heroin and cocaine addicts in the United States typically purchase from many suppliers (Riley et al. 1997). Superficially this is odd. All else being equal, conducting illegal transactions with a larger number of people increases the risk of detection. However, two factors may combine to override that consideration. One is that retailers are unreliable because they are subject to sudden arrest or injury and, mostly being addicts themselves, are from time to time not operationally competent. The second is that buyers of addictive drugs have urgent needs and poor impulse control. They manage the latter by buying frequently, even though there are very large quantity discounts. But when they wish to purchase they want immediate delivery, so to speak; having many suppliers when individual suppliers are unreliable, is critical.

As a second example, consider the observation that many persons selling cocaine and heroin are dependent users of those drugs. Dependence is conceptually distinct from intoxication; it involves systematic and lasting changes in neuroreceptors and reward pathways. The architecture underpinning tastes and choices has been altered. In particular, dependence primes individuals to experience powerful cravings for the drug and to be prone to binges. In other words, the sales force is singularly inept at holding inventory responsibly.

Why do such participants drive out others, and not vice versa? As Moore (1990) observed, drug-using sellers are advantaged over abstinent sellers in that they receive part of their compensation in the form of discounted drugs, which they presumably value at some price between wholesale and retail; non-users must incur the risks of selling all of their drugs in order to obtain the full return. Since the markets have a reputation for involving physical risk, those who require less compensation for that risk will enter before others with similar skills. This has other consequences; if attitudes toward physical risk are correlated with risk-taking more generally, we can expect a market primarily of risk lovers. An additional source of transaction risk is that participants are subject to random removal from the market through arrest or injury. That contracts are unenforceable in courts may add further to risks.

2.5.2   Some Consequences of Participant Characteristics for Policy

Drug enforcement does not work primarily through incapacitation or rehabilitation; most dealers who are incarcerated or reformed can be replaced easily. Rather, drug enforcement works via deterrence. In particular, drug enforcement deters people from selling drugs at a low price, convincing the sellers collectively to provide the drug only for a higher profit at a higher price.

All deterrence, both the conventional form applicable to nonconsensual crimes and the "risks and prices" version applicable to black market distribution, depends on the object of the deterrent threat perceiving and responding to incentives. Since Becker's (1968) seminal work it has been common to presume that criminals respond to those incentives rationally, but many living things respond to their environment in nonrational ways. Even plants stems grow up toward light (phototropism) and roots grow down (geotropism). If drug sellers are systematically different, might their response to deterrent sanctions also be systematically different than would be predicted by conventional economic models?

Caulkins and MacCoun (2003) have developed a model of bounded rationality that aims "to show that even modest departures from the classical model of decision-making are sufficient to break the link between drug enforcement and drug prices. To the extent that in reality the decision to sell drugs is even more spontaneous, emotional, and idiosyncratic than we describe, then the conclusion holds with even greater force" (p. 439). As suggested already, we believe that there is ample evidence that the assumption of consistent and rational behavior is particularly strained in these markets.

This may also be a set of participants who are hard to deter in that they do not interpret signals from the criminal justice system well. In this respect they are not different from other chronic violent and property crime offenders as a population. For a review of that literature, see Nagin (1998). However, the nature of the potential response is different; rather than a decision about whether to desist from the criminal activity or reduce intensity in face of increased sanction severity or risk of apprehension, they make price decisions, even if only through manipulation of purity. Pricing decisions seem inherently more complex.

One important factor influencing (lack of) exit from dealing is a little-noted observation by Boyum (1992) about profits in illegal markets. Even if a drug-dealing business is operating at an economic loss, when one takes into account risk compensation, it will be showing a positive cash flow, indeed probably a very positive one. The entrepreneur will have to pay agents at levels that reflect their valuation of the risks they face, but there are no accounting books that record the entrepreneur's own estimate of risk. Moreover there is a growing body of interviews with dealers that suggest they systematically underestimate the length of sentences they face (e.g., Decker 2008).

The market is also characterized by extremely weak feedback about quality. The chain from heroin refiner in Afghanistan to final consumer in London may have eight links: sales to traffickers in Afghanistan, Iran, and then Turkey; sale to an importer in Britain (10 kilograms) and then three more sales to dealers within the United Kingdom (1 kilogram, 100 grams, 10 grams). Each link in the chain knows only the ones immediately above and below. Only the final user knows whether the purity was less than expected, and he does not know which party is responsible for higher than expected dilution.

The links of the chain get broken randomly; the chain that delivered a particular bundle may not be fully operational three months later because one participant was arrested or killed. Information about unexpectedly low purity will be transmitted back up the chain slowly and imperfectly.

2.6 Concluding Comments

This chapter aims more to encourage a line of inquiry than to provide a resolution of the specific puzzles that motivated its writing. The focus on participant characteristics surely will not explain all the differences, but it points to a set of variables that might play a prominent role in the analysis.

If economists are to contribute usefully to an understanding of drug markets, they will have to invest in learning about the distinctive characteristics of the participants that they attract and the environment in which they operate. Our conjecture is that these markets will turn out to have distinct features and that the puzzles above (and many others) will be resolved not by turning drug dealers into simply another group of tough risk takers but by learning about decision-making in the face of chronic dependence, massive uncertainty about the product and high risks of nearly catastrophic events such as incarceration, injury, and impoverishment.

A recent paper by Cook et al. (2007) on gun markets in Chicago offers a model of this kind of research. Working with an ethnographer and a criminologist, two well-known economists (Philip Cook and Jens Ludwig) showed that a combination of illegality, infrequent transactions, and ignorant buyers created a market that worked poorly. The relative strength of the drug market had an effect as well; leaders of the drug-dealing organizations that had many competitive advantages in supplying illegal guns chose to stay away from that business because of the lengthy sentences faced for gun offenses that would imperil their drug selling.

Most of the economics literature on drug markets has aimed at finding clever theoretical solutions to problems that trouble academic economists, without investing in an understanding of how the markets operate or what makes them distinctive. We believe that investment is essential.

Notes

1. The UN Office on Drugs and Crime estimates a total of almost 322 billion USD in retail sales; 94 billion USD in wholesale revenues; and 13 billion USD in producer sales (UNODC 2005: 127). This is likely an overestimate, particularly of the marijuana revenues and of the share going to wholesalers. A more recent and better documented study estimated that the global marijuana market at the retail level was probably only half as large as the figure estimated by the UNODC; it did not attempt a global estimate for cocaine and heroin, but for the countries it did consider, the figures were generally lower than the UNODC estimates (Kilmer and Pacula 2009).

2. We do not take up here the circumstances under which market power becomes possible. Reuter (1983) suggests that corrupt enforcement agencies with a sole franchise may provide a unique opportunity for some form of monopoly in illegal markets.

3. Illegal drugs increase in value within the United States by roughly 50 billion USD per year (60 billion USD retail minus roughly 10 billion USD in import costs). If the 500,000 people incarcerated for drug law violations demanded an average of 40,000 USD per year of incarceration, that risk compensation would account for 40 percent of that 50 billion USD markup.

4. We thank Martin Bouchard for this observation.

5. Even the classic exception to this rule, used cars, has eroded since Akerlof's classic (1970) paper, with statutory warranties in the European Union and the Magnuson–Moss warranty act in the United States, dealer warranties, and ubiquitous vehicle history checks.

6. "What exactly is in street heroin, how pure it is and what the effects of different cuts are is the subject of much discussion on the street. . . . Assays of street-level heroin in New York City found that among a sample of 40 bags, at least 27 types of adulterants and cuts had been added to produce heroin . . .." (Wendel and Curtis 2000; citing Strategic Intelligence Section 1996).

7. The film *Traffic* portrayed this. Fuentes, having researched Colombian cocaine import organizations in the United States Fuentes (1998, personal communication) reports not

having heard of any systematic testing; refunds and replacements were available for bad shipments.

References

Akerlof, G. 1970. The market for lemons: Product quality and market uncertainty. *Quarterly Journal of Economics* 84: 488–500.

Becker, G. 1968. The economics of crime and punishment. *Journal of Political Economy* 76 (2): 169–217.

Bennett, T. H., and R. Sibbitt. 2000. *Drug Use among Arrestees. Research Findings No. 119. Home Office Research and Statistics Directorate*. London: Home Office.

Boyum, D. A. 1992. Reflections on economic theory and drug enforcement. Unpublished PhD thesis in public policy. Harvard University, Cambridge.

Caulkins, J. P., and S. Chandler. 2006. Long-run trends in incarceration of drug offenders in the US. *Crime and Delinquency* 52 (4): 619–41. doi:10.1177/0011128705284793.

Caulkins, J. P. 2007. Price and purity analysis for illicit drugs: Data and conceptual issues. *Drug and Alcohol Dependence* 90S: S61–S68.

Caulkins, J. P., and N. Nicosia. 2010. What economics can contribute to the addiction sciences. *Addiction (Abingdon, England)* 105 (7): 1156–63.

Caulkins, J. P., and P. Reuter. 1998. What price data tell us about drug markets. *Journal of Drug Issues* 28 (3): 593–612.

Caulkins, J., and P. Reuter. 2010. How drug enforcement affects drug prices. In M. Tonry, ed., *Crime and Justice: A Review of Research*, vol. 39. Chicago: University of Chicago Press, 213–72.

Caulkins, J., P. P. Reuter, and L. Taylor. 2006. Can supply restrictions lower price? Violence, drug dealing, and positional advantage. *Contributions to Economic Analysis and Policy* 5 (1), article 3. http://www.bepress.com/bejeap/contributions/vol5/iss1/art3.

Caulkins, J. P., and R. J. MacCoun. 2003. Limited rationality and the limits of supply reduction. *Journal of Drug Issues* 33 (2): 433–64.

Caulkins, J. P., R. Liccardo Pacula, J. Arkes, P. Reuter, S. Paddock, M. Iguchi, and J. Riley. 2004. The price and purity of illicit drugs: 1981 through the second quarter of 2003. Report prepared by RAND and published by the Office of National Drug Control Policy as Publication NCJ 207768, November.

Caulkins, J. P., G. Feichtinger, J. Haunschmied, and G. Tragler. 2006. Quality cycles and the strategic manipulation of value. *Operations Research* 54 (4):666–677.

Cook, P. J., J. Ludwig, S. A. Venkatesh, and A. Braga. 2007. Underground gun markets. *Economic Journal* 117 (524):F588–F618.

Costa Storti, C., and P. De Grauwe. 2009. Globalization and the price decline of illicit drugs. *International Journal of Drug Policy* 20 (1): 48–61.

Decker, S., and M. Chapman. 2008. *Drug Smugglers on Drug Smugglin:g Lessons from the Inside*. Philadelphia: Temple University Press.

De Silva, N. 2005a. *Sentencing Statistics 2003. Home Office Statistical Bulletin 05/05.* London: Home Office.

De Silva, N. 2005b. *Sentencing Statistics 2004. Home Office Statistical Bulletin 15/05.* London: Home Office.

Fuentes, J. R. 1998. Life of a cell: Managerial practice and strategy in Colombian cocaine distribution in the United States. PhD dissertation. City University of New York.

Galenianos, M., Pacula, R. L., and N. Persico. 2009. A search theoretic model of the retail market for illicit drugs. Working paper 14980. NBER, Cambridge, MA. http://www.nber.org/papers/w14980.

Grossman, M. 2004. Individual behaviors and substance abuse: The role of price. Working paper 10948. NBER, Cambridge, MA.

Kilmer, B., and R. Pacula. 2009. Estimaating the size of the global drug market: A demand side approach. In P. Reuter and F. Trautmann, eds., *Assessing the Operations of the Global Illicit Drug Markets, 1998–2007* Brussels: Report for the European Commission. http://ec.europa.eu/justice/doc_centre/drugs/doc_drugs_intro_en.htm.

Kilmer, B, J. P. Caulkins, B. M. Bond, and P. Reuter. 2010. Reducing drug trafficking revenues and violence in Mexico: Would legalizing marijuana in California help? RAND OP-325-RC, Santa Monica, CA.

Kuziemko, I., and S. Levitt. 2004. An empirical analysis of imprisoning drug offenders. *Journal of Public Economics* 88: 2043–66.

Levitt, S., and S. A. Venkatesh. 2000. An economic analysis of a drug-selling gang's finances. *Quarterly Journal of Economics* 115 (3): 755–89.

MacCoun, R. J., and P. Reuter. 2001. *Drug War Heresies: Learning from Other Vices, Times and Places.* Cambridge: Cambridge University Press.

Matrix Knowledge Group. 2007. The illicit drug trade in the United Kingdom. Home Office Online Report 20/07. London.

Moore, M. H. 1990. Supply control and drug law enforcement. In M. Tonry and J. Q. Wilson, eds., *Drugs and Crime.* Chicago: University of Chicago Press, 109–58.

Moore, T. J., J. P. Caulkins, A. Ritter, P. Dietze, S. Monagle, and J. Pruden. 2005. *Heroin Markets in Australia: Current Understanding and Future Possibilities.* DPMP Monograph Series. Fitzroy: Turning Point Alcohol and Drug Centre.

Nagin, D. S. 1998. Criminal deterrence research: A review of the evidence and a research agenda for the outset of the 21st century. In M. Tonry, ed., *Crime and Justice: An Annual Review of Research.* Chicago: University of Chicago Press, 1–42.

National Institute of Justice. 2003. *Preliminary Data on Drug Use & Related Matters Among Adult Arrestees & Juvenile Detainees 2002.* Washington, DC: U.S. Department of Justice.

ONDCP. 2001. What America's users spend on illicit drugs 1988–2000. Executive Office of the President, Washington, DC.

ONDCP. 2009. Annual Report Arrestee Drug Abuse Monitoring Program II. Executive Office of the President, Washington, DC. *ADAM* II: 2009.

Paoli, L., V. Greenfield, and P. Reuter. 2009. *The World Heroin Market: Can Supply Be Reduced.* New York: Oxford University Press.

Rasmussen, D., and B. Benson 1994. *The Economic Anatomy of a Drug War: Criminal Justice in the Commons*. Lanham, MD: Rowman and Littlefield.

Reuter, P. 1983. *Disorganized Crime: The Economics of the Visible Hand*. Cambridge: MIT Press.

Reuter, P., and M. A. R. Kleiman. 1986. Risks and prices: An economic analysis of drug enforcement. In M. Tonry and N. Morris, eds., *Crime and Justice: An Annual Review of Research*, vol. 7. Chicago: University of Chicago Press, 289–340.

Reuter, P., R. MacCoun, and P. Murphy. 1990. *Money from Crime: A Study of the Economics of Drug Dealing in Washington, D.C.* Santa Monica: RAND.

Reuter, P., and A. Stevens. 2007. *An Analysis of U.K. Drug Policy*. London: UK Drug Policy Commission.

Rigter, H. 2006. What drug policies cost: Drug policy spending in the Netherlands in 2003. *Addiction (Abingdon, England)* 101:323–329.

Riley, K .J. 1997. *Crack Powder Cocaine and Heroin: Drug Purchase and Use Patterns in Six U.S. Cities*. Washington, DC: National Institute of Justice and Office of National Drug Control Policy.

Rydell, C. P., and S. S. Everingham. 1994. *Controlling Cocaine*. Santa Monica, CA: RAND Corporation.

Sevigny, E., and J. P. Caulkins. 2004. Kingpins or mules? An analysis of drug offenders incarcerated in federal and state prisons. *Criminology and Public Policy* 3 (3): 401–34.

Strumpf, K. 2003. Illegal sport bookmakers. Mimeo. University of North Carolina.

Thoumi, F. 2003. *Illegal Drugs, Economy and Society in the Andes*. Washington, DC: Woodrow Wilson Center.

UNODC. 2005. *World Drug Report 2004*. Vienna: United Nations Office on Drugs and Crime.

Walsh, J. 2004. Fuzzy logic: Why the White House drug control budget doesn't add up. *Federation of American Scientists Drug Policy Analysis Bulletin*.

Wendel, T., and R. Curtis. 2000. The heraldry of heroin: "Dope stamps" and the dynamics of drug markets in New York City. *Journal of Drug Issues* 30 (2): 225–60.

Zinberg, N. 1984. *Drug, Set and Setting*. New Haven: Yale University Press.

3 The Hidden Financial Flows of Organized Crime: A Literature Review and Some Preliminary Empirical Results

Friedrich Schneider

3.1 Introduction

Until 2009 the economic development of the world economy and globalization made enormous gains in economic well-being possible, but this development has always contained risks, too. One of them is transnational or organized crime, which rose remarkably in the last twenty years.[1] Among others this raises the following two questions: (1) How is organized crime financed, and what do we know about this financing? (2) Which economic implications does organized crime have? In this chapter question 2 will be very briefly answered, the main focus lies on providing a much more detailed answer on the financing of organized crime—question 1. Moreover a detailed analysis of the finances of organized crime organizations is crucial to reduce their financial possibilities, so that the basis of their operations is at least limited. Such an analysis is also a goal of this chapter.

The chapter is structured as follows: Section 3.2 provides an literature review at about the kinds of organized crime financing. Section 3.3 shows the infiltration of the organized crime and the Hawala banking system. In section 3.4 some conclusions and policy recommendations are drawn.

3.2 The Kinds of Organized Crime Financing: A Preliminary Literature Review

The literature review of this section is supposed to meet the two objectives: to widen the knowledge of this subject and the understanding of the main issues under debate and to focus on the literature closely related to the research topic. The body of literature on organized crime financing, and their mechanisms, is diverse and quite often very descriptive; hence I summarize only some that, in my opinion, are important contributions. But while my selection is subjective, I think most areas are covered. The literature review cannot be separated from the analysis of the finances of the terrorist organization because they often work closely together.[2] Hence I start with common aspects and then consider differences.

3.2.1 Some Common Aspects of Transnational Crime and Terrorist Groups Financing

Similarities between transnational crime and terrorist groups are fully described by Schneider (2008a, b, 2009), Sanderson (2004); Gilmore (2004), Shelley (2005), Wilkinson (2005), Makarenko (2002, 2003a, b, c), and Koh (2006):

1. Both are generally rational actors.
2. Both use extreme violence and the threat of reprisals.
3. Both use kidnappings, assassinations, and extortion.
4. Both operate secretly, though at times publicly in friendly territory.
5. Both defy the state and the rule of law, except when there is state sponsorship.

According to Masciandaro (2004, 2005, 2006), Picarelli (2006), Shelley (2005), and Yepes (2008) the issues of transnational crime, money laundering, and the financing of terrorism have the following common aspects:

1. Wire transfers or electronic payment systems are used to move money through multiple jurisdictions.
2. A variety of criminal activities are engaged like traffickers and other criminal syndicates.

However, the line is now becoming less defined, since terrorists often resort to crime and cooperate with criminals in generating money, obtaining arms and explosives. According to Makarenko (2003a, b) criminals are likely to use terrorism tactics and random violence in pursuits of revenues:

1. drug, arms, and human trafficking,[3] trading in precious stones (demands), and other commodities;
2. smuggled cash, cigarettes, and other addictive goods;
3. counterfeit goods; and
4. kidnapping.

Both groups benefit from shell companies and offshore bank facilities. Money laundering experts,[4] for instance, argue that both groups use a technique known as a "starburst": a deposit of dirty money is made in a bank with standing instructions to wire it in small random fragments to hundreds of other bank accounts around the world, in both onshore and offshore financial centers. Tracking down the money becomes very difficult, since getting legal permission to pursue bank accounts in multiple jurisdictions can take years. Napoleoni (2005, p. 33) argues, "You build a long chain of representative offices at the end of which there is a shell company registered offshore, and you are lucky if you get to the end of the chain. Financial investigations often run into a blind alley always through, somewhere, in a tiny offshore office."

3.2.2 The Main Differences between Organized Crime and Terrorist Groups' Financing

It is obvious that there are many differences between organized crime and terrorist groups with respect to financing. To some extend it is possible to make a distinction in the roots and operational characteristics between terrorist financing and money laundering by organized (transnational) criminals.

Terrorist Financing A number of scholars (Napoleoni, Krueger, Yepes) explain terrorism through religion, development of sociopolitical causes, and even the economy is sometimes important. Typical operational characteristics of terrorist groups and their financing are:

1. low costs/low technology made possible some recent attacks with a great impact on human lives, on nations, and on economies (e.g., 9/11 New York, Madrid, London, and Mumbai);
2. flexible and decentralized organizations with independent decisions and actions;
3. common ideology with indiscriminate targets (no purpose related to profit);
4. financial means are needed to plan and execute (future) terrorist attacks; there is only a limited need to hide assets; and
5. self-financing with possible criminal activities but also obtaining money from legal sources (e.g., donations and charity organizations).

Terrorists use different sources of money, depending on their motivations, their mode of operations, and the resistance they face from law enforcement. Quite often the money starts off clean, becoming "dirty" only when the terrorist crime is committed later on. Hence terrorist enterprises use clean money to commit crimes. The money sometimes consists of legally obtained resources that are used for a limited period of time and of smaller amounts of money to prepare attacks.

Organized (Transnational) Crime Turnover and Money Laundering

Dirty money is earned through various criminal activities, like drug, weapon, and human trafficking.[5] How much illicit crime money in all its forms can be observed? Baker (2005) estimates the illicit money to range between 1.0 and 1.6 trillion USD a year. This estimate has been adopted by the World Bank. Moreover Baker estimates that half—500 to 800 USD a year—comes out of developing and transitional economies. These are countries that often have the weakest legal and administrative structures, the largest criminal gangs of drug dealers, and, far too often, economic and political elites who want to take their money out by any means possible.

In table 3.1 the global flows from illicit activities worldwide are shown. In cross-border illicit financial flows, the proceeds of bribery and theft are the smallest, at only perhaps 3 percent of the global total. Criminally generated funds account for some 30 to 35 percent of the

Table 3.1
Global flows from illicit activities worldwide, 2000 to 2001

Global flows	Low (billion USD)	Percent of GDP	High (billion USD)	Percent of GDP
Drugs	120	11%	200	12.5%
Counterfeit goods	80	7.5%	120	7.5%
Counterfeit currency	3	0.2%	3	0.2%
Human trafficking	12	1.1%	15	0.9%
Illegal arms trade	6	2.0%	10	0.6%
Smuggling	60	5.6%	100	6.3%
Racketeering	50	4.7%	100	6.3%
Crime subtotal	*331*	*31.2%*	*549*	*34.3%*
Mispricing	200	18.9%	250	15.6%
Abusive transfer pricing	300	28.3%	500	31.2%
Fake transactions	200	18.9%	250	15.6%
Commercial subtotal	*700*	*66.0%*	*1,000*	*62.5%*
Corruption	*30*	*2.8%*	*50*	*5.1%*
Grand total	*1,061*	*100.0%*	*1,599*	*100.0%*

Source: Baker (2005).

global total. Commercially tax evading money, driven in particular by abusive transfer pricing and faked transactions as well as mispricing is by far the largest component, at some 60 to 65 percent of the global total.

In the next step the main characteristic of money laundering is to make dirty money appear legal (compare Walker 1999, 2000, 2004, 2007). There are numerous methods of money laundering; in table 3.2 the twelve most important methods are shown. Which of these methods is mostly used depends on the crime activity and on the specific institutional arrangements in a country where the criminal money is "earned." For example, in the drug business method 8, business ownership, is quite often used. In the drug business and in big cities smaller amounts of cash are earned by drug dealers in a lot of different spaces, which they infiltrate into cash-intensive operations such as restaurants which are especially well suited for money laundering purposes. But also cash deposits (the so-called smurfing method) or illegal gambling is quite often used. Obviously, as these methods clearly show, there are a number of ways to launder money. It might be more efficient to reduce the crime activities then to fight against these methods.

Schneider (2008a, b) estimates with the help of the MIMIC estimation procedure that money laundering from organized transnational crime has increased form 273 billion USD (1.33 percent of official GDP) in 1995 to 603 billion USD (or 1.74 percent of the official GDP) in 2006 for twenty OECD countries (Australia, Austria, Belgium, Canada, Denmark, Germany, Finland, France, Greece, Great Britain, Ireland, Italy, Japan, Netherlands, New Zealand, Norway, Portugal, Switzerland, Spain, and the United States). On a worldwide basis in 2006, 600 billion USD are estimated to be laundered coming only from the drug (crime) business.

Unger (2007) estimates the amount of laundered money and their top twenty destinations, which is shown in table 3.3 over the time span 1997 to 2000. Here two estimates are presented, one by Walker (1999, 2007) and one by the IMF. The Walker figure is with 2.850 billion USD much larger then the IMF figure with 1.500 billion USD (both figures are for the year 2005). Walker's figures have been criticized as much too high, which was one reason why the IMF estimates have been chosen. Table 3.3 clearly shows that two-thirds of worldwide money laundering was sent to the top twenty countries listed. One should realize that most of these countries are very established, well developed, and have sizable legal/official economies. What is also amazing

Table 3.2
Methods of money laundering

1	Wire transfers or electronic banking	Primary tool of money launderers to move funds around in the banking system. These moves can conceal the illicit origins of the funds or just place the money where the launderers need them. Often the funds go through several banks and even different jurisdictions.
2	Cash deposits	Money launderers need to deposit cash advances to bank accounts prior to wire transfers. Due to anti–money-laundering regulations they often "structure" the payments (i.e., break down large to smaller amounts). This is also called "smurfing."
3	Informal value transfer systems (IVTS)	Money launderers need not rely on the banking sector, other transfer providers, such as the *hawala* or *hindi* are readily available to undertake fund transfers. These systems consist of shops (mainly selling groceries, phone cards, or other similar items) that are also involved in transfer services. IVTSs enable international fund transfers, as these shops are present in several jurisdictions.
4	Cash smuggling	Money launderers might mail, Fedex, or simply carry cash with them from one region to another, or even to different jurisdictions.
5	Gambling	Casinos, horse races, and lotteries are ways of legalizing funds. The money launderer can buy (for "dirty" cash) winning tickets—or in the case of casinos chips—and redeem the tickets or the chips in a "clean" bank check. Afterward the check can be easily deposited in the banking sector.
6	Insurance policies	Money launderers purchase single premium insurance (with "dirty" cash), redeem early (and pay some penalty) in order to receive clean checks to deposit. Longer term premium payments might make laundering even harder to detect.
7	Securities	Usually used to facilitate fund transfers, where underlying security deals provide cover (and legitimate looking reason) for transfers.
8	Business ownership	Money might be laundered through legitimate businesses, where laundering funds can be added to legitimate revenues. Cash-intensive operations, such as restaurants, are especially well suited for laundering.
9	Shell corporations	Money launderers might create companies exclusively to provide cover for fund moves without legitimate business activities.
10	Purchases	Real estate or any durable good purchases can be used to launder monies. Typically the item is bought for cash and resold for clean monies, like bank checks.
11	Credit card advance payment	Money launderers pay money in advance with "dirty" money, and receive clean checks on the balance from the bank
12	ATM operations	Banks might allow other firms to operate their ATMs (i.e., to maintain and fill them with cash). Money launderers fill ATMs with "dirty" cash, and receive clean checks (for the cash withdrawn) from the bank.

Source: Unger (2007, pp.195–96).

Table 3.3
Amount of laundered money and top twenty destinations of laundered money, 2005

Rank	Destination	Percent of worldwide money laundering	Walker estimate 2.85 trillion, amount in billion USD	IMF estimate of 1.5 trillion worldwide, amount in billion USD
1	United States	18.9%	538,145	283,500
2	Cayman Islands	4.9%	138,329	73,500
3	Russia	4.2%	120,493	63,000
4	Italy	3.7%	105,688	55,500
5	China	3.3%	94,726	49,500
6	Romania	3.1%	89,595	46,500
7	Canada	3.0%	85,444	45,000
8	Vatican City	2.8%	80,596	42,000
9	Luxembourg	2.8%	78,468	42,000
10	France	2.4%	68,471	36,000
11	Bahamas	2.3%	66,398	34,500
12	Germany	2.2%	61,315	33,000
13	Switzerland	2.1%	58,993	31,500
14	Bermuda	1.9%	52,887	28,500
15	Netherlands	1.7%	49,591	25,500
16	Liechtenstein	1.7%	48,949	25,500
17	Austria	1.7%	48,376	25,500
18	Hong Kong	1.6%	44,519	24,000
19	United Kingdom	1.6%	44,478	24,000
20	Spain	1.2%	35,461	18,000
	SUM	67.1%	1,910,922	1,006,500

Source: Unger (2007, p. 80).

is that there are only a few microstate offshore countries (OFCS) and tax havens among them (Cayman Islands, Vatican City, Bermuda, and Liechtenstein).[6] The majority of countries that attract money laundering flows are economic prepotencies at not tiny unimportant countries. The United States has the largest worldwide share of money laundering of almost 19 percent, followed by the Cayman Islands (4.9 percent), Russia (4.2 percent), Italy (3.7 percent), but also smaller countries like Switzerland (2.1 percent of worldwide money laundering), Liechtenstein (1.7 percent), and Austria (1.7 percent) are also quite attractive. If one takes the lower IMF value for Austria, Switzerland, and in the United Kingdom, roughly 5.5 percent of the total amount is laundered, which comes close to roughly 10 percent of official GDP of the three countries However, it should be stated that it is not clear whether this money is only laundered in these countries or stays in these countries. It might leave these countries when it was laundered. In general, as table 3.3 demonstrates, the amount of laundered money is important and two-thirds of that money is concentrated in twenty countries.

Bagella, Busato, and Argentiero (2009, p. 881) use a theoretical two-sector dynamic general equilibrium model to measure ML for the United States and the EU-15 macro areas over the sample 2000:01 to 2007:01 at a quarterly frequency. Their series are generated through a fully microfounded dynamic model, which is appropriately calibrated to replicate selected stochastic properties of the two economies. Their model (and the analysis) has a short-run perspective, and for this reason, this chapter discusses the stochastic properties of the Hodrick–Prescott filtered series. Bagella et al. (2009, p. 881) got the following results: First the simulations show that ML accounts for approximately 19 percent of the GDP measured for the EU-15, while it accounts for 13 percent in the US economy, over the sample 2000:01 to 2007:04. Second, the simulated ML appears less volatile than the corresponding GDP. As regards the EU-15 macro area, the simulated statistics suggest that ML volatility is one-third of the GDP; for the US economy, the same statistics produce a figure of two-fifths. These estimates are certainly high, and unfortunately, no consistent check was done by Bagella et al. as to whether such figures are plausible.

From a global perspective for 2000, the IMF (2003, 2001) as well as the World Bank estimate that 2 to 4 percent of the world GDP stem from illicit (criminal) sources. Agarwal and Agarwal (2006) estimate from economic intelligence units, that global money laundering amounts to more than 2.0 to 2.5 trillion USD annually or about 5 to 6 percent of World GDP in 2006 (4,444 trillion USD in 2006) to be contrasted against an observed figure of 500 billion to one trillion USD in 2004 from the same authors (Agarwal and Agarwal 2004). Recent IMF estimates on money laundering by the drug traffickers, who "introduce" the proceeds gained through the selling of drugs into the legitimate financial market, amount to 600 billion USD annually. The IDB (2004) reaches the conclusion that for Latin America a rough estimate appears to be somewhere between 2.5 and 6.3 percent of annual GDP of Latin American countries.

In their latest study again Walker and Unger (2009, p. 821) undertake an attempt, measuring global money laundering and the proceeds of transnational crime that are pumped through the financial system worldwide. They criticize those methods such as case studies, proxy variables, or models for measuring the shadow economy all tend to under- or overestimate money laundering. They present a model, which is a gravity model, that makes it possible to estimate the flows of illicit funds from and to each jurisdiction in the world and worldwide. This "Walker model" was first developed in 1994, and used and updated recently. The authors show that it belongs to a group of gravity models that have recently become popular in international trade theory. Using triangulation, they demonstrate that the original Walker model estimates are compatible with recent findings on money laundering. Once the scale of money laundering is known, its macroeconomic effects and the impact of crime prevention, regulation, and law enforcement effects on money laundering and transnational crime can also be measured. Walker and Unger (2009, pp. 849–50) conclude, that their model still seems to be the most reliable and robust method to estimate global money laundering, and thereby the important effects of transnational crime on economic, social, and political institutions. Rightly they argue, that the attractiveness and distance indicator in the Walker model are a valid first approximation but are still quite ad hoc. A better microfoundation for the Walker model will be needed in the future. For this, the behavior of money launderers, and in particular what makes them send their money to a specific country, is important. Hence Walker and Unger (2009, p. 850) argue that an economics of crime microfoundation for the Walker model would mean that similarly to international trade theory, behavioral assumptions about money launderers have to be made. The gravity model must be the (reduced form) outcome of the launderers' rational calculus of sending their money to another country and possibly getting caught, but potentially making large profits.

3.2.3   The Sources of Organized Crime Financing

Drug Trafficking   According to Yepes (2008), in May 2002 a report called "Global Overview of Narcotics-Funded Terrorist and Other Extremist and Transnational Crime Groups" was launched, prepared by the Federal Research Division of the Library of Congress and the US Department of Defense. The report examined connections between extremist groups and narcotics trafficking in the following regions: in Latin America: the triborder region of Argentina, Brazil, and Paraguay, and also Colombia and Peru; in the Middle East: Lebanon; in southern

Europe: Albania and Macedonia; in Central Asia: Kyrgyzstan, Tajikistan, and Uzbekistan; and in East Asia: The Philippines.

Oil Smuggling   According to Johnson (2001) and Napoleoni (2005) another business is oil smuggling, where terror, criminal, and legitimate economies interact. Countries, where oil smuggling is a significant problem are Thailand, China, Russia, Cambodia, Iran, and Tanzania. In all these countries oil smuggling earns for themselves significant profits, a substantial portion of which enters the laundering cycle. Oil smuggling is also related to arms trade.

Arms/Diamonds Trafficking   Besides drugs trafficking, according to Levi and Gilmore (2002), Schneider (2004, 2008a, b, 2009), and Yepes (2008) arms trafficking and illegal diamonds trade are some of the most important illegal sources of funding of organized crime groups. The illicit arms trade demonstrates how comparatively easy it is to obtain false documentation accompanying arms shipments, especially end-user certificates. Inconsistent documentation requirements between states, and inefficient control in customs and port authorities in many states, have created an environment in which the illicit arms trade does not need to rely entirely on criminal activities:

1. When a state is involved in supplying arms to an embargoed state, payments often come in the form of commercial payments, such as "oil for arms" deals to avoid bank involvement.
2. When an arms broker supplies weapons to an embargoed state, banks are often used because shipments are usually paid for in the form of letters of credit of by the direct transfer of hard-currency funds. In this case money laundering becomes an important factor to ensure that the final arms destination is disguised. It is at this point that offshore banks play an important role because their facilities can ensure that any deposit or transfer is routed via several intermediary institutions; and deposits or transfers can be conducted in the name of a series of shell companies. Both of these techniques are used to hide the financial trail behind multiple administrative layers.
3. In situations where access to normal banking channels is very difficult (e.g., as with most non-state actors), the financing of arms deals often takes a different form, most often through commodity exchanges. According to Smillie et al. (2000), illicit arms transfers to Liberia

and Sierra Leone were often financed with diamonds and timber concessions.

3.3   The Infiltration of Organized Crime and the Informal Money Transfer (*Hawala*) System

3.3.1   The Infiltration of Organized Crime
In figure 3.1 the various channels of the infiltration of the organized crime groups are summarized. As the figure shows, in the use of financial resources, the financial means/flows stand on five pillars ranking from legal investments to classical criminal activities.

3.3.2   The Informal Money Transfer (*Hawala*) Banking System
Especially during the 1990s international concern grew over the "underground banking" and its abuse by serious offenders. Some academic works by Williams (2007), Savona (1997), and El-Quorchi et al. (2003) have explained how informal systems operate, including their risks. The informal value transfers systems (IVTS) changes from region to

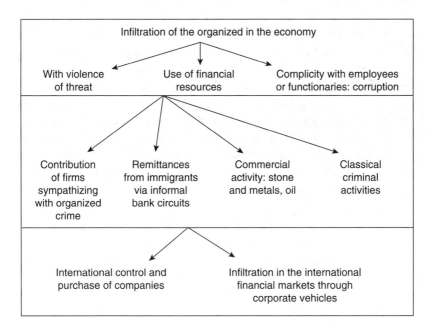

Figure 3.1
Infiltration of the organized crime in the economy. Source: Yepes (2008) with own remarks.

region (*hawala*, or door to door). Some scholars (Williams 2007; El-Quorchi et al. 2003) argue that *hawala* is vulnerable to criminal abuse, and like the other financial institutions, there is evidence that money derived from drug trafficking, illegal arms sales, body part trade, corruption, tax evasion, and all kinds of fraud have indeed moved through *hawala* networks.

Hawala banking still takes place up to now and there is some of literature (e.g., Bunt 2007) about the *hawala* banking system, where these authors point to the need for a regulation of the *hawala* system. As argued, another way to transfer criminal financial flows is the *hawala* banking. According to Bunt (2007), *hawala* bankers[7] are financial service providers who carry out financial transactions without a license and therefore without government control. They accept cash, checks, or other valuable goods (diamonds, gold) at one location and pay a corresponding sum in cash or other remuneration at another location. Unlike official banks, *hawala* bankers disregard the legal obligations concerning the identification of clients, record keeping, and the disclosure of unusual transactions, to which these official financial institutions are subject.

To summarize: Through the *hawala* system that forms an integral part of the informal black market economy, underground bankers ensure the transfer of money without having to move it physically or electronically. When a payment needs to be made overseas, the underground banker will get in touch with a courier (or more recently using email, fax, or phone) in that country informing him of the details of making the payment. If the recipient of the payment wishes to personally obtain the money, a code referring to the underground banker in the country of payment is given to the recipient. Such a system is almost untraceable because it leaves little if any paper trail. Transaction records are, if they are kept at all, being kept only until the money is delivered, at which time they are destroyed. Even when there is a paper or electronic record of sorts, it is often in dialects and languages that serve as de facto encryption system.

According to Fischer (2002, p.17), the annual turnover of the *hawala* banking system in the early 1970s was already 60 billion USD in the Arabic countries; for example, six million foreign laborers in Saudi Arabia, who are sending home 40 billion USD a year home, make substantial use of the "ethnic" *hawala* system. Fletcher and Baldwin (2002, p. 119) estimate with regard to Pakistan that 2.5 billion USD inherit the country in remittances via the *hawala* system in 2001; the amount of money in India´s Hindi system was 50 billion USD in 1971. Despite the growing competition by formal remittance services, the use of *hawala* banking has probably not declined. According to a recent estimate by the IMF, migrants (especially Asian) transfer 100 billion dollars per annum to family members and relations in their country of origin through the official financial system. In addition a similar amount of money is transferred in the form of goods, cash, and through underground bankers (IMF 2007).

According to Bunt (2007), there are at least two different perspectives on *hawala* banking. From the first point of view, *hawala* banking is regarded as a centuries-old institution that has not yet outlived its usefulness. Low-income workers and migrant workers, in particular, supposedly put more trust in *hawala* bankers than in formal banks. This viewpoint emphasizes the problem associated with subjecting *hawala* banking to the same rules as formal banks. Regulation either through registration or licensing is seen as ineffective because it will simply push the system further into the underground, further complicating the already problematic task of controlling *hawala* transactions (Razavy 2005, p. 292; Perkel 2004, pp. 210–11). Hence *hawala* banking might be the closest thing of a free market banking, without government regulation and it functioned well for centuries. One should clearly emphasize these advantages of *hawala* banking when criticizing it. From the opposite point of view, Bunt (2007) argues that *hawala* banking is described as "underground banking," a system that flies under the radar of modern supervision of financial transactions. Underground banking is considered a threat to the effectiveness of anti–money laundering measures and the fight against terrorist financing. To prevent underground bankers from becoming a safe haven for criminals and terrorists, they should be subject to the standard regulations regarding record keeping, disclosure of unusual transactions, and identification of clients.[8]

3.3.3 The Principal Sources of Organized Crime Financing

The sources of organized crime financing, which are channeled through formal and informal systems, come from a variety of origins, some criminal, some not. As discussed the most important are:

1. domestic (individual and corporate): black mail and corruption;
2. diaspora-migrant communities: contributions for protection;
3. high-level organized crime: fraud, illegal production and smuggling of drugs, kidnapping, armed robbery, trafficking in human beings; and

4. investments and legitimate business: money as used to acquire enterprises and engage in trade, with profits being used to finance terrorism.

3.4 Summary and Conclusions

In this chapter an attempt is made to review the literature of the finances of organized crime, the aspect of and to tackle the quite difficult topic of estimating the volume of the finances of organized crime. The chapter reaches the following two major results:

First, the necessity of money laundering is obvious as a great number of illegal (criminal) transactions are done by cash. Hence this amount of cash from criminal activities must be laundered in order to have some "legal" profit, to do some investment or consumption, in the legal world. Also first estimates are shown.

Second, to get a figure of the extent and development of the amount of the financial means of organized crime over time is even more difficult. This chapter collects most of the available findings and shows that money laundering from organized crime has increased from 1995 273 billion USD (or 1.33 percent of official GDP) to 603 billion USD (or 1.74 percent of official GDP) in 2006 for twenty OECD countries (Australia, Austria, Belgium, Canada, Denmark, Germany, Finland, France, Greece, Great Britain, Ireland, Italy, Japan, Netherlands, New Zealand, Norway, Portugal, Switzerland, Spain, and the United States). On a worldwide basis in 2006, 600 billion USD were estimated to be laundered coming only from the total drug (crime) business. These figures are very preliminary with a large error but give a clear indication how important money laundering and the turnover of organized crime nowadays is.

From these preliminary results I draw the following three conclusions:

• The revenues of organized crime are scientifically extremely difficult to tackle. Organized crime is defined differently in almost every country, the measures taken against it are different and vary from country to country, and it is not so all clear what really money laundering from the revenues of organized crime are.

• To fight against organized crime is extremely difficult, as there are no efficient and powerful international organizations that can effectively fight against organized crime.

• This chapter should be seen as a first start/attempt to shed some light on the gray area of the revenues of organized crime and to provide some better empirical bases.

Notes

1. For an example, see Walker and Unger (2009). In Schneider (2010) similar emperical findings and results are published.

2. Compare Schneider (2008a, b, 2009), Makarenko (2002, 2003a, b, c), Koh (2006), and Masciandaro (2004).

3. Makarenko (2003a, p. 66) writes: "The most common criminal activity terrorist groups have been involved in is the illicit drug trade. Since the 1970s groups such as FARC, Basque Fatherland and Liberty (Euzkadi Ta Askatasuna—ETA), the Kurdistan Workers Party (Partiya Karkaren Kurdistan—PKK) and Sendero Luminoso have all been linked to the drug trade by well-documented evidence. Since the early 1990s additional groups such as Hizbullah and the IMU have also realized the financial utility of participating in the illicit drugs trade. It is alleged that Hizbullah continues to protect heroin and cocaine laboratories in the Bekaa Valley; and evidence strongly indicated that the IMU—prior to the Afghan campaign—controlled drug trafficking routes into Central Asia from northern Afghanistan."

4. See Koh (2006), Schneider (2004, 2008a, b, 2009), and Masciandaro (2004).

5. For a detailed analysis, see Schneider (2008a, b, 2009), Schneider and Windischbauer (2008), Schneider, Dreer, and Riegler (2006), and Takats (2007).

6. Compare also Masciandaro (2005, 2006), Zdanowicz (2009), Truman and Reuter (2004), and Walker and Unger (2009).

7. Several traditional terms, like *hundi* (India) and *fei-ch'ein* (China) remind one of the fact that *hawala* banking came up independently in different parts of the world. At present, a range of other terms is used to refer to the same phenomenon, such as "informal banking," "underground banking," "ethnic banking," or "informal value transfer system."

8. Compare also Richard (2005) and Rider (2004).

References

Agarwal, J. D., and A. Agarwal. 2004. Globalization and international capital flows. *Finance India* 19 (1): 65–99.

Agarwal, J. D., and A. Agarwal 2006. Money laundering: New forms of crime, and victimization. Paper presented at the National Workshop on New Forms of Crime. Victimization, Department of Criminology, University of Madras, India.

2009. Bagella, M., F. Busato, and A. Argentiero. 2009. Money laundering in a microfounded dynamic model: Simulations for the U.S. and the EU-15 economies. *Review of Law and Economics* 5 (2): 879–902.

Baker, R. W. 2005. *Capitalism's Athilles Heel: Dirty Money and How to Renew the Free-Market System*. Hoboken, NJ: Wiley.

Bunt, H. van D. 2007. The relation between organized crime and informal markets: The role of *hawala* bankers in the transfer of proceeds from organized crime. Discussion paper. CRIMPREV, Gant University, Gant, Belgium.

El Quorchi, M., et al. 2003. *Informal Funds Transfer Systems: an Analysis of the Informal Hawala System*, 1–53. Washington, DC: International Monetary Fund.

Fischer, H. S. 2002. Hawala—What is it and how to emasculate it. California, Beverly Hills, Study.

Fletcher, N., and J. Baldwin. 2002. Money laundery counter measures with primary focus upon terrorism and the U.S. Patriot Act 2001. *Journal of Money Laundering Control* 6 (2): 105–36.

Gilmore, W. C. 2004. *Dirty Money: The Evolution of International Measures to Counter Money Laundering and the Financing of Terrorism.* Strasbourg: Council of Europe.

IDB. 2004. A first estimation of illicit flows in Latin America. Report. Washington, DC.

IMF. 2001. Financial system abuse, financial crime and money laundering. IMF Report. Monetary and Exchange Affairs and Policy Department, Washington, DC.

IMF. 2003. Money laundering: New facts. IMF Study. Washington, DC.

Johnson, J. 2001. In pursuit of dirty money: Identifying weaknesses in the global financial system. *Journal of Money Laundering Control* 5 (2):122–33.

Koh, J.-M. 2006. *Suppressing Terrorist Financing and Money Laundering.* Berlin: Springer.

Levi, M., and W. Gilmore. 2002. Terrorist finance, money laundering and the rise of mutual evaluation: A new paradigm for crime control. In *Financing Terrorism.* Dordreicht: Kluwer Academic, 87–115.

Makarenko, T. 2002. A model of terrorist-criminal relations. Jane's Intelligence Review 11 (2): 101–18.

Makarenko, T. 2003a. Tracing the dynamics of the illicit arms trade. Jane's Intelligence Review 12 (2): 223–41.

Makarenko, T. 2003b. A model of terrorist-criminal relations. Janes's Intelligence Review 12 (4): 341–49.

Makarenko, T. 2003c. Transnational terror and organized crime: Blurring the lines. *Sais Review* 24 (1): 49–61.

Masciandaro, D. 2004. *Global Financial Crime: Terrorism, Money Laundering and Off Shore Centres.* Burlington, VT: Ashgate.

Masciandaro, D. 2005. Financial supervisory unification and financial intelligence units. *Journal of Money Laundering Control* 8 (4): 354–71.

Masciandaro, D. 2006. Offshore financial centres and international soft laws: Explaining the regulation gap. *Second Annual Conference: Società Italiana di Diritto ed Economia*, Rome, 1–49.

Napoleoni, L. 2005. *Terror Incorporated: Tracing the Dollars behind the Terror Networks.* New York: Seven Stories Press.

Perkel, W. 2004. Money laundering and terrorism: Informal value transfer systems. *American Criminal Law Review* 41 (2): 183–211.

Picarelli, J. 2006. The turbulent nexus of transnational organised crime and terrorism: A theory of malevolent international relations. *Global Crime* 7 (1): 1–24.

Razavy, M. 2005. Hawala: An underground haven for terrorist of social phenomenon? *Crime, Law, and Social Change* 44 (2): 277–99.

Richard, A. C. 2005. *Fighting Terrorist Financing: Transatlantic Cooperation and International Institutions*. Baltimore: Johns Hopkins University Press.

Rider, B. 2004. The war on terror and crime and the offshore centres. In D. Masciandaro, ed., *Global Financial Crime: Terrorism, Money Laundering and Offshore Centres*. Aldershot, UK: Ashgate, 61–95.

Sanderson, T. M. 2004. Transnational terror and organized crime: Blurring the lines. *Sais Review* 24 (1): 49–61.

Savona, E. U., and ISPAC. 1997. *Responding to Money Laundering: International Perspectives*. Amsterdam: Harwood Academic.

Schneider, F. 2004. The financial flows of Islamic terrorism. In D. Masciandaro, ed., *Global Financial Crime: Terrorism, Money Laundering and Offshore Centres*. Aldershot, UK: Ashgate, 97–126.

Schneider, F. 2008a. Turnover of organized crime and money laundering: Some preliminary empirical findings. Discussion paper. Department of Economics, University of Linz.

Schneider, F. 2008b. Money laundering from revenues from organized crime: Some preliminary empirical findings. Revised version of a paper presented at the Conference "Illicit Trade and Globalization," CES-ifo Venice Summer Workshop, Venice National University, San Servolo, July 14–15, 2008.

Schneider, F. 2009. Die Finanzströme von Organisierter Kriminalität und Terrorismus: Was wissen wir (nicht)? *Vierteljahreshefte zur Wirtschaftsforschung* 78 (4): 73–87.

Schneider, F. 2010. Turnover of organized crime and money laundering: Some preliminary emperical findings. *Public Choice* 144 (3–4): 473–86.

Schneider, F., E. Dreer, and W. Riegler. 2006. *Geldwäsche: Formen, Akteure, Größenordnung— Warum die Politik machtlos ist*. Wiesbaden: Gabler.

Schneider, F., and U. Windischbauer. 2008. Money laundering: Some facts. *European Journal of Law and Economics* 26 (4): 387–404.

Shelley, L. 2005. The nexus between terrorism and organized crime. In *Confronting Terrorism Financing*. Lanham, MD: University Press of America, 29–33.

Smillie, D., et al. 2000. *The Heart of the Matter: Sierra Leone, Diamonds and Human Security*. Ontario: Partnership Africa.

Takats, Ilöd. 2007. A theory of "crying wolf": The economics of money laundering enforcement. Paper presented at the *Conference* "Tackling Money Laundering," University of Utrecht, November 2–3, 2007.

Truman, E. M., and P. Reuter 2004. Chasing dirty money: Progress on anti-money laundering. Institute for International Economics, Washington, DC.

Unger, B. 2007. *The Scale and Impacts of Money Laundering*. Cheltenham, UK: Edward Elgar.

Walker, J. 1999. How big is global money laundering? *Journal of Money Laundering Control* 3 (1): 64–85.

Walker, J. 2000. Money laundering: Quantifying international patterns. *Australian Social Monitor* 2 (6): 139–47.

Walker, J.. 2004. *A Very Temptative Exploration of the Relationship between Shadow Economy and the Production and Transit of Illicit Drugs*. New York: UNODC.

Walker, J. 2007. Measuring global money laundering. Paper presented at the conference "Tackling Money Laundering," University of Utrecht.

Walker, J., and B. Unger. 2009. Measuring global money laundering: The Walker gravity model. *Review of Law and Economics* 5 (2): 821–53. doi:10.2202/1555-5879.1418.

Wilkinson, P. 2005. International terrorism: The changing threat and the EU's response. *Cahier de Chaillot* (84): 81–89.

Williams, P. 2007. Warming indicators and terrorist finances. In P. Williams, ed., *Terrorism Financing and State Responses: A Comparative Perspective*. Stanford: Stanford University Press.

Yepes, V. 2008. International cooperation in the fight against terrorist financing. Dissertation. Universitat de Barcelona.

Zdanowicz, J. 2009. Trade-based money laundering and terrorist financing. *Review of Law and Economics* 5 (2): 854–78.

4 Gotcha! A Profile of Smuggling in International Trade

Helge Berger and Volker Nitsch

4.1 Introduction

In principle, international trade statistics should match so that a country's exports to a particular partner are identical to the partner's recorded imports from that supplier. In practice, however, these numbers differ, for various reasons. For instance, a major source of discrepancy is the conceptual difference in valuation. Exporting countries report the value of goods at the initial point of departure (FOB), while import values refer to the value at the point of final destination, thereby including the costs of freight and insurance (CIF). As a result the CIF/FOB ratio has been frequently used in the literature as a measure of transportation costs. Limão and Venables (2001) provide a recent application of this approach; see Hummels and Lugovskyy (2006) for a detailed critique.

Apart from the different treatment of shipping costs, however, there are also other methodological difficulties when exploring matched partner trade statistics.[1] For instance, the correct identification of the source or destination country might be a problem. When the country of final destination is not known at the time of exportation, the exporter declares the country of last shipment; the country of final destination, in contrast, classifies its imports by country of origin. Another potential issue of importance is timing. Since there are often notable time lags between the departure and arrival of a shipment (e.g., due to long-distance sea cargo, a delay in customs declaration, or temporary storage in a warehouse), trade could be recorded in different calendar years. More important, statistical offices in the source and destination country may value goods at different prices and/or exchange rates. Finally, recorded trade on the commodity level may differ due to the omission of individual transactions in one of the partner countries (e.g., because of varying trade thresholds across countries), the exclusion of certain product groups in a country's trade statistics (e.g., military material or repair trade), or differences in commodity classification (e.g., a regrouping of a transaction into chapter 99 for reasons of confidentiality). In view of all these difficulties, the European Union, though aiming to reduce the declaration burden on businesses, still refrains from using mirror (single-flow) trade statistics.[2]

Most recently Fisman and Wei (2009) have emphasized another possible explanation for the observed differences in matched partner trade statistics. They argue that the gap between exports and imports may (partly) reflect systematic (criminal) behavior by traders. In particular, they argue that for products with sharp export restrictions in the source country and no barriers to import in the destination country, traders have a strong incentive to underreport exports (i.e., to smuggle the good out of the country), while properly declaring imports (because of no constraints for entry, in combination with the risk of seizure when there is false declaration). Analyzing trade gaps for a product category that is likely to display those characteristics, antiques of an age exceeding one hundred years (Harmonized System [HS] product code 9706), Fisman and Wei (2009) find that underreporting is indeed strongest for countries for which survey-based measures indicate a high level of corruption, and thus ignorance of legal rules and procedures (also in trade) may be relatively easy. Moreover they find no such association for a product category with no (or less strict) restrictions for exportation, such as toys, scale models, puzzles, and parts (HS code 9503), which appears reassuring.

In this chapter, we examine the discrepancies in pairwise trade statistics for a much broader set of product categories. In particular, we aim to identify countries that systematically underreport export activities in international trade statistics and thus apparently suffer strongly from smuggling. Further we explore differences in trade gaps across individual product categories. This allows analyzing, for instance, whether there are products other than cultural objects that are prone to illicit trade. In sum, we develop a profile of smuggling that identifies both major source countries and important product categories for smuggling.

To preview our results, we find that pairwise discrepancies in official trade statistics are highly correlated across both countries and products. Moreover country-specific trade gaps are strongly associated with the level of corruption, especially in the source country. Also product-specific trade gaps vary systematically with the level of protection in the destination country. Taken together, these findings suggest that at least part of the discrepancy in international trade figures is due to smuggling.[3]

The remainder of the chapter is organized as follows: Section 4.2 briefly reviews the relevant literature on misreporting in trade. In section 4.3 we then describe our methodology and the data, followed by a presentation in section 4.4 of the empirical results. Section 4.5 summarizes our findings and concludes.

4.2 Misinvoicing in Trade

The finding that official trade statistics may suffer from misreporting and faked declarations is a well-known fact, not only to statisticians of international trade. Bhagwati (1964, 1967) provides an early economic discussion of incentives for misinvoicing in trade; Bhagwati and Hansen (1973) develop a trade model to examine the welfare effects of smuggling. Also there are a number of papers that focus on regional experiences in the accuracy of trade statistics. Deardorff and Stolper (1990), among others, examine illegal trade in Africa; see also Yeats (1990). Baldwin (2006, pp. 57–61) provides an extensive discussion of problems in the collection of trade data in Europe, including a detailed description of fraudulent trade activities by criminals.

While Fisman and Wei (2009) focus on the strongest reason for misreporting exports, an outright export embargo, there are other incentives for underinvoicing exports or smuggling goods out of the country. A first group of reasons covers export restrictions in general. Apart from the prohibition of exports, there may be other, less strict hindrances to sales abroad, such as export taxes, export quotas, and various regulatory hurdles. Misdescription or misdeclaration of cargo is an obvious solution to circumvent these trade restrictions.

Another set of reasons focuses on incentives to hide export sales. For instance, underreporting of exports allows firms to acquire foreign exchange that is not disclosed to national authorities; the foreign currency can then be freely used by exporters without complying with any controls and regulations (e.g., a potential option may be the sale of foreign currency in the parallel exchange rate market). Authorities further may use information on firms' export activities to infer on their production. As a result firms that seek to hide output (e.g., to evade domestic taxes) will automatically also seek to hide exports. Dabla-Norris, Gradstein, and Inchauste (2008) provide a description of informal activities by firms.

Most important for our purposes, a number of papers have already shown that reporting incentives may have measurable effects on aggregate trade figures. Celasun and Rodrik (1989) argue that a sizable share of the increase in Turkish exports after 1980 is due to a change in invoicing practices of domestic entrepreneurs (in order to take advantage of generous export subsidies). Baldwin (2006) notes that in the early 2000s, the effect of VAT fraud on trade was so large that the United Kingdom had to restate its national accounts. More generally, McDonald (1985) provides several case studies on the size of trade data discrepancies for individual countries.

4.3   Methodology and Data

Our main measure of interest is the difference in recorded trade flows between the exporting and the importing country. Following Fisman and Wei (2009), we define the reporting gap in official trade statistics as:

$$\text{Gap}^k_{ijt} = \ln(1 + \text{Imports}^k_{jit}) - \ln(1 + \text{Exports}^k_{ijt}), \tag{4.1}$$

where Imports^k_{jit} denotes country j's imports of product k from country i in year t and Exports denotes the corresponding exports from i to j as recorded in the source country.

In our empirical analysis we aim to explain the observed variation in trade gaps. Fisman and Wei (2009) highlight that for some product categories, discrepancies in trade statistics reflect extra-legal activities and thus are associated with measures of corruption; we examine the effect of various determinants on trade gaps for all types of products. In particular, we apply the following very general regression framework:

$$\text{Gap}^k_{ijt} = \alpha + \beta X_{it} + \gamma M_{jt} + \delta P_{ijt} + \phi Z^k_t + \varepsilon^k_{ijt}, \tag{4.2}$$

where X_{it} is a vector of exporter-specific variables that may be correlated with the reporting gap (such as, for instance, corruption), M_{jt} is a corresponding set of importer-specific attributes, P_{ijt} collects various pair-specific variables (e.g., bilateral distance as a proxy for transportation costs), Z is a set of product-specific controls (e.g., including the tariff rate in the destination country), and ε is a well-behaved residual.

We estimate this equation using conventional OLS with year effects, computing standard errors that are robust to clustering.

Relevant country-specific attributes we consider include the level of corruption, the level of economic development, country size, and land-lockedness. Fisman and Wei (2009) argue that smuggling is more prevalent in countries with corrupt bureaucracies. More specifically, they argue that hiding exports should be easier in a country where it is customary to bribe government officials than in countries where export controls are strictly enforced. As a result corruption in the source country should be associated with a larger underreporting of exports, thereby widening trade gaps in pairwise trade statistics. Similarly, though working in the opposite direction (i.e., reducing the trade gap), the incentive to properly declare imports is lower when it is relatively easy to persuade customs officials in the destination country to disregard the law. In addition smuggling may be related to a country's level of economic development. Poor countries often have a less effective customs administration; they also produce less reliable official statistics. Moreover low income may force people into illegal activities. The geographic size of a country may be another proxy for the effectiveness of border controls, since large countries may find it more difficult to enforce trade restrictions. To control for the effect of shipping costs on differences in matched partner trade statistics, we include a dummy variable for landlockedness. Most landlocked countries face a cost disadvantage in international trade, having to cope with the costs of overland transport to neighboring ports and the costs of crossing of at least one additional international border; see Radelet and Sachs (1998). In addition we include two country-pair specific measures of transportation costs that are standard in the "gravity" model of trade: the bilateral distance between the two trading partners, and a dummy variable for sharing a common land border. Finally, we enter some measures of product-specific characteristics, such as the applied tariff and the value-to-weight ratio. Low levels of trade protection possibly imply fewer incentives for misreporting; smuggling may be particularly attractive for products with high value-to-weight ratios.

Our data are mainly taken from standard sources. In line with previous work, we use the United Nations Comtrade database to obtain exports and imports data at the four-digit (HS) product level. The database contains detailed (annual) trade statistics reported by statistical authorities of close to 200 countries or territories and standardized by the UN Statistics Division; we examine the records of shipments to the five largest importing nations in the world (United States, Germany, China, United Kingdom, and Japan).[4] At the four-digit level, there are more than 1,200 product categories. We use the most recent commodity classification (HS-2002); the data are available for five years, covering the period from 2002 to 2006.

Our measure of corruption is taken from the World Bank's Worldwide Governance Indicators project; see Kaufmann, Kraay, and Mastruzzi (2007). This project combines various variables into an aggregate "control of corruption" score; the score lies between −2.5 and 2.5, with higher scores corresponding to better outcomes (i.e., a less corrupt bureaucracy). As a check, we also use the Corruption Perceptions Index from Transparency International; see http://www.transparency.org. Other data are mainly obtained from the World Bank's World Development Indicators and the CIA World Factbook. Average import tariffs at the four-digit level are provided by the UNCTAD/WTO International Trade Centre (and obtained from http://www.macmap.org). A data appendix describes the variables and sources in more detail.

4.4   Empirical Results

We begin by exploring the full sample of annual country pair-specific trade differences at the four-digit product level. For illustration, table 4.1 lists the five largest (percentage) discrepancies in bilateral trade by importer. Interestingly, a few empirical regularities already emerge from this rough tabulation. For instance, most experiences where recorded import values strongly exceed corresponding exports appear to be concentrated in a single product category, "petroleum oils, crude" (HS code 2709). As Yeats (1978) notes, this discrepancy is often due to problems in valuing petroleum, and the frequent diversion of petroleum exports from its original destination en route. For other product categories, in contrast, export values (despite disregarding shipment costs) are considerably larger than imports in mirror statistics; these categories include "other aircraft (e.g., helicopters, aeroplanes), spacecraft" (8802), "cruise ships, excursion boats, ferry-boats, cargo ships, barges, and similar vessels for the transport of persons or goods" (8901), and "gold (including gold plated with platinum)" (7108). A possible explanation is that, especially for bulky items with low-frequency trading, the time lag between exportation and importation may be of particular importance. Also, to the extent that there is any geographical pattern in misreporting, overinvoicing

Table 4.1
Largest trade gaps, 2004

Underreporting of exports

Importer

United States			Germany			China			United Kingdom			Japan		
Exporter	Product	Gap	Exporter	Product	Gap	Exporter	Product	Gap	Exporter	Product	Gap	Exporter	Product	Gap
SAU	2709	23.8	LBY	2709	22.0	PHL	8542	22.4	BWA	7102	21.5	SAU	2709	23.4
VEN	2709	23.7	GBR	8803	21.2	AGO	2709	22.3	SAU	2710	20.6	QAT	2709	22.4
NGA	2709	23.5	DNK	9999	21.2	SAU	2709	22.3	KWT	2710	20.4	IDN	2711	22.3
IRQ	2709	22.9	SAU	2709	20.7	OMN	2709	22.2	PHL	8542	20.3	KWT	2709	22.1
AGO	2709	22.2	SYR	2709	20.7	IRN	2709	22.0	EGY	2709	19.7	ARE	2711	21.6

Overreporting of exports

Importer

United States			Germany			China			United Kingdom			Japan		
Exporter	Product	Gap	Exporter	Product	Gap	Exporter	Product	Gap	Exporter	Product	Gap	Exporter	Product	Gap
DEU	8901	-19.9	CHN	8901	-20.3	HKG	8703	-20.8	USA	8803	-21.2	SWE	8802	-18.9
FIN	8901	-19.9	BEL	8803	-19.8	HKG	4101	-19.3	DEU	8802	-21.0	SGP	2204	-18.5
PRT	8802	-19.2	AUT	8901	-19.7	HKG	7108	-19.2	HKG	7108	-20.8	SGP	2208	-18.0
MEX	8602	-19.1	DNK	2716	-19.1	JPN	7108	-18.6	CAN	7108	-20.7	NZL	2709	-17.9
KOR	8901	-18.7	BLR	2709	-18.7	ARE	9999	-18.5	USA	8802	-20.7	BHR	7604	-17.6

of exports appears to be a more frequent problem in trade with neighboring countries.

To further analyze the geographical pattern in misreporting, we examine differences in trade gaps across countries in more detail. In particular, we aim to identify countries that consistently understate their exports (and thus appear to be particularly prone to smuggling). In a first exercise, we compute for each exporter the average trade gap across all products. Since there may be sizable product-specific differences in reported trade values between the exporting and the importing country, taking the arithmetic mean of these reporting gaps over often hundreds of products is a simple way to (hopefully) identify country-specific differences in trade reporting. Table 4.2 lists the five countries with the largest average percentage share of missing exports by importer. As shown, we find indeed a strong and consistent mismatch in international trade statistics, with continuous underreporting, for instance, by Equatorial Guinea, Indonesia, and the Philippines. More important, reviewing the full distribution of exporting countries, it turns out that the extent to which countries tend to misreport exports is broadly similar across trade destinations. The correlation of exporter-specific average trade gaps across importing countries is astonishingly high, on the order of about 0.9. Table 4.3 reports a set of simple bivariate correlation coefficients; (unreported) Spearman rank correlations provide similar results.

4.4.1 Benchmark Results

To analyze the country pair-specific discrepancies in matched partner trade statistics in more detail, we next apply rigorous econometric techniques. In particular, we are interested in the extent to which gaps in official trade statistics are perhaps the result of illicit trade. Fisman and Wei (2009) argue that, for selected product categories, the difference in recorded trade flows is due to smuggling. For antiquities, they find that the extent of underreporting of exports is closely related to the (perceived) level of corruption in the exporting country. We examine whether this association also holds for the whole range of products traded internationally.

Table 4.4 presents our benchmark results. In the first column we report the estimation results for the most basic specification of equation (4.2); that is, we regress the observed average pairwise trade gap on our variable of interest, corruption in the exporting country, and add a comprehensive set of importer and year fixed effects. The estimated

Table 4.2
Underreporting of exports by country, 2002 to 2006

Importer											
United States		Germany		China		United Kingdom		Japan		All five importers	
Exporter	Gap	Exporter	Gap	Exporter	Gap	Exporter	Gap	Exporter	Gap	Exporter	Gap
Libya	14.5	Equatorial Guinea	12.1	Equatorial Guinea	14.9	Indonesia	12.1	Iraq	16.3	Equatorial Guinea	12.6
Lesotho	13.5	Indonesia	11.9	Congo	13.5	Lao PDR	11.5	Equatorial Guinea	14.0	Indonesia	12.4
Indonesia	13.3	Ukraine	11.4	Democratic Republic of Congo	12.7	Myanmar	11.5	Western Sahara	13.7	Philippines	11.6
Philippines	12.7	Philippines	11.2	Tchad	11.8	Bouvet Island	11.4	Indonesia	13.2	Iraq	11.4
Iraq	12.5	Serbia and Montenegro	11.0	Rwanda	11.8	Falkland Islands	11.2	Botswana	12.8	Western Sahara	11.3

Table 4.3
Correlation of exporter-specific average trade gaps

	United States	Germany	China	United Kingdom	Japan	All
United States	1.0000					
Germany	0.9245	1.0000				
China	0.8357	0.7824	1.0000			
United Kingdom	0.9368	0.9571	0.7986	1.0000		
Japan	0.9015	0.8572	0.8963	0.8582	1.0000	
All five importers	0.9700	0.9494	0.9120	0.9564	0.9548	1.0000

Note: 202 observations.

Table 4.4
Does exporter corruption matter?

Corruption (WB) exporter	−1.96*	−1.89*	−1.47*	−1.41*	
	(0.21)	(0.22)	(0.48)	(0.48)	
Corruption (TI) exporter					−0.53**
					(0.22)
(Log) distance		0.81*		0.62**	0.42
		(0.26)		(0.26)	(0.28)
Common border dummy		−0.38		−0.52	−0.65
		(0.74)		(0.74)	(0.72)
Landlocked dummy exporter		−0.59		−0.65	−0.74
		(0.74)		(0.74)	(0.80)
(Log) GDP per capita exporter			−0.65**	−0.65**	−0.69**
			(0.31)	(0.31)	(0.33)
(Log) area exporter			−0.51*	−0.49*	−0.26**
			(0.10)	(0.10)	(0.13)
Observations	4,774	4,774	4,366	4,366	3,324
Adjusted R^2	0.17	0.18	0.25	0.26	0.20

Notes: OLS estimation. Dependent variable is the average pairwise trade gap. Importer and year fixed effects included, but not reported. Standard errors robust to clustering by exporter in parentheses; * and ** denote significant at the 1 and 5 percent level, respectively.

coefficient on the corruption measure is −1.96, with a robust standard error of 0.21. This coefficient is not only consistent with the hypothesis that more corruption (i.e., a lower score) is associated with a broader underreporting of exports; with a t-statistic of 9.4, the coefficient is also highly significant statistically. Moreover the effect is economically large; a better corruption rating by one index point is associated with a lower trade gap by about 2 percentage points, thereby reducing the discrepancy in corresponding trade figures by about one-half. The estimated coefficient is even slightly larger in magnitude than the analogous estimate for antiquities in Fisman and Wei (2009). Also our default specification fits the data reasonably well, explaining almost 20 percent of the variation in trade gaps. In sum, our results suggest that smuggling activities are not restricted to a small set of products where there is a strong asymmetry in reporting incentives, but rather seem to affect a large range of products dependent on the norms of corruption in the exporting country.

4.4.2 Robustness Analysis

In the remaining columns of table 4.4, we present a number of sensitivity checks. We begin our robustness analysis by adding various control variables that may affect the bilateral gap in trade reporting. In column 2 we include various measures for transportation costs. Except for landlockedness, which is found to be associated, if anything, with smaller (instead of larger) trade gaps, the coefficients take on the expected sign; the discrepancy between recorded exports and imports grows with the geographic distance among the trading partners and is smaller for neighboring countries. However, only the distance variable enters the regression significantly different from zero. More important, the estimated coefficient on exporter corruption remains virtually unchanged with this extension. In column 3, instead of adding measures of shipping costs, we include potential proxies for smuggling other than corruption. Of these variables, the coefficient on per capita income in the exporting country is indeed negative and significant, indicating that poorer countries tend to understate exports. The negative coefficient on country size, in contrast, implies that trade gaps are on average larger for geographically small exporters, suggesting that possible "natural" restrictions on the effectiveness of border controls may be of less importance for the observed discrepancies in corresponding trade figures. Reassuringly, our finding of a negative association between exporter corruption and misreporting in trade is again

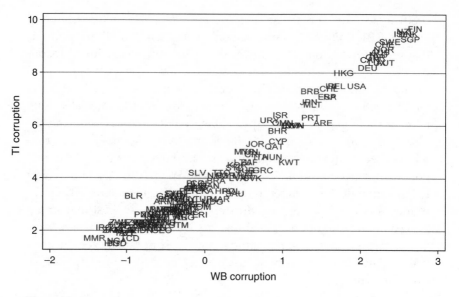

Figure 4.1
Corruption measures, 2004

basically unaffected by this extension, though the estimated coefficient is slightly smaller in magnitude. Next, we include the two sets of controls jointly, without much effect. Finally, in the column on the extreme right of table 4.4, we replace our World Bank corruption variable with a measure taken from Transparency International. This score is available only for a smaller number of countries. However, we still find a significant negative relationship between corruption in the exporting country and the share of exports that is also recorded in the importing country, perhaps reflecting the high correlation between both corruption ratings; see figure 4.1 for a scatter plot.[5]

Table 4.5 presents another set of robustness checks. We divide the sample along various lines and report coefficient estimates on exporter corruption, obtained for these subsamples. In particular, we tabulate results for individual years, for separate importing countries, and for various groups of exporting countries. Of these perturbations, only restrictions on the sample of exporting countries included in the empirical analysis have a significant impact on the key coefficient. Not surprisingly, the effect of corruption on the discrepancy in trade statistics disappears for shipments from OECD member countries and trading partners nearby to importers (in our sample), since both groups of countries (often) have low corruption ratings.

Table 4.5
Robustness checks for exporter corruption

	Corruption (WB) exporter	Observations	Adjusted R^2	Corruption (TI) exporter	Observations	Adjusted R^2
2002	−1.63* (0.48)	883	0.33	−0.36 (0.28)	500	0.36
2003	−1.85* (0.57)	891	0.27	−0.53*** (0.30)	637	0.19
2004	−1.44** (0.64)	884	0.19	−0.52*** (0.29)	703	0.14
2005	−1.34** (0.61)	878	0.19	−0.72* (0.28)	750	0.18
2006	−0.89 (0.60)	830	0.29	−0.35 (0.28)	734	0.23
Importer: United States	−1.44* (0.54)	881	0.25	−0.57** (0.25)	665	0.19
Importer: Germany	−1.25* (0.44)	883	0.34	−0.47** (0.21)	666	0.27
Importer: China	−1.31** (0.55)	849	0.19	−0.47** (0.22)	665	0.16
Importer: United Kingdom	−1.07** (0.47)	877	0.26	−0.41*** (0.22)	664	0.19
Importer: Japan	−2.05* (0.50)	876	0.31	−0.80* (0.23)	664	0.25
Exporter: OECD	0.20 (0.27)	730	0.23	0.08 (0.11)	730	0.23
Exporter: GDPpc > 1,000 USD	−1.26*** (0.67)	2,900	0.24	−0.55** (0.27)	2,347	0.16
Exporter: Distance < 5,000 km	−0.28 (0.55)	1,068	0.32	0.04 (0.23)	869	0.30

Notes: OLS estimation. Dependent variable is the average pairwise trade gap. The specification is similar to column 4 in table 4.4; that is, the regression includes the following (unreported) controls: (log) distance, common border dummy, landlocked dummy exporter, (log) GDP per capita exporter, (log) area exporter. Importer and year fixed effects included, but not reported. Standard errors robust to clustering by exporter in parentheses. *, **, and *** denote significant at the 1, 5, and 10 percent level, respectively.

Table 4.6
Product-level evidence for exporter corruption

	Full sample		Gap > 0	Exports and imports > 0
Corruption (WB) exporter	−0.42 (0.37)		−0.45 (0.38)	−0.08*** (0.04)
Corruption (TI) exporter		−0.07 (0.13)		
(Log) distance	0.20 (0.16)	0.14 (0.15)	0.29*** (0.16)	0.06 (0.04)
Common border dummy	−0.94*** (0.51)	−0.84*** (0.47)	−0.83*** (0.43)	−0.43** (0.19)
Landlocked dummy exporter	−0.67 (0.49)	−0.62 (0.48)	−0.43 (0.39)	0.21*** (0.11)
(Log) GDP per capita exporter	−0.71** (0.28)	−0.82* (0.26)	−1.06* (0.26)	−0.03 (0.04)
(Log) area exporter	−0.10 (0.09)	−0.03 (0.09)	−0.45* (0.10)	0.06 (0.04)
Observations	1,226,793	1,185,092	686,112	729,553
Adjusted R^2	0.06	0.06	0.19	0.02

Notes: OLS estimation. Dependent variable is the pairwise trade gap at the four-digit product level. Importer, product and year fixed effects included, but not reported. Standard errors robust to clustering by exporter in parentheses. *, **, and *** denote significant at the 1, 5, and 10 percent level, respectively.

In a next experiment, instead of splitting the sample, we now sizably increase the number of observations. More specifically, we substitute the average pairwise trade gap across all traded products with individual product-specific trade gaps between pairs of countries. Table 4.6 reports the results. For this extension the point estimate on the corruption measure decreases in magnitude and even loses statistical significance (though it remains negative). However, it seems generally difficult to explain variation in trade gaps at the product level. Neither the bilateral distance term remains important, nor does the size effect. The empirical fit of our framework is much lower; the adjusted R-squared falls to 0.06. Moreover, in unreported results, we find that the estimated coefficient on corruption remains negative and significant when the control for per capita income in the exporting country is dropped; that is, for the large sample of individual product-specific trade gaps by exporter, the effect of corruption on the reporting gap seems to work mainly through its correlation with income. Figure 4.2 graphs the association between per capita income and corruption.

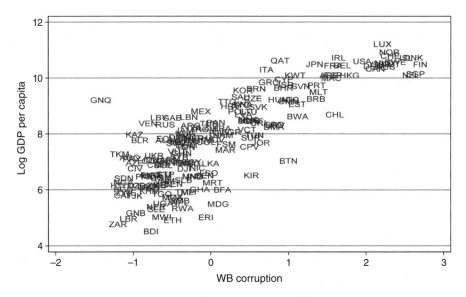

Figure 4.2
Corruption and income, 2004

We also explore two reasonable slices of the sample; results are tabulated in the last two columns (on the right) of table 4.6. First we drop observations with negative trade gaps (i.e., where exports exceed imports). Then we explore a sample where both partner countries, exporter and importer, have a data entry for a trade flow; previously we have imposed a trade value of zero when information from one partner was missing. As shown, both restrictions yield interesting results. Excluding episodes of over-reported exports improves the fit of the regression markedly. With this modification, many coefficients increase in size and significance; the adjusted R-squared jumps to 0.19. When episodes of missing trade are dropped, the point estimate on corruption becomes of borderline significance (with a p-value of 0.059), while the coefficient on per capita income becomes statistically indifferent from zero.

4.4.3 Extensions

We have also performed a set of other extensions to identify the possible effect of corruption on trade. Table 4.7 varies our measure of trade gaps. Instead of trade values, we exploit information on the recorded weights and quantities of shipments. For smuggled goods the choice of the trade measure should be irrelevant for the estimation results; these goods are moved out of the country illegally and unreported.

Table 4.7
Does exporter corruption matter only for values?

	Weight		Quantity	
Corruption (WB) exporter	−0.89** (0.35)		−0.89* (0.32)	
Corruption (TI) exporter		−0.24 (0.16)		−0.24*** (0.14)
(Log) distance	0.36*** (0.19)	0.29 (0.21)	0.32*** (0.17)	0.23 (0.18)
Common border dummy	−0.34 (0.61)	−0.45 (0.59)	−0.47 (0.59)	−0.43 (0.59)
Landlocked dummy exporter	−0.51 (0.51)	−0.70 (0.54)	−0.39 (0.46)	−0.47 (0.49)
(Log) GDP per capita exporter	−0.44*** (0.22)	−0.59** (0.24)	−0.41** (0.20)	−0.54** (0.21)
(Log) area exporter	−0.28* (0.07)	−0.14 (0.09)	−0.23* (0.06)	−0.09 (0.08)
Observations	4,366	3,324	4,366	3,324
Adjusted R^2	0.22	0.19	0.22	0.18

Notes: OLS estimation. Dependent variable is the average pairwise trade gap in the measure that is reported in the first row of the table. Importer and year fixed effects included, but not reported. Standard errors robust to clustering by exporter in parentheses. *, **, and *** denote significant at the 1, 5, and 10 percent level, respectively.

However, if corruption mainly implies that customs officials are bribed to underinvoice export values, then the weight and quantity of a good may still be properly recorded at customs, which would reduce the estimated impact of corruption. As shown, the coefficient estimates on exporter corruption indeed decrease in magnitude (by about one-third) when we substitute (nominal) trade values by real trade measures. Still most estimates remain statistically different from zero at conventional levels.

Previous research focuses exclusively on trade restrictions (and the incentives to misreport trade) in the exporting country. A similar reasoning, however, applies for the importing country as well. For certain import sanctions and duties, traders may find it profitable to underinvoice goods (which may or may not have been properly declared in the source country) upon entry. As a result, while corruption in the exporting country is associated with larger trade gaps, we could observe the opposite effect of lower trade gaps for corruption in the importing country. Table 4.8 provides estimates for importer-specific

Table 4.8
Does importer corruption matter?

Corruption (WB) importer	0.20** (0.06)	0.22** (0.07)	−0.14*** (0.05)	−0.01 (0.08)	
Corruption (TI) importer					−0.01 (0.05)
(Log) distance		0.31** (0.07)		0.37* (0.05)	0.37* (0.05)
Common border dummy		−0.65** (0.21)		−0.53*** (0.24)	−0.53*** (0.23)
(Log) GDP per capita importer			0.29** (0.06)	0.09 (0.10)	0.10 (0.12)
(Log) area importer			−0.23* (0.01)	−0.19* (0.02)	−0.19* (0.03)
Observations	5,295	5,287	4,800	4,800	4,800
Adjusted R^2	0.67	0.67	0.67	0.67	0.67

Notes: OLS estimation. Dependent variable is the average pairwise trade gap. Exporter and year fixed effects included, but not reported. Standard errors robust to clustering by importer in parentheses. *, **, and *** denote significant at the 1, 5, and 10 percent level, respectively.

determinants of pairwise discrepancies in trade statistics; these estimates are analogues to table 4.4. Although our sample covers only five importing countries that have, except for China, almost similar corruption ratings, we find convincing evidence that corruption also matters for imports.[6] The positive coefficient indicates that a more corrupt bureaucracy in the importing country (i.e., a lower corruption index) is associated with a smaller trade gap (and thus less recorded imports). The effect disappears once we control for other importer characteristics (especially country size). However, given the small number of importing countries in our sample, this finding is perhaps not terribly disturbing.

In our final exercise we explore differences in trade gaps across products. Fisman and Wei (2009) argue that one particular (four-digit) product category, antiques of an age exceeding one hundred years (product code 9706), exhibits specific features so that smuggling becomes highly attractive; exports of cultural objects is often strongly restricted, while there are no measurable barriers to imports. We examine, applying the same basic methodology, whether other product categories perhaps display similar features. Table 4.9 tabulates product categories for which we find the largest reported trade gaps. The top

Table 4.9
Underreporting of exports by product, 2002 to 2006

Importer											
United States		Germany		China		United Kingdom		Japan		All five importers	
Product	Gap	Product	Gap	Product	Gap	Product	Gap	Product	Gap	Product	Gap
9999	10.6	7112	7.0	2709	10.7	9999	7.8	2709	9.9	2709	6.9
9706	8.6	9704	6.7	8908	9.6	8411	6.8	2619	8.9	6110	5.0
2709	7.2	2709	6.6	2615	7.2	2620	6.5	9999	8.2	4403	4.8
6110	6.5	2607	6.3	8601	7.0	9706	6.1	2305	7.0	9999	4.8
6102	6.2	9302	5.8	2518	6.8	7112	5.6	2711	6.5	6204	4.5
Position of product code 9706 (1,241 products)											
2.	8.6	100.0	3.4	1,214.	−5.0	4.	6.1	191.	2.3	53.	3.1

Table 4.10
Correlation of product-specific average trade gaps

	United States	Germany	China	United Kingdom	Japan	All
United States	1.0000					
Germany	0.4347	1.0000				
China	0.1858	0.0558	1.0000			
United Kingdom	0.3426	0.2910	0.1581	1.0000		
Japan	0.4562	0.4685	0.2251	0.2539	1.0000	
All five importers	0.7292	0.6516	0.5376	0.6157	0.7381	1.0000

Notes: 1,240 observations.

categories appear to differ widely across importers. There are only three product groups for which we observe a large share of underreported exports in more than one destination country. For two of these categories, however, "petroleum oils, crude" (code 2709) and "commodities not specified according to kind" (9999), the discrepancy is likely to be unrelated to smuggling. The third top-ranked category is the product category chosen by Fisman and Wei, antiquities. For this group, we report, for comparison, also the rank and the recording gap in other countries. Again, there are sizable differences across importing countries, with China even recording import values that are considerably smaller than worldwide reported exports (i.e., a negative trade gap).

Table 4.10 reports the pairwise correlation coefficients that describe the full ranking of products. Similar to our results for exporters, we also find that product-specific trade gaps are significantly correlated across importers, though the correlation coefficients are much lower than before, especially for bilateral pairs that include China.

Still we aim to characterize differences in trade gaps across products. For instance, one measure for which we explore its association with the discrepancy between recorded imports and exports is the level of import protection, as proxied by the total ad valorem equivalent tariff. To the extent that reporting incentives matter, one would expect that traders report import values more correctly (and thus reporting gaps in trade statistics are smaller) when barriers to imports are low. We also exploit two other product-specific measures provided in the UN Comtrade database: the weight and quantity of pairwise trade. Based on these variables, we compute the (average)

Table 4.11
Does importer protection matter for product-level trade gaps?

	Pairwise product-level trade gaps		Average importer-specific product-level trade gaps	
Level of protection importer	−0.008* (0.002)	−0.007* (0.002)	−0.013* (0.004)	−0.012* (0.004)
Value/weight importer	4.14*** (2.42)		−7.91* (5.87)	
Unit value importer	1.89 (1.85)		−3.34* (7.24)	
Value/weight exporter		1.36** (0.57)		2.47 (3.77)
Unit value exporter		−2.63* (0.92)		−4.17* (1.13)
Observations	804,452	733,507	25,192	29,067
Adjusted R^2	0.39	0.11	0.06	0.05

Notes: OLS estimation. Dependent variable is reported in the first row of the table. Year fixed effects always included, but not reported. When appropriate, importer or country pair fixed effects are included, but not reported. Standard errors robust to clustering by product in parentheses. *, **, and *** denote significant at the 1, 5, and 10 percent level, respectively.

value-to-weight and value-to-quantity ratios of product-level trade, supposing that high-value goods, such as antiquities, are more attractive for smuggling.

Again, we apply a variant of (4.2), which includes a comprehensive set of either importer- or country pair-specific fixed effects to capture country (pair)-related determinants of trade gaps, including corruption. Table 4.11 presents the results. We report two sets of estimation results. The first two columns tabulate the estimates for individual product-level trade gaps; the remaining two columns show the results when trade gaps are averaged across exporters for individual importers and products. We also report separate results for characteristics in product-level trade recorded by exporting and importing countries, documenting minor differences in statistical significance. Interestingly, we find strong and consistent evidence that trade gaps decrease with the level of import protection. The estimated coefficient on the import tariff is negative and highly significant in all specifications, supporting the view that reporting incentives measurably affect the accuracy of trade statistics. The estimation results for product characteristics are less convincing, possibly as a result of aggregation to the four-digit product level. Specifically, our findings suggest that trade gaps tend to be larger, if anything, for products with low value-to-quantity ratios. Thus it appears that underreporting of exports is more prevalent in bulky mass shipments, so that antiquities are an exception rather than the rule, an issue that deserves our future attention.

4.5 Conclusions

Discrepancies in international trade statistics have been frequently analyzed in the past. Statisticians often aim to identify (and quantify) potential reasons for the differences in pairwise trade statistics to perhaps properly adjust their national trade figures. Economists occasionally exploit the difference between recorded exports and imports as a proxy for bilateral transaction costs.

In this chapter we examine another potential explanation for the observed discrepancy in trade statistics, (illegal) nondeclaration. Similar to Fisman and Wei (2009) for antiquities, we find that the reporting gap in bilateral trade is strongly associated with the level of corruption, especially in the source country. In countries with corrupt bureaucracies, it should be easier (and perhaps even common practice) to ignore legal rules and procedures. To the extent that this misbehavior also affects international trade transactions, our findings suggest that reporting gaps in official trade statistics partly reflect smuggling activities.

Acknowledgments

We thank Mohammad Reza Farzanegan, Dorothe Singer, Andrey Stoyanov, anonymous referees, and participants at various conferences for helpful comments and Verena Arendt, Lena-Maria Dörfler, and Svenja Hector for valuable research assistance.

Notes

1. Morgenstern (1950), in a classic paper, provides a very detailed analysis of discrepancies in officially reported exports and imports figures. See Rozanski and Yeats (1994) for a more recent treatment.

2. For an early attempt, see the European Commission's "Simpler Legislation for the Internal Market (SLIM)" initiative, which is documented at http://ec.europa.eu/internal_market/simplification/index_en.htm.

3. In reality, customs offices already apply such profiles to assess risks. In the European Union, for example, a risk information form is used to exchange information among the customs administrations of member states; see http://ec.europa.eu/taxation _customs/customs/customs_controls/risk_management/implementing/index_en.htm. In Germany, a central office for risk analysis (Zentralstelle Risikoanalyse, ZORA) has been established in 2002; see http://www.bundesfinanzministerium.de/cln_06/ nn_17844/DE/Aktuelles/Monatsbericht__des__BMF/2006/englisch/060918agmb009 .html.

4. See table I.8 of the WTO's International Trade Statistics 2007, available at http://www .wto.org/english/res_e/statis_e/its2007_e/its07_world_trade_dev_e.pdf.

5. In another (unreported) robustness check we examine the association between the trade gap and individual components of the World Bank's "Control of Corruption" measure. For 18 of the 22 variables we obtain a negative coefficient; most of these coefficients are statistically different from zero at conventional levels of significance.

6. In 2006 the World Bank corruption indexes were as follows: United States 1.30; Germany 1.78; China -0.53; United Kingdom 1.86; Japan 1.31. The average score for the full sample is zero.

References

Baldwin, R. 2006. The euro's trade effects. Working paper 594. European Central Bank.

Bhagwati, J. 1964. On the underinvoicing of imports. *Bulletin of the Oxford University Institute of Economics and Statistics.* 26 (August): 389–97.

Bhagwati, J. 1967. Fiscal policies, the faking of foreign trade declarations, and the balance of payments. *Bulletin of the Oxford University Institute of Economics and Statistics* 29 (February): 61–77.

Bhagwati, J., and B. Hansen. 1973. A theoretical analysis of smuggling. *Quarterly Journal of Economics* 87 (May): 172–87.

Celasun, M., and D. Rodrik. 1989. Debt, adjustment, and growth: Turkey. In J. D. Sachs and S. M. Collins, eds., *Developing Country Debt and Economic Performance: Country Studies.* Chicago: University of Chicago Press, 615–808.

Dabla-Norris, E., M. Gradstein, and G. Inchauste. 2008. What causes firms to hide output? The determinants of informality. *Journal of Development Economics* 85 (February): 1–27.

Deardorff, A. V., and W. F. Stolper. 1990. Effects of smuggling under African conditions: A factual, institutional and analytic discussion. *Weltwirtschaftliches Archiv* 126 (1): 116–41.

Fisman, R., and S.-J. Wei. 2009. The smuggling of art, and the art of smuggling: Uncovering the illicit trade in cultural property and antiques. *American Economic Journal: Applied Economics.* 1 (July): 82–96.

Hummels, D., and V. Lugovskyy. 2006. Are matched partner trade statistics a usable measure of transportation costs? *Review of International Economics* 14 (February): 69–86.

Kaufmann, D., A. Kraay, and M. Mastruzzi. 2007. Governance matters VI: Governance indicators for 1996–2006. Policy research working paper 4280. World Bank.

Limão, N., and A. Venables. 2001. Infrastructure, geographical disadvantage, transport costs, and trade. *World Bank Economic Review* 21: 451–79.

McDonald, D. C. 1985. Trade data discrepancies and the incentive to smuggle: An empirical analysis. *International Monetary Fund Staff Papers* 32 (December): 668–92.

Morgenstern, O. 1950. *The Accuracy of Economic Observations.* Princeton: Princeton University Press.

Radelet, S., and J. Sachs. 1998. Shipping costs, manufactured exports, and economic growth. Working paper. Harvard University.

Rozanski, J., and A. J. Yeats. 1994. On the (in)accuracy of economic observations: An assessment of trends in the reliability of international trade statistics. *Journal of Development Economics* 44 (June): 103–30.

Yeats, A. J. 1978. On the accuracy of partner country trade statistics. *Oxford Bulletin of Economics and Statistics* 40 (November): 341–61.

Yeats, A. J. 1990. On the accuracy of economic observations: Do Sub-Saharan trade statistics mean anything? *World Bank Economic Review* 4 (May): 135–56.

Data Appendix

Trade gap
Difference between log of import value (in current USD) recorded in the importing country and the corresponding log of exports (in current US dollar) recorded in exporting country at the 4-digit HS level
Source: computed from UN Comtrade (http://comtrade.un.org)

Corruption (WB)
Control of corruption score
Source: World Bank Worldwide Governance Indicators project (http://www.governance.org)

Corruption (TI)
Corruption perceptions index
Source: Transparency International (http://www.transparency.org)

(Log) Distance
Log of bilateral distance (in km) based on coordinates for the geographic center of countries
Source: based on data from CIA World Factbook (http://www.cia.gov/library/publications/the-world-factbook/)

Common border dummy
Dummy variable that takes the value of 1 when two countries share a common land border (and zero otherwise)
Source: based on data from CIA World Factbook (http://www.cia.gov/library/publications/the-world-factbook/)

Landlocked dummy
Dummy variable that takes the value of 1 when two countries share a common language (and zero otherwise)
Source: based on data from CIA World Factbook (http://www.cia.gov/library/publications/the-world-factbook/)

(Log) GDP per capita
Log of GDP per capita (in current USD)
Source: World Bank World Development Indicators

(Log) Area
Log of surface area (in sq km)
Source: World Bank World Development Indicators

Level of protection
Total ad valorem equivalent tariff at the 4-digit HS level (in %)
Source: UNCTAD/WTO International Trade Centre
(http://www.macmap.org)

Value/weight
Trade value (in current USD) / Net weight (in kg)
Source: computed from UN Comtrade (http://comtrade.un.org)

Unit value
Trade value (in current USD) / Trade quantity (in units)
Source: computed from UN Comtrade (http://comtrade.un.org)

5 Dark Side of Trade in Iran: Evidence from a Structural Equation Model

Mohammad Reza Farzanegan

5.1 Introduction

Smuggling, as an economic crime, is the hidden export and/or import of products without payment of the legal duties and taxes. Smuggling involves illegal trade in both legal and illegal goods. In this chapter, I examine the smuggling of legal goods, which can be imported or exported upon paying of taxes and duties. I do not consider illegal trafficking of human beings, such as illegal immigrants and/or sex slaves, or smuggling of weapons and illegal drugs. To investigate the concept of smuggling, I select the economists' way to undercover the main incentives behind the illegal trade. The main carrots (e.g., black market premiums, tariffs, subsidies, weak governance, trade openness, and increasing disposable income of clients) and sticks (e.g., higher penalty rate, well-functioning institutions, efficient education system, sound and well-targeted social security system, and decreasing disposable income of clients) are examined in a statistical model to measure the magnitude of smuggling and factors that are important to understand it. In taking such an approach, I follow the dictate of Fisman and Miguel (2008, p. 55), who recommend that "Rather than engaging in abstract theorizing and speculation, we need to figure out how to measure the scale of illicit activity and then see how it responds to economic carrots and sticks out in the real world of smugglers and gangsters."

The global magnitude of illegal trade is, however, difficult to measure. There are some estimates by international organizations. IMF (2003, 2001) and the World Bank estimate that about 2 to 4 percent of the global gross domestic product in 2000 originated from illegal trade activities. Money laundering is an option to legalize the illegal funds from smuggling among other illegal activities. Agarwal and Agarwal

(2006, 2004) estimated the amount of global money laundering, amounting to 5 to 6 percent of world GDP in 2006. Schneider (2010) estimated the amount of money laundering in twenty OECD countries. Based on his examination, the amount of money laundering increased from 273 billion USD in 1995 to 603 billion USD in 2006.

My focus is on the case of Iran. In this chapter, I analyze the incentives for illegal trade in Iran and the consequences for the macro-economy. A highly regulated foreign exchange market, frequent governmental interventions in trade, and protective policies implemented in this area are common features of developing countries such as Iran. The aforementioned shortages along with other bottlenecks in the structure of the Iranian economy and the political system provide a unique opportunity for such an experiment. The effect of smuggling on the economy has been a topic of hot debate in Iran and is extensively discussed in the Iranian media. Table 5.1 summarizes some of the information in the media about the magnitude of smuggling in Iran.

Smugglers engage in illegal trade after comparing the costs of such an engagement with its potential benefits. Similar to other trades, if the benefits of illegal trade exceed its costs, then smuggling flourishes. Table 5.2 shows that smuggling in Iran is not risky. Let us calculate the rate of success in smuggling based on the presented information in this table. I assume (on the basis of my estimations in this chapter) that the

Table 5.1
Media information on the amount of smuggling in Iran

Source	Estimated amount of smuggling
Mehdi Karbasian, the former head of Iran's customs. *Akhbar-e Eqtesadi, 7 Bahman 1378* (January 27, 2000)	1.5 to 2 billion USD worth of goods was smuggled into the country
Hosayn Nasiri, the former Secretary of the Supreme Council of Free Trade Zones. *Radio Free Europe/Radio Liberty 3* (September 18, 2000)	3 billion USD
Bonyan, 25 Bahman 1380 (February 14, 2002)	3.5 billion USD
Iran daily citing government sources. *Iran Daily,* Febuary 28, 2001	3 to 5 billion USD
Eqtesad-e Iran (Iran's version of *The Economist*). *Eqtesad-e Iran 360 (Bahman 1380* [January–February 2002])	4 billion USD worth of goods are smuggled or "legally smuggled" into Iran
Wall Street Journal, December 7, 1998	Two-thirds of sold goods in Tehran Bazaar are smuggled

Source: Based on information in Keshavarzian (2007).

Table 5.2
Smuggling cases in the Judiciary system of Iran, 2000 to 2005

Description	2000	2001	2002	2003 (first 7 months)	2004 (first 6 months)	2005 (first 6 months)
Number of total investigated cases at judiciary system	46,675	37,547	57,716	45,416	38,973	34,170
Value of all investigated cases (billion rials)	624.5	1687	1,743.8	952.5	641.3	761.6
Number of investigated cases under 1,000 USD value	39,999	29,077	47,583	39,714	34,588	29,865
Share of petty smuggling in investigated smuggling	86%	77%	82%	87%	88%	87%
Value of investigated cases under 1,000 USD value (billion) rials	249.8	49	237.2	154.5	123	120.2
Share of petty smuggling value in total value of investigated smuggling	40%	2.90%	13.6%	16.22%	19%	15%
Realized fines (billion rials)					12.3	59
Predicted fines (billion rials)					1,038.5	1,027.2
Share of realized to predicted fines					1.2%	5.7%

Source: Seif (2008, p. 183).

total amount of smuggling in Iran, on average, is 3 billion USD and 1 USD =10,000 rials. For the year 2002, I can calculate the ratio of value of total investigated smuggling cases to value of assumed smuggling: (174,400,000 USD/3,000,000,000 USD) × 100 = 5.8 percent. This means that only about 6 percent of all smuggled goods are investigated (or confiscated). In other words, the rate of success in the smuggling business is about 95 percent.

Pervasive corruption is another major contributor to increasing smuggling in Iran. Illegal traders know corrupt bureaucrats in governmental organizations (e.g., customs, police, and ports) through their networking. The high perception of corruption is an indicator for a fertile situation to smuggle. The Transparency International produces the Corruption Perception Index (CPI) every year, measuring the degree of perception of corruption among the public officials and politicians. This index covers both administrative and political corruption. Scores of countries in the TI-CPI are from 0 (highly corrupt) to 10 (least corrupt). The CPI index of Iran reduced from 3 in 2003 to 2.3 in 2009. Therefore Iran is located at the bottom part of the CPI ranking with a pervasive corruption.[1] Another indicator that ranks different aspects of institutions is the World Governance Indicators (WGI) published by the World Bank. One of these indicators is the regularity quality (from −2.5 to 2.5). Iran shows weak scores in this index, which measures the ability of government in providing sound policies and regulation for the development of the private sector. The score has reduced from −1.10 in 2003 to −1.62 in 2008. The score on rule of law from WGI regarding the quality of contract enforcement, property rights, the police, the courts, and judiciary system is also negative. It fluctuated around −0.8 between 2003 and 2008. The WGI also provides an index for corruption that measures both petty and grand corruption, and capture of state by private agents. This indicator has likewise been negative from 1996 to 2008. While the best instance was in 2002 (reformist government with a score of −0.2), the worst may be observed in 2008 (Ahmadinejad government with a score of −0.8) and 1996 (Hashemi Rafsanjani government with a score of −0.9) (for more details, see Kaufmann et al. 2009).

The other reason behind businesses' engaging in illegal trade is the high burden of operating in legal parts of trade. High costs to import and export due to high taxes, duties, and a complicated administrative process, as well as different and sometimes contradictory regulations, encourage illegal trade. The World Bank (2010a) Doing Business project provides interesting insights in relative position of Iran's foreign trade to other control groups. This information shows relatively high costs of legal trade in Iran. For example, from 2008 to 2010, costs to export and import have increased from 860 to 1,061 (USD per container) and from 1,330 to 1,706 (USD per container), respectively. The number of documents necessary for exports and imports did not show any changes during the past three years. The total ranking of Iran within category of international trade is also weak (134th of 183 countries). Most countries in the Middle East region perform better than Iran in terms of

Table 5.3
Costs of legal trade in Iran

Good practice economies	Documents to export	Time to export (days)	Costs to export (USD per container)	Documents to imports	Time to imports (days)	Costs to imports (USD per container)
Denmark		5				
France	2			2		
Malaysia			450			
Singapore					3	439
Iran	7	25	1,061	8	38	1,706
Comparative economies						
Iraq	10	102	3,900	10	101	3,900
Jordan	7	17	730	7	19	1,290
Oman	10	22	821	10	26	1,037
Saudi Arabia	5	17	681	5	18	678
UAE	4	8	593	5	9	579

Source: World Bank (2010a).

general ranking in international trade categories (e.g., Oman, 123; Jordan, 71; Saudi Arabia, 23; and UAE, 5). Table 5.3 illustrates the latest comparative position of Iran in international trade. The financial costs of imports in Iran are much higher than the average of time and monetary costs of imports in the Middle East and North Africa (MENA) and OECD countries. The average costs to imports in the MENA and OECD region are 1,221 and 1,145 USD per container, respectively. These costs for the case of Iran are 1,706 USD. While traders in the OECD and the MENA regions need on average between 11 and 26 days, in Iran one needs 38 days. Incentives to smuggling products are not limited to higher costs of legal trade but are also due to official prohibitions of consumption of several goods. One of the most demanding consuming products is alcoholic beverages, which are forbidden to trade in Iran. Alcoholic beverages have been the most important detected smuggled products in terms of value in the past years.

Table 5.4 shows the 10 largest detected smuggled goods in Iran during the first 11 months of 2009 and 2008. The highest share belongs to alcoholic beverages with 24.9 percent of total detection. There are some significant increases in smuggling of specific goods such as cars (growth of 345 percent and cosmetics with increase of 108 percent). An

Table 5.4
Ten largest detected (export and import) smuggled goods in Iran

	Smuggled goods	First 11 months of 2009/10		First 11 month of 2008/09		
		Value (million rials)	Share of total (%)	Value (million rials)	Share of total (%)	Percentage of changes
1	Alcoholic bevergaes	604,549.49	24.90	618,154.75	20.86	−2.20
2	Piece (cloths)	428,594.38	17.65	254,090.32	8.57	68.68
3	Car	150,077.44	6.18	33,696.80	1.14	345.38
4	Mobile	128,410.01	5.29	105,626.69	3.56	21.57
5	Textile	104,315.94	4.30	61,322.74	2.07	70.11
6	Gasoil	83,993.97	3.46	192,303.98	6.49	−56.32
7	Shoes	68,217.05	2.81	40,957.56	1.38	66.56
8	Machinery	60,475.32	2.49	38,791.83	1.31	55.90
9	Rice	38,768.46	1.60	50,799.31	1.71	−23.68
10	Cosmetics	27,722.11	1.14	13,273.39	0.45	108.85
11	Others	732,944.44	30.19	1,554,191.01	52.45	−52.84
Total		2,428,068.61	100	2,963,208.38	100	

Source: Iran Customs Administration (2010).
Note: One USD is about 10,000 rials.

interesting observation is the reduction of illegal exports of gasoil. A reduction of 56 percent of illegal exports of this product may be related to a significant reduction of subsidies on a group of oil products such as gasoline and gasoil in 2008 and 2009. Another characteristic of the Iranian economy is a massive subsidy on energy and nonenergy products. The government uses the oil rents to "buy off" the population by offering costly subsidies. These subsides, especially on petroleum products, have created a large distortion in the price system. Large price disparities between Iran and its neighbors have fostered export smuggling of fuel in Iran, putting a heavy burden on the government budgets. In 1997, energy subsidies accounted for about 18 percent of Iranian GDP, and in 2002, these subsidies reached 16.9 billion USD or 14.5 percent of GDP (International Institute for Energy Studies 2005).

Table 5.5 presents the relative prices of different kinds of oil products in Iran to import prices (free on board [fob] prices of the Persian Gulf). Note in the table, for example, that the local price of gasoline in Iran on average has been about 0.27 of the import prices.

Table 5.5
Ratio of Iranian oil products prices and FOB prices of Persian Gulf

Products	1996	1997	1998	1999	2000	2001	2002	2003	2004	2005	2006
LPG	0.06	0.05	0.03	0.02	0.02	0.02	0.02	0.02	0.02	0.01	0.01
Gasoline-normal	0.27	0.26	0.24	0.27	0.21	0.34	0.34	0.38	0.31	0.23	0.21
Kerosene	0.05	0.07	0.08	0.08	0.07	0.1	0.09	0.1	0.06	0.04	0.04
Gasoil	0.06	0.07	0.09	0.04	0.03	0.04	0.03	0.03	0.02	0.02	0.01

Source: Institute for International Energy Studies (IIES) (http://eia.iies.org/economic/price4.asp).

Besides these economical factors behind smuggling in Iran, there is the role of certain military organizations to consider. Para-state organizations and military bodies undermine Iran's ability to reduce smuggling. The most controversial debates are about the revolutionary guard's economic and trading activities since the end of the war with Iraq in 1988. Dealing with such bodies' extensive discretion and a lack of accountability present difficulties for any reformist government in Iran (see Farzanegan 2009 for more figures on the role of paramilitary bodies in smuggling).

In view of the presented background on the political economy of Iran, I will investigate the dark side of trade and quantify the economic value of import and export smuggling in Iran. The contributions of this study are the following:

1. This study is the first to apply both structural equation modeling and foreign trade statistics to trace the causes and consequences of smuggling and quantify its relative size in Iran.
2. The main direct effects of hypothesized causes on smuggling are examined by way of the indirect effects of causal variables through interaction terms. In contrast to classic regression analysis, I use interaction terms and examine the effects of main causal variables through relevant institutional quality factors; this is a novel approach to the multiple indicators multiple causes (MIMIC) model in economics
3. A theoretical background for the applied causal and indicator variables is provided to help evaluate the importance of the Iranian results for other studies on smuggling.
4. Prresented is the first combined index of quality of political-economic institutions for the case of Iran, and this may be useful for further empirical investigations on political economy of Iran.

The rest of this chapter is organized as follows. In section 5.2, I review the theoretical and empirical literature on illegal trade. Methodology is explained in section 5.3. Causal and indicator variables are discussed in section 5.4. I discuss the results in section 5.5, and I draw some conclusions in section 5.6.

5.2 Review of the Literature

5.2.1 Theoretical Literature

The welfare aspects of smuggling have attracted some attention of economists. Bhagwati and Hansen (1973) study the welfare levels under tariffs with and without smuggling. They conclude that the achievement of a given degree of protection to domestic importable production, in the presence of smuggling, leads to lower levels of welfare than if smuggling were absent.

Pitt (1981) proposes a model of smuggling consistent with the coexistence of smuggling, legal trade, and price disparity. By his definition, price disparity can be calculated by comparing the domestic price of the goods (P^d, in domestic currency units) to the quantity of domestic exchange that can be earned through legal trade (i.e., the world price, P^f, which has quoted in USD times the legal effective exchange rate for the exportables, EER).The price disparity is then $((P^d/P^f \times \mathrm{EER}) - 1) \times 100$. The presence of a price disparity can be an indicator of smuggling. Pitt considers the case of "technical smuggling" domination in Indonesia, and postulates that the greater the legal trade, the easier it is to hide smuggling from enforcement agencies, by which naturally smuggling becomes less costly. Where the quantity of legal trade and subsequently governmental tax revenues from the smuggling operations exceed those from nonsmuggling, he concludes that the policy of complete and effective enforcement against smuggling would not maximize the level of legal trade. This is in contrast to Bhagwati and Hensen (1973) conclusion that smuggling causes a lower level of welfare due to a reduction in public revenues. Pitt tests his theoretical construct using a simple OLS model for the case of export smuggling of rubber in Indonesia during 1949 to 1972. He establishes a linear relationship for the legal export of rubber as dependant on the variable rainfall, with incentive to smuggling defined as the rupiah return to a dollar's worth of smuggling relative to the rupiah return to a dollar's worth of legal trade, which is the ratio of the black market exchange rate to the legal effective exchange rate for rubber export. He compares the domestic price of rubber to price of its domestic competing activity (rice). So the dominant share of the explaining variances in legal trade of rubber belongs to the incentive to smuggle with a negative coefficient.

Martin and Panagariya (1984) show that increased enforcement of anti-smuggling laws raises real per unit costs of smuggling and also the domestic price of imports but lowers the absolute quantity and the share of illegal imports in total imports. However, their model does not illustrate an unambiguous effect of smuggling on the welfare.

Norton (1988) provides a theoretical model for smuggling of agricultural goods within EEC countries, but mainly the Republic of Ireland and Northern Ireland. He enters the transport cost for smuggling as well as the probability of detection into his model, and shows that an increase in the tax rate will increase the optimal choice of smuggled goods and the number of firms that are involved in this operation. As tax rates increase, intramarginal smugglers will increase their expected rents from smuggling, and the distance margin for worthwhile smuggling will be extended. However, there are some firms that depending to their transport costs will not smuggle goods. His model shows that increasing the fines on smuggling can reduce the expected value of the profits. Nevertheless, the Norton model can be used to show a negative relationship between increased fine rates on smuggling and the amounts of smuggled goods, on one side, and a positive relationship between increased taxes and tariffs on legal imports and the amount of smuggled products, on the other side.

Thursby et al. (1991) propose a model where smuggling is camouflaged by legal sales. They evaluate the effects of market structure and enforcement of law on smuggling and welfare. In their model, if the price effect of smuggling is greater than its cost, then it is possible that smuggling improves the welfare. They show that in increasing law enforcement against smugglers, government reduces the welfare of society. The case they model is cigarette smuggling in the United States during 1975 to 1982.

5.2.2 Empirical Literature

Because of its hidden and illegal nature, smuggling is difficult to measure. Those who engage in illegal imports and exports of products are a part of larger shadow economy. Fortunately, some economists have succeeded in developing a way to measure corruption and the shadow economy that traces smuggling through the official

international trade statistics. The trade discrepancy, the so-called
smuggling gap, is used to uncover irregularities in foreign trade and
thus to detect smuggling. In theory, export (import) of country A
should equal the import (export) of country B. The trade discrepancy
method aims to find significant gaps between registered export and
import figures in a country with its trading partners. Of course, there
are some important considerations and adjustments before implementing such an investigation. The possible discrepancies in trade statistics
of a country with its trading partners may due to different measure of
pricing exports and imports. In most countries import prices are presented in CIF (cost, insurance, and freight) while exports are in FOB
(free on board). That means that country A reported its exports to
country B in FOB prices and country B reports the same amount of
imports from country A in CIF prices that is higher than the FOB
prices. It is important to adjust export figures (in FOB prices), taking
into account the insurance and transportation costs. Most countries use
a unique CIF/FOB ratio to make the adjustment. Such an approach is
an accepted norm in practice due to its simplicity. However, it is not
always appropriate to use the same CIF/FOB ratio for all imports and
exports from/to different countries. The best option is to use different
CIF/FOB ratios depending on the country of origin and the destination of product. Nevertheless, when in world trade the insurance and
transportation data are missing or difficult to locate, most countries
use their unique adjustment ratio.[2] Before the import/export figures
can be compared, the figures have to translated into a similar basis.
The IMF (1993) recommends adding 10 percent to export figures as an
approximate adjustment for insurance and transportation costs (or
deducting 10 percent from import values).[3]

Morgenstern (1963) was among the first scholars to use the trade
data discrepancy method to detect smuggling. The technique was next
adapted and refined by Bhagwati (1964) to the case of Turkey and by
Naya and Morgan (1969) to the case of South East Asian counties.
McDonald (1985) used this method for ten developing countries,
finding a close association between export underinvoicing, export
taxes, and black market premium (BMP). Fisman and Wei (2004) used
this technique to study "missing imports" in China; a short time later
Fisman and Wei (2007) studied and found illegal trade in China's cultural goods. Hsieh and Moretti (2006) used foreign trade data to uncover
corruption by the government of Iraq, whereby under the "oil for food"
program oil exports were systematically underinvoiced in return for

bribes from oil buyers. Berger and Nitsch (2008) examined the foreign trade data discrepancies of the world's five largest importers from 2002 to 2006 and found a positive relationship between estimated discrepancies and level of corruption in both partner countries. Yavari (2000) applied the methodology of Bhagwati (1964) and estimated overvaluation of imports in Iran from 1977 to 1997. His calculation of import misinvoicing shows a different pattern before and after the final year of Iran's war with Iraq (1988). Beja (2008) applied the trade data gap method for the case of China and estimated the value of unrecorded trade around $1.4 trillion from 2000 to 2005.

Structural equation models (SEM) based on the theory of latent variables have been applied to measure the nonobservable economic concepts such as the shadow economy and corruption. One variant of SEM is the multiple indicators multiple causes (MIMIC) model. In the MIMIC approach the latent variable is connected to its theoretical causes and indicators. For the application of the MIMIC methodology in the shadow economy and corruption literature, see Schneider (2005) and Dreher et al. (2007), respectively. The application of the MIMIC models in the smuggling literature is new. Farzanegan (2009) uses trade discrepancy and the structural equation model to estimate the size of smuggling in Iran. Madah and Pajoyan (2005) also examine smuggling in Iran using a structural equation approach. They calculate an ordinal trend of import smuggling using only three causal variables, namely the rate of fines, the ratio of the official to the black market exchange rates, and import tariffs, and find a negative effect of fine rates on smuggling but a positive effect of exchange rates and tariffs. They did not, however, estimate the relative size and value of smuggling. To accomplish this, information is required on the value of smuggling in one of the years of the sample through another technique such as foreign trade data discrepancy. This complementary estimation enables the calculated MIMIC ordinal index of smuggling to be transformed to a relative index and thereby a meaningful value. Madah and Pajoyan also do not control for the effects of other key variables such as GDP per capita, trade openness, human capital, quality of political and economic institutions, and a range of important interaction terms. Thus their estimations are biased by the omitted variable problem. By focusing their study only on import smuggling, they neglects the important phenomenon of export smuggling. Export smuggling of fuel products from Iran results in a large divergence of government revenue.

Buehn and Farzanegan (2011) also use trade discrepancy approach within a structural model. They estimate an ordinal index of smuggling for 54 countries, and they are first to rank smuggling worldwide. They do not, however, estimate the relative size of smuggling for two reasons. First, their study is a cross-sectional analysis for 54 countries over the period 1990 to 1999. As such, the transformation of the MIMIC index into an index in USDs or percentage of official GDP would also provide a ranking of countries. Given the cross-sectional character of the sample, it was not possible to provide insight into the development of smuggling over time. Second, the aim of their study was primarily to provide an index of smuggling similar to the corruption index presented in Dreher et al. (2007). Their result should thus be seen as a first step to arrive at a broad index that can be used for further empirical analysis of smuggling. Buehn and Eichler (2009) calculate misinvoicing of trade in a study of illegal trade between Mexico and the United States. They conclude that export misinvoicing is positively correlated to a real peso depreciation and Mexican taxes on income/profits.

5.3 Methodology

As was mentioned in the preceding section, the MIMIC model, which is a specific form of SEM, is used to estimate the ordinal index of smuggling. I have one endogenous latent variable, which is smuggling. Because smuggling is not directly observable, from literature I have identified a robust set of causes and indicators of smuggling. This enables me to use the MIMIC model to analyze the relationship between smuggling and its determinants and, by accounting for the different indicators for smuggling, to reduce the possibility of error in the variables. Thus I use the MIMIC model to confirm the theoretical influence of a set of casual variables on smuggling.[4]

5.3.1 The Variables and Determinants

The MIMIC model consists of two parts: structural and measurement equations. The structural part of model examines the relationship between the latent variable of smuggling with its determinants (causes). The measurement part of model analyzes the link between the latent variable of smuggling and its indicators. The MIMIC estimates the relationship between observable variables (causes and indicators) and the latent variable by minimizing the distance between the sample covariance matrix **S** and the covariance matrix $\Sigma(\theta)$ predicted by the model.

The structural model is given by

$$\eta = \gamma'x + \zeta, \tag{5.1}$$

where η is a latent variable (smuggling), x is a vector of causal variables: $x' = (x_1, x_2, \ldots, x_q)$, γ is a vector of coefficients which shows the effects of causal variables on latent variable: $\gamma' = (\gamma_1, \gamma_2, \ldots, \gamma_q)$. These causal variables explain some of the variations in the latent variable; the unexplained part of the variations is reflected in the error term ζ. Of course, we could include the interaction terms in the structural part of model to investigate the conditional effects of causal variables on the latent variable.

The measurement part of model examines the link between the latent variable and its indicators. Since the latent variable of smuggling is not directly observable, we need a set of sound indicators to represent some part of smuggling effects on the macroeconomy. None of these indicators, however, is a perfect proxy for the latent variable of smuggling. Thus in the measurement model we consider also error terms for each of these indicators. The measurement model is given by

$$y = \lambda\eta + \varepsilon, \tag{5.2}$$

where y is a p vector of indicators of smuggling: $y' = (y_1, y_2, \ldots, y_p)$. η is the latent variable, λ is a vector of coefficients in the measurement part of model and represents the response of respected indicator to a unit change in the latent variable, and ε is the error term.

We substitute equation (5.1) into equation (5.2) to get a reduced form of multivariate regression model, where the endogenous dependent variable is an indicator of the latent variable of smuggling and the exogenous variables are its causes. The reduced form of model is given by

$$y = \Pi x + z, \tag{5.3}$$

where $\Pi = \lambda\gamma'$ is a matrix with rank equal to 1 and $z = \lambda\varsigma + \varepsilon$. The error term z in equation (5.3) is a p vector of linear combinations of the white noise error terms ς and ε from the structural and the measurement model, that is, $z \sim (0, \Omega)$. The covariance matrix Ω is given as $\text{Cov}(z) = E[(\lambda\varsigma + \varepsilon)(\lambda\varsigma + \varepsilon)'] = \lambda\lambda'\psi + \Theta_\varepsilon$ and similarly constrained like Π (Buehn and Farzanegan 2011). To estimate the model's parameters and identification of model, we need to find a reference variable. Since the latent variable is unobservable by definition and has no scale of its own, its unit of measurement has to be defined. The reference variable does this task. It is recommended that the value for the observed variable should be fixed, since the observed variable should represent the major effect of the latent variable (see Diamantopoulos and Siguaw 2000 for more details).

The estimation procedure minimizes the following fitting function:

$$F = \ln|\Sigma(\theta)| + \text{tr}\left[S\Sigma^{-1}\left(\hat{\theta}\right)\right] - \ln|S| - (p+q), \tag{5.4}$$

where $\Sigma(\theta)$ is the MIMIC model's covariance matrix. It is the function of parameters λ, γ. The values for the parameters and covariances are chosen in order to produce an estimate for $\Sigma(\theta)$, $\hat{\Sigma} = \Sigma(\hat{\theta})$, that is, as close as possible to the sample covariance matrix S of the observed causes and indicators, consisting of the x's and y's.

The first step in the MIMIC model estimation is to confirm the hypothesized relationships between the latent variable and its causes and indicators. Once these relationships and the parameters are identified and estimated the MIMIC model results can be used to calculate the latent variable scores. Next, with the help of the exogenous calculation of the relative size of smuggling in trade through the trade discrepancy approach, the ordinal scores of smuggling transform to cardinal scores, and so, finally, the estimate of the value of smuggling can be obtained.

5.3.2   The Empirical MIMIC Model of Smuggling

Following the theoretical presentation of the MIMIC model in previous section, I discuss and present the specific MIMIC model with the name of causes and indicators of smuggling, as will be explained in the subsequent section. The following causes are employed in the structural part of model: penalty rate on smuggling, black market premium, tariff burden, GDP per capita, unemployment rate, trade openness, literacy rate, quality of political and economic institutions, and interaction terms between real GDP per capita with black market premium, trade openness, and tariffs. Also included are interaction terms of education with black market premium, trade openness, institutions, and tariffs. The indirect effect of income through the quality of institutions is considered in the structural part of model. The structural equation (5.1), using the above-mentioned causal variables, is given by

$$[\text{Smuggling}] = [\gamma_1, \gamma_2, \gamma_3, \gamma_4, \gamma_5, \gamma_6, \gamma_7, \gamma_8, \gamma_9, \gamma_{10}] \times$$

$$\begin{bmatrix} \text{Penalty rate} \\ \text{Black market premium} \\ \text{Tariffs} \\ \text{Trade openness} \\ \text{Education} \\ \text{GDP per capita} \\ \text{Unemploymnet} \\ \text{GDP per capita growth} \\ \text{Quality of institutions} \\ \text{Interaction terms} \end{bmatrix} + [\varsigma]. \qquad (5.5)$$

The measurement part of model has three indicators to capture some parts of smuggling effects on the macroeconomy: petroleum goods consumption growth rate, import prices, and real government revenues. The applied measurement model (5.2) is given by

$$\begin{bmatrix} \text{Petroleum goods consumption} \\ \text{Import prices} \\ \text{Real government revenues} \end{bmatrix} = \begin{bmatrix} \lambda_1 \\ \lambda_2 \\ \lambda_3 \end{bmatrix} \times [\text{Smuggling}] + \begin{bmatrix} \varepsilon_1 \\ \varepsilon_2 \\ \varepsilon_3 \end{bmatrix}. \qquad (5.6)$$

The applied path diagram of the MIMIC models is illustrated in figure 5.1. The expected theoretical sign of causes and indicators are presented in the small squares.

5.4   Data

In this section, I explain the causes and indicators that I use to estimate the size of smuggling in Iran from 1970 to 2002.

5.4.1   Causes of Smuggling

Penalty Rate   Cost–benefit analysis is also applicable in smuggling related activities. The potential benefits for smugglers are due to evasion of trade taxes, tariffs, and duties. Thus in the local market the smuggled goods have a more competitive position compared to legally imported goods. The costs depend on the level of risk in illegal business. Furthermore the quality of judiciary system, monitoring of police forces, and the degree of legal punishment may increase the costs. In the countries

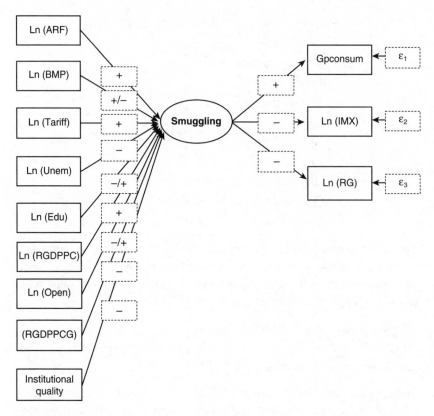

Figure 5.1
Hypothesized path diagram (without interactions). Source: Farzanegan (2009). Reprinted with permission from Elsevier.

with a weak judiciary system and low penalties, we can expect the industry of smuggling to thrive. In the theoretical literature on smuggling, one of the key variables is enforcement of law and penalty rate (see Martin and Panagariya 1984; Norton 1988). High penalties can change the culture of corruption. Fisman and Miguel (2007) examine the effect of law enforcement on the behavior of the UN diplomats who illegally park their cars. Their results confirm the effectiveness of penalizing illegal behavior, and this may have some cultural aspects as well.

In this chapter, I adjust for inflation a penalty rate on smuggling that equals one Iranian rial for every US dollar of smuggled goods. The adjustment of this variable is based on Madah and Pajoyan (2005). Figure 5.2 shows the penalty rates in Iran.

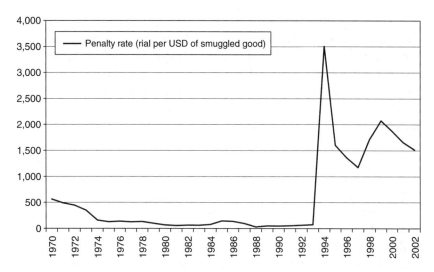

Figure 5.2
Development of penalty rate on smuggling in Iran. Source: Madah and Pajoyan (2005).

The real rate of penalty before the revision of smuggling punishment codes by the Expediency Council of Iran in 1994 was very low and negligible. The real rate of penalty in 1994 increased by 46 times its rate in the previous year.

Thus there can be expected a negative effect of the penalty rate on the amount of smuggling. The penalty rate on smuggling is entered into the model in its log of inverse form. This was done to make the variable's distribution normal.[5]

Black Market Premium (BMP)   A high premium in the black market of foreign exchange (mainly USD) signals a go-ahead for illegal traders. They can underinvoice their real amount of exports and sell the unreported US dollars from their exports in the domestic black market for US dollars. However, a high black market premium can also discourage some illegal traders by increasing their costs. Illegal importers who do not have access to the subsidized foreign exchange in the banking system face higher financing costs of their imports. They have to buy the foreign exchange in the black market at a higher price. Thus a higher BMP can discourage import misinvoicing. Of course, if the illegal importers have access to the official banking system and subsidized foreign exchange, then we can expect them to consider overinvoicing their real imports. In overinvoicing their real imports, the import smugglers gain subsidized foreign exchange from the banking system. They can sell the extra acquired foreign exchange in the local black market and obtain an attractive profit (for more on the theoretical aspects of BMP effects on smuggling, see Barnett 2003; De Macedo 1987). McDonald (1985) also includes evidence on the BMP effect on underinvoicing of exports and overinvoicing of imports. Kiguel and O`Connel (1995) discuss the negative effects of higher BMPs on exports, since exporters are encouraged to engage in misinvoicing their real amount of exports and thus falsify the official data on exports. Figure 5.3 illustrates the trend of BMP in Iran. We can consider that the black market for the US dollar was a post-revolutionary phenomena in Iran. The post-revolutionary economy was accompanied by a histori- cally record high black market for the US dollar. The unusually large premium in the black market (see figure 5.3) was achieved under strict foreign exchange control during most years after the revolution. An importer with access to a subsidized official exchange rate 22 times below the black market rate had great incentive to overinvoice imports or underinvoice exports for an easy and immediate profit (Farzanegan 2009). The Khatami government implemented some key economic reforms that reduced rent-seeking opportunities. One of those reforms was unification of different exchange rates in 2002. Khatami

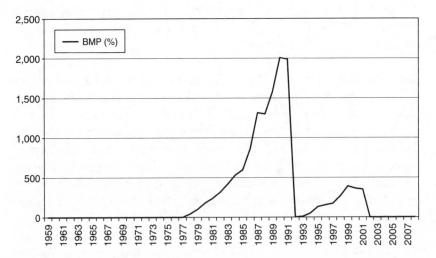

Figure 5.3
Black market premium in Iran (percent, USD/IRR). Source: CBI (2010).

government reforms in the foreign exchange market were intended to control smuggling and the mismanagement of scare resources by increasing transparency. However, such an institutional reform had its own costs as well. Increased inflation was one of the costs due to higher import prices following unification of exchange rates. It is estimated that fiscal costs of this reform amounted to 3 to 6 percent of GDP (for more details on trade reforms under Khatami, see an excellent review by Alizadeh 2003).

Theincreasing BMPs can be expected to provide attractive incentives for illegal traders to increase their activities. To show this, I use a logarithmic transformation of data obtained from the Iranian Central Bank.

Tariff Burden on Imports   Tariffs and taxes on trade are one of the standard determinants of engaging in smuggling and the shadow economy. It is defined as the taxes and duties on imports divided by total imports. Higher taxes on imports encourage importers to under-invoice their real amount of imports. Such a misinvoicing reduces the amount of paid taxes. In a case study for Chile, Phylaktis (1991) finds that tariffs have an increasing effect on smuggling. Pitt (1981) shows that trade restrictions such as trade taxes and duties can cause price disparities among countries, encouraging illegal traders to use such price gaps to their advantage. Figure 5.4 shows the import taxes burden

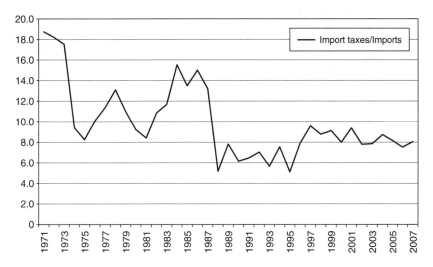

Figure 5.4
Import taxes burden (percent). Source: CBI (2010).

from 1970 to 2008 in Iran. Notice the overall decreasing trend in tariffs. A significant decrease is evident at the end of war with Iraq (1988–89) and at start of a reconstruction of economy and the liberalization policies under the Hashemi Rafsanjani government. The average share of import taxes in total imports during three periods (before revolution, 1971–1978; Iran–Iraq war, 1979–1987; and postwar period, 1988–2008) are 13, 12, and 8 percent, respectively.

The same decreasing trend can be observed in the share of import taxes in total taxes from 1970 to 2008. The average share of import taxes in total taxes during three periods (before revolution, 1971–1978; Iran–Iraq war, 1979–1987; and postwar period, 1988–2008) are 40, 32, and 26 percent, respectively. Clearly, there can be expected an increasing effect of the higher tariff burden on the smuggling size.

GDP Per capita and the Unemployment Rate   An increasing GDP per capita (as a proxy for disposable income of consumers) and /or a reduction of the unemployment rate can raise the effective demand for both legal and illegal imported goods, encouraging higher consumption. Increasing income can also boost corruption-related activities when rent-seeking opportunities are present (see Braun and Di Tella 2004; Fréchette 2006). Braun and Di Tella (p. 93) explain this as due to the pro-cyclical nature of corruption-related activities, where "moral standards are lowered during booms, as greed becomes the dominant force for economic decision."

The effect of changes in the unemployment rate on smuggling depends on the relative weight of "income effects" and "substitution effects." Increasing unemployment or decreasing GDP per capita in the official economy may encourage people to find alternative economic activities in the shadow economy and illegal trade. This is called the "substitution effect." On the other side, increasing unemployment and/or a decrease of GDP per capita may reduce the purchasing power of consumers. Thus their demand for both legal and illegal goods in the market will fall. This is called the "income effect." Thus, besides including the level of GDP per capita, I have controlled for the growth rate of GDP per capita. An increasing growth rate pushes economic agents into economic activity. The negative connection between the growth rate of income and the shadow economy related activities is already discussed in the literature (see Frey and Weck-Hannemann 1984; Loayza 1997; Kaufmann and Kaliberda 1996; Eilat and Zinnes 2002; Schneider and Enste 2000). Figure 5.5 shows the development of

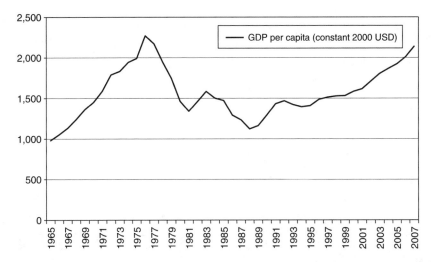

Figure 5.5
Trend of real GDP per capita (USD). Source: World Bank (2010b).

income per capita in constant prices for Iran. The average real GDP per capita (USD) during three periods (before revolution, 1971–1978; Iran–Iraq war, 1979–1987; and postwar period, 1988–2008) are 1,941, 1,455, and 1,571 USD, respectively. The real income per capita during the post-revolutionary years is, on average, behind the record growth in the pre-revolution year of 1979. Figure 5.6 shows the unemployment trend in Iran.

Trade Openness Trade openness is defined as the share of total trade (imports and exports) in GDP. Usually a reduction of tariffs can be expected to lead to higher levels of legal trade. Thus lower amounts of smuggling can be expected in times of higher trade openness. However, the positive effect of higher trade openness in this context depends on the quality of institutions and monitoring system. The Iranian experience of increased illegal imports through Free Trade Zones suggests a connection between institutions and trade openness (Arabmazar 2007). It is estimated that for every $100,000 in legal imports, smugglers import $300,000 through official customs. Investigations also show that at least 90 percent of import smuggling is through Free Trade Zones[6]. In the theoretical literature, we can abide by the observation (of Pitt 1981) that the greater the legal trade, the easier it is to hide smuggling from enforcement agencies, and

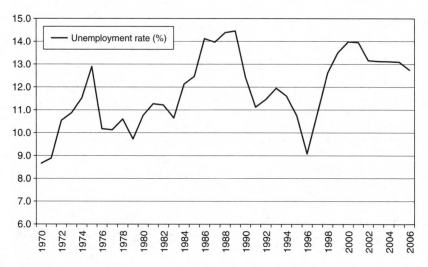

Figure 5.6
Unemployment rate (percent) in Iran. Source: Amini et al. (2007).

smuggling will therefore be less costly. Indeed trade liberalization without an effective monitoring system creates new rent-seeking opportunities for well-connected traders. It is necessary to design instruments to reduce corruption besides implementing trade liberalization (For debates on trade openness and corruption, see Ades and Di Tella 1999; Sung and Chu 2003). Figure 5.7 shows the trend of trade openness (in current prices) in Iran.

The average trade openness (percent) during three periods (before revolution, 1971–1978; Iran–Iraq war, 1979–1987; and postwar period, 1988–2008) is 56, 31, and 42 percent, respectively.

Education There are two different schools of thought regarding the effects of education (expenditures) on aggregated indicators such as economic growth. One group believes that the government spending on education and health care can increase economic growth and reduce income inequality and poverty (e.g., see Barro 1991; Tanzi and Chu 1998; Sylwester 2002). The other group of researchers undermines the positive and significant effect of education (spending) on aggregated indicators such as growth and poverty. Jimenez (1986) suggested that the poor do not benefit from education spending and such spending does not reduce income inequality. Fields (1980) and Ram (1989) also have a similar view. Pritchett (2001) and Benhabib and Spiegel (1994)

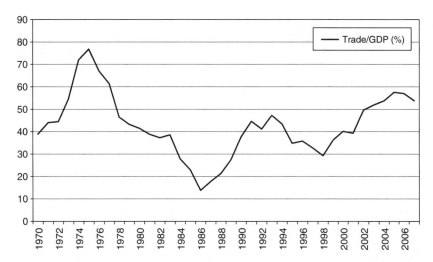

Figure 5.7
Trade openness in Iran (percent). Source: CBI (2010).

suggest that the effectiveness of education and education spending on growth depends on the quality of institutions in the economy. As long as the other bottlenecks remain in the economy, increasing education may not lead to higher growth.

Increasing education of people may increase opportunities for employment in the legal and official economy. However, where institutions are weak and extensive rent-seeking exists in the economy, educated people may take advantage of such opportunities for personal gain. Also it is well known that increased education usually leads to higher income, and that wealthier people are usually risk lovers. Hence a positive attitude toward risky activities may be what encourages people to engage in illegal trade for higher profits.

High on the agenda of the Iranian government after the revolution of 1979 was expanding public education and eradicating illiteracy. There came also a significant increase in the quantitative aspects of schooling after the revolution. While the average years of schooling were 0.63 in 1960, this figure reached 4.66 years in 2000 (Barro and Lee 2001). The literacy rate, as a further example, was only 50 percent in 1978; this reached 87 percent in 2005. While the share of government expenditures for education in total government expenditures decreased from about 20 percent in 1960 to 13 percent in the last year of the Pahlavi monarchy, it experienced a steady increasing trend in the

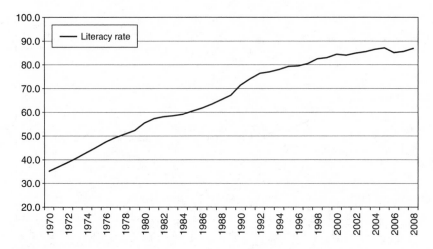

Figure 5.8
Literacy rate in Iran. Source: CBI (2010).

post-revolutionary government. Figure 5.8 illustrates the trend of literacy rate in Iran.

Quality of Economic and Political Institutions Political and economic institutions define the rules and framework for economic agents. These institutions not only directly affect the incentives of traders but also are crucial for the effects of other variables on illegal trade related activities. For example, higher penalties rates are expected to reduce the incentives to engage in smuggling. However, in the case of weak monitoring institutions and judiciary system, such penalties will be useless. Another example is effectiveness of education, and trade openness on reduction of smuggling. Higher education may change citizens' attitudes toward illegal activities, but weak economic institutions, extensive corruption, and rent-seeking opportunities may negate the positive effects of education.

In my analysis, I use three indicators for political institutions and one indicator for economic institutions. The polity index, the Vanhannen indicators (democracy, competition, and participation) measure the degree of democracy and political openness in Iran. The indicator for the quality of economic institutions is called "contract-intensive money (CIM)." This is an objective measure of the enforceability of contracts and the security of property rights. This indicator defined as ratio of noncurrency money to total money supply (M2-C)/M2). A

Table 5.6
Correlation among different measures of institutional quality

Institutional quality indicators	Polity	CIM	Van_comp	Van_index	Van_part
Polity	1.00				
CIM	0.35	1.00			
Van_comp	0.65	0.02	1.00		
Van_index	0.79	0.10	0.94	1.00	
Van_part	0.84	0.20	0.48	0.70	1.00

Source: Farzanegan (2009). Reprinted with permission from Elsevier.

higher level of CIM is associated with a larger amount of money in a less liquid form, indicating a "transaction-friendly" environment. This index was introduced by Clague et al. (1999). The data for constructing the index is from CBI (2008). I also construct an index based on the different political and economic institutions using factor analysis. The rationale behind factor analysis is that different measures of institutional qualities all measure the same concept, for example, good governance and democracy. So there should be a relatively high correlation between these different measures (see table 5.6). The final calculated index of institutional quality (IQ) reflects the underlying concept being measured through the various observed institutional quality measures (see figure 5.9 and appendix B for underlying data of IQ).

5.4.2 Indicators of Smuggling

Indicators of smuggling are meant to capture some parts of smuggling effects on the economy. Based on the previous literature and characteristics of the Iranian economy, I use the following indicators:

Government Revenues   Monetary costs of smuggling are due to tax and tariff evasion. Tax revenues are the predominant source of government revenues in most countries. While developed countries rely more on direct taxes such as taxes on income, profits, and capital gains, developing countries depend more on indirect taxes, including taxes on international trade (Askari 2006, p. 135). Higher reliance on indirect taxes (taxes on imports and consumption) is due to lower administrative costs of such taxes. Smugglers by evading these legal taxes put a heavy burden on the government annual budgets. Thus I expect that a

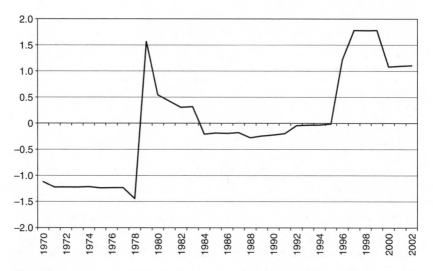

Figure 5.9
Institutional quality index for Iran. The lower the value is, the lower the quality of the political and economic institutions. Source: Farzanegan (2009). Reprinted with permission from Elsevier.

higher level of smuggling reduces international trade tax revenues and consequently general government revenues. Iranian government revenues depend mostly on oil and gas revenues and tax revenues. Oil revenues cover crude oil and refinery products. However, massive subsideies have caused petrochemical goods to be exported illegally. Before a rationing system was set in place, gasoline comprised up to 90 percent of all smuggling from Iran. The source of government revenues is CBI (2008).

Import Price Index The import price index measures the price changes of imported products into Iran. This index is computed based on a basket of imported goods in the local market. The imported goods can be both legally and illegally imported products. Since smugglers evade taxes and duties, they can sell their products at lower prices than their legal competitors in the local market. Depending on the size of smuggled goods in the market, their prices will influence the final market equilibrium prices of all products. One example of this is the mobile phone set market in Iran and the decision of the Ahmadinejad government to increase tariffs on mobile phone imports. In 2006, with domestic demand for mobile phone sets in Iran for 10 million mobile phones, and domestic production at only 1 million mobile phones, the government decided to raise the tariff on mobile phone imports from 4 to 60 percent. The main reason given for the high tariff hike was that the funds were to be invested in domestic mobile phone production. The share of smuggled mobile phone sets in recent years approached 80 percent of the local market. The tremendous increase in tariffs on legal imports of this product, besides the imposition of technical controls on the registration of illegally imported mobile phones sets in national telephone network, significantly increased the import prices for this product. The import tariff for this mobile phones, within two years of increased from 4 to 60 percent, only to decline back again to 4 percent in 2008 (Farzanegan 2009). Fisman and Miguel (2008, p. 66) provide insight on the Chinese government anticorruption programs affecting the import prices: " . . . official imports into Guangdong province jumped by 10 percent as smuggling declined. But exports plummeted 12 percent as the province's factories struggled to deal with higher priced imported inputs, like oil and raw materials, which could no longer be smuggled in tariff-free . . .." The theoretical debates on the effect of smuggling on import prices are presented in Thursby et al. (1991) and Martin and Panagariya (1984).

Petroleum Products Consumption Growth Rate   This variable is selected as another indicator for smuggling effects. The main reason behind selection of this variable is the high price disparity between Iran and its neighbors in oil and refinery products. The massive smuggling of petroleum products is the concern of General Ali Soltani, director of the campaign against economic crimes, who maintains that: "Every year, 1.8-billion litres of refined oil products worth 10.8 billion rials [$1.18 billion] are smuggled abroad."[7] Table 5.7 gives a comparison the prices of gasoline in Iran and some of its neighbors. In 2006, for example,

Table 5.7
Pump price for gasoline (USD per liter) in Iran and its neighbors

	1998	2000	2002	2004	2006
Afghanistan			0.34	0.53	0.68
Iran	0	0.05	0.07	0.09	0.09
Oman	0.31	0.31	0.31	0.31	0.31
Pakistan	0.46	0.53	0.52	0.62	1.01
Turkey	0.78	0.88	1.02	1.44	1.88

Source: World Bank (2010b).

while the price of gasoline in Iran was about 10 cents per liter, in Turkey it was sold at about 2 USD per liter. Such a significant pride disparity is due to smuggling.

5.5   Results

The estimation results of the MIMIC models are presented in table 5.8 for eleven different specifications. The main differences among these specifications are due to the various political and economical institutional quality measures and inclusion of various interaction terms. The ordinal index of smuggling can be calculated based on the significant variables in the structural part of models. In order to estimate the cardinal index of smuggling and meaningful size of illegal trade, I used a "trade discrepancy" method as a complementary estimation. The trade discrepancy methodology allows the estimated ordinal index of smuggling to be transformed into cardinal and meaningful numbers.

First, I discuss the estimated results on the structural part of the MIMIC models. The penalty rate (in its inverse form[8]) has an increasing effect on smuggling. Mathematically speaking, its direct effect has a decreasing effect on smuggling. This effect is also statistically significant in all specifications at 1 percent level. The effect of the black market premium for the US dollar on smuggling is positive and significant in specifications 1, 3, 4, 5, 6, 10, and 11. This positive effect means that increasing black market premium provides attractive opportunities for the illegal traders. This result is in line with the theoretical literature discussed in this chapter. Increasing unemployment reduces the smuggling-related activities, while higher levels of GDP per capita increase smuggling. This shows that "income effects" are stronger than "substitution effects" in Iran. Increasing income per capita increases demand for all legal or illegal goods in the local market. Higher trade liberalization in Iran is accompanied by higher illegal trade; this is the so-called Pitt effect (see Pitt 1981). The higher quality of political and economic institutions discourages engagement of economic agents in the illegal trade. Better political institutions provide more transparency in all aspects of society, including trade. The free media, however, highlight the corruption cases in the economy, increasing the risk of engagement in the illegal trade. The negative effects of political and economic institutional quality on smuggling are statistically significant at 1 percent level in all models. Higher levels of literacy in Iran have expanded smuggling. This shows to some extent the unproductive system of

Table 5.8
Estimations of MIMIC-model

Specification	S1	S2	S3	S4	S5	S6	S7	S8	S9	S10	S11
Causes	Standardized solutions with (t statistucsstatistics)										
Ln (inverse of penalty rate)	0.12 (4.0)	0.13 (5.1)	0.13 (4.1)	0.09 (3.4)	0.09 (3.0)	0.12 (4.0)	0.12 (4.4)	0.13 (4.6)	0.13 (4.8)	0.09 (3.3)	0.08 (3.0)
Ln (black market premium)	0.10 (2.4)	−0.09 (−1.5)	0.13 (2.9)	0.13 (3.5)	0.16 (3.8)	0.12 (3.3)	0.03 (0.7)	−0.03 (−0.5)	−0.04 (−0.9)	0.12 (1.8)	0.16 (6.0)
Ln (tariff burden)	0.04 (1.7)	−0.00 (−0.1)	−0.01 (−0.2)	0.04 (1.8)	0.04 (1.7)	0.03 (1.3)	−0.0 (−0.5)	−0.01 (−0.5)	−0.01 (−0.5)	0.06 (2.7)	0.02 (1.4)
Ln (unemployment)	−0.03 (−2.1)	−0.00 (−0.0)	−0.04 (−2.5)	−0.09 (−4.9)	−0.08 (−4.4)	−0.03 (−2.1)	−0.02 (−1.2)	−0.00 (−0.1)	0.00 (0.0)	−0.05 (−2.1)	−0.07 (−4.6)
Ln (education)	0.32 (0.5)	2.66 (3.5)	0.14 (0.2)	0.83 (1.6)	1.13 (2.0)	0.50 (0.9)	2.34 (3.2)	2.98 (3.6)	3.21 (4.4)	−0.73 (−8.0)	−0.74 (−19.2)
Ln (real GDP per capita)	0.88 (4.1)	0.32 (1.8)	0.69 (3.1)	0.84 (4.7)	0.73 (4.0)	0.76 (4.3)	0.39 (2.8)	0.03 (1.4)		0.69 (3.8)	0.81 (5.8)
Ln (trade openness)	0.13 (3.4)	0.08 (2.4)	0.13 (3.7)	0.11 (3.3)	0.12 (3.6)	0.11 (3.9)	0.07 (2.4)	0.06 (2.4)	0.04 (1.1)	0.11 (3.4)	0.10 (4.3)
GDP per capita growth rate	−0.87 (−4.2)	−0.30 (−1.8)	−0.70 (−3.2)	−0.84 (−4.8)	−0.71 (−4.0)	−0.75 (−4.4)	−0.36 (−2.6)		0.03 (0.8)	−0.69 (−3.8)	−0.82 (−6.1)
Polity index	−0.09 (3.1)					−0.09 (−3.0)					
CIM		−0.21 (−4.6)					−0.14 (−3.5)	−0.22 (−4.2)	−0.22 (−6.3)		

Table 5.8
(continued)

Specification	S1	S2	S3	S4	S5	S6	S7	S8	S9	S10	S11
Causes	Standardized solutions with (t statistucsstatistics)										
Van_part			-0.08 (-2.1)								
Van_index				-0.09 (-4.4)							
Van_comp					-0.07 (-3.8)						
IQ										-0.13 (-2.0)	-0.12 (-4.7)
Ln (bmp)*ln(rgdppc)	0.11 (0.8)	0.03 (0.2)	0.10 (0.6)	0.04 (0.3)	-0.06 (-0.4)					0.18 (0.9)	
Ln (open)*ln(rgdppc)	-0.8 (-4.7)	-0.4 (-3.3)	-0.6 (-3.78)	-0.7 (-4.9)	-0.6 (-4.2)	-0.7 (-4.6)	-0.4 (-3.1)			-0.6 (-3.4)	-0.7 (-5.7)
Ln (tariff)*ln(rgdppc)	0.09 (0.7)	0.2 (2.2)	0.3 (1.9)	0.09 (0.7)	0.06 (0.4)	0.09 (0.6)		-0.02 (-0.9)		0.14 (1.0)	
Ln (bmp)*gdppcg	-0.1 (-0.8)	-0.03 (-0.2)	-0.11 (-0.7)	-0.03 (-0.2)	0.06 (0.4)				0.03 (1.2)	-0.18 (-0.9)	
Ln (tariff)*gdppcg	-0.08 (-0.6)	-0.2 (-2.2)	-0.3 (-1.9)	-0.07 (-0.6)	-0.04 (-0.2)	-0.07 (-0.5)			-0.01 (-0.3)	-0.11 (-0.8)	

Table 5.8
(continued)

Specification	S1	S2	S3	S4	S5	S6	S7	S8	S9	S10	S11
Causes	Standardized solutions with (t statistucsstatistics)										
Ln(open)*gdppcg	0.7 (4.6)	0.4 (3.3)	0.6 (3.6)	0.6 (4.8)	0.5 (4.0)	0.6 (4.5)	0.3 (3.0)		-0.0 (-0.09)	0.5 (3.3)	0.6 (5.8)
Ln(edu)*ln(bmp)	0.05 (0.8)	0.1 (1.9)	0.02 (0.3)	0.00 (0.08)	-0.03 (-0.5)	0.0 (0.07)		0.02 (0.5)		0.03 (0.3)	
Ln (edu)*CIM	-1.0 (-1.5)	-3.3 (-4.6)	-0.9 (-1.3)	-1.6 (-3.0)	-1.9 (-3.4)	-1.3 (-2.2)	-3.13 (-4.5)	-3.7 (-4.9)	-4.2 (-5.7)		
Ln (edu)*ln(open)	0.09 (2.0)	0.09 (2.2)	0.12 (2.5)	0.08 (2.0)	0.05 (1.2)	0.07 (1.8)	0.02 (0.7)			0.10 (1.8)	0.10 (3.9)
Ln (edu)*ln(tariff)	0.14 (3.5)	0.10 (3.0)	0.14 (3.1)	0.15 (4.3)	0.11 (3.0)	0.12 (3.2)	0.04 (1.2)			0.12 (2.8)	0.15 (5.3)
Ln(edu)*IQ										-0.1 (-1.3)	
Ln (open)*IQ										-0.07 (-1.3)	
Ln (rgdppc)*IQ										-0.1 (-0.9)	
GDPPCG*IQ										0.05 (0.5)	

Table 5.8
(continued)

Indicators

Petroleum consumption	0.5 (3.9)	0.4 (2.8)	0.4 (3.3)	0.5 (4.1)	0.5 (4.2)	0.5 (3.7)	0.3 (2.7)	0.3 (2.5)	0.3 (2.5)	0.5 (3.9)	0.5 (3.7)
Ln (import price index)*	−0.96	−0.97	−0.96	−0.96	−0.96	−0.95	−0.96	−0.97	−0.97	−0.97	−0.97
Ln (government revenues)	−0.6 (−4.3)	−0.6 (−4.7)	−0.6 (−4.8)	−0.5 (−4.1)	−0.5 (−4.0)	−0.6 (−4.6)	−0.6 (−4.9)	−0.6 (−4.8)	−0.6 (−4.8)	−0.5 (−4.0)	−0.6 (−4.2)

Goodness-of-fit indexes

RMSEA[a]	0.00	0.00	0.00	0.00	0.00	0.00	0.00	0.00	0.00	0.00	0.00
GFI[b]	0.87	0.86	0.87	0.87	0.87	0.87	0.84	0.83	0.84	0.88	0.85
AGFI[c]	0.85	0.84	0.85	0.85	0.85	0.85	0.82	0.80	0.81	0.87	0.83
NFI[d]	0.94	0.94	0.94	0.94	0.94	0.94	0.92	0.90	0.89	0.95	0.90

Source: Farzanegan (2009). Reprinted with permission from Elsevier.
Note: The * indicates a scale variable.
a. The RMSEA shows how well the model, with unknown but optimally chosen parameter values, would fit the population covariance matrix if it were available. Values less than 0.05 are indicators of a good fit.
b. This index ranges between 0 and 1. The GFI > 0.90 is usually taken as reflecting acceptable fits.
c. GFI adjusted for a degree of freedom.
d. Normed fit index (NFI), which has the range of 0 to 1. The larger amount is better.

education in Iran. The interaction of education and quality of economic institutions nevertheless shows a negative effect on smuggling. This negative effect is highly significant in most specifications. It means that education may discourage youths from engaging in illegal trade provided that the quality of the economic institutions is good.

On the side of measurement model, increased smuggling has a significant and negative effect on import prices. As can be expected, high levels of smuggling also raise consumption of petroleum products. Furthermore tax evasion by smugglers burdens the government budget. This is shown in negative effects of smuggling on government revenues. The goodness-of-fit indicators show satisfactory performance of all specifications.

As I mentioned earlier, the MIMIC models in table 5.8 provide necessary information for ordinal index of smuggling in Iran. To make this ordinal index to meaningful economic terms, we need estimation of smuggling through another methodology at one of the years of our sample (1970–2002). I use the trade discrepancy method to estimate the total misinvoicing in Iran. I compare my estimations to those of Yavari (2000). The trade discrepancy method is already explained in the empirical literature section of this chapter and Farzanegan (2009); for import, export, and total misinvoicing in Iran, see Farzanegan (2009). Yavari (2000) also calculated import misinvoicing in Iran for the period of 1988 to 1997. The figures in his calculation are quite close to my calculations of import misinvoicing for the same period, in particular for 1993. The differences may be due to different trade weights and trade partners used in his and my analysis.

I use the figure from 1993 as the share of total misinvoicing in Iran's total trade. This leads to a relative size of misinvoicing in Iran's foreign trade of 12.74 percent. This figure will be used for calibrating the ordinal smuggling index derived from structural equations. The relative size of smuggling in total trade for all specifications is illustrated in table 5.9a; also shown in table 5.9a is the absolute amount of smuggling for each specification. The average size of smuggling in trade and the average amount of smuggling across all specifications is about 13 percent, or $2.65 billion. This is the first estimation of the amount of smuggling in Iran based on the SEM and trade discrepancy method. The estimated relative size of smuggling (table 5.9a) enables me to calculate the absolute amount of illegal trade in Iran. Table 5.9b presents the estimated amount of smuggling over 1988 to 2002 for all specifications. According to table 5.9b, the highest amount of

Table 5.9a
Size (percent of trade) and amount of smuggling (million USD)

Year/ specifications	S1	S2	S3	S4	S5	S6	S7	S8	S9	S10	S11
1970	9.1	13.7	13.2	15.4	13.6	15.9	15.1	13.4	14.4	16.0	15.6
1971	11.5	14.2	13.3	15.4	13.9	16.0	15.5	13.5	14.4	16.1	15.7
1972	10.7	14.0	13.2	15.1	13.7	15.7	15.2	13.5	14.3	15.7	15.3
1973	12.2	14.1	13.4	15.0	13.8	15.6	15.3	13.7	14.2	15.6	15.3
1974	13.0	13.9	13.4	14.9	13.8	15.5	15.2	14.3	14.3	15.4	15.2
1975	13.2	14.2	13.1	14.8	14.2	15.3	15.3	14.6	14.3	15.2	15.1
1976	12.0	13.9	13.0	14.6	14.1	14.9	14.7	14.1	14.2	14.9	14.8
1977	14.3	14.0	13.2	14.6	14.2	15.0	15.1	14.3	14.1	15.1	14.9
1978	14.1	12.9	13.2	14.4	14.0	14.7	13.5	12.3	13.0	15.0	14.8
1979	15.8	13.4	12.4	14.2	13.0	14.8	14.0	12.8	13.4	14.7	14.7
1980	17.0	13.7	13.1	14.1	13.0	14.7	14.6	13.5	13.5	14.7	14.6
1981	16.1	13.7	13.2	14.0	13.0	14.5	14.2	13.7	13.6	14.5	14.4
1982	14.8	13.6	13.1	13.9	12.9	14.2	13.9	13.5	13.6	14.3	14.2
1983	15.9	13.7	13.1	13.9	12.9	14.3	14.1	13.9	13.6	14.4	14.3
1984	15.7	13.6	12.8	14.0	13.5	14.2	13.9	13.5	13.6	14.5	14.3
1985	14.8	13.5	12.8	13.8	13.4	14.1	13.7	13.2	13.5	14.1	14.2
1986	12.5	13.3	12.7	13.6	13.2	13.8	13.2	13.2	13.5	13.8	13.8
1987	14.6	13.6	12.8	13.6	13.4	14.0	13.7	13.4	13.5	13.9	14.0
1988	12.7	13.5	12.9	13.4	13.2	13.7	13.5	13.6	13.7	13.5	13.7
1989	13.0	13.6	12.8	13.3	13.2	13.6	13.4	13.4	13.5	13.4	13.5
1990	13.0	13.7	12.9	13.1	13.2	13.3	13.4	13.3	13.3	13.2	13.3
1991	13.0	13.7	12.9	13.0	13.2	13.1	12.7	12.9	13.1	13.1	13.2

Table 5.9a
(continued)

Year/ specifications	S1	S2	S3	S4	S5	S6	S7	S8	S9	S10	S11
1992	10.3	13.0	12.7	12.7	12.9	12.6	11.9	12.3	12.9	12.6	12.7
1993	12.7	12.7	12.7	12.7	12.7	12.7	12.7	12.7	12.7	12.7	12.7
1994	7.6	11.8	12.4	12.4	12.5	12.2	11.2	10.7	11.9	12.0	12.2
1995	5.5	11.4	12.3	12.2	12.4	11.9	10.8	10.5	11.8	11.7	11.9
1996	5.7	11.3	12.0	12.1	11.7	11.8	10.2	10.2	11.7	11.6	11.7
1997	4.4	11.0	11.9	11.9	11.6	11.6	9.9	10.1	11.7	11.3	11.4
1998	4.8	11.2	12.0	11.8	11.6	11.6	10.1	9.8	11.5	11.1	11.3
1999	3.8	11.0	11.9	11.7	11.6	11.4	9.7	9.7	11.5	11.0	11.2
2000	2.9	10.7	11.5	11.8	12.3	11.2	9.5	9.2	11.2	10.9	11.1
2001	3.6	10.7	11.6	11.8	12.3	11.3	9.4	9.2	11.2	11.0	11.2
2002	5.1	10.6	11.6	11.8	12.2	11.3	9.7	9.1	11.0	11.1	11.2
Max	17.0	14.2	13.4	15.4	14.2	16.0	15.5	14.6	14.4	16.1	15.7
Min	2.9	10.6	11.5	11.7	11.6	11.2	9.4	9.1	11.0	10.9	11.1
Average	11.07	12.94	12.69	13.49	13.04	13.66	12.98	12.45	13.08	13.59	13.57
Average amount of smuggling (million USD, 1988–2002)	1,824	2,744	2,798	2,825	2,841	2,784	2,555	2,535	2,777	2,742	2,772

Source: Farzanegan (2009). Reprinted with permission from Elsevier.

Table 5.9b
Value of smuggling (million USD)

Year/specifications	S1	S2	S3	S4	S5	S6	S7	S8	S9	S10	S11
1988	1,547	1,642	1,560	1,628	1,603	1,661	1,639	1,651	1,666	1,635	1,667
1989	2,293	2,409	2,269	2,352	2,335	2,395	2,370	2,362	2,386	2,372	2,391
1990	3,554	3,763	3,527	3,596	3,614	3,649	3,663	3,642	3,657	3,609	3,654
1991	4,146	4,353	4,098	4,147	4,189	4,162	4,049	4,105	4,166	4,175	4,200
1992	3,402	4,281	4,174	4,197	4,243	4,170	3,932	4,048	4,244	4,153	4,194
1993	3,093	3,093	3,093	3,093	3,093	3,093	3,093	3,093	3,093	3,093	3,093
1994	1,438	2,225	2,347	2,347	2,363	2,297	2,114	2,024	2,243	2,271	2,304
1995	1,010	2,094	2,259	2,248	2,281	2,184	1,983	1,923	2,172	2,143	2,184
1996	1,285	2,530	2,697	2,708	2,633	2,656	2,296	2,293	2,632	2,595	2,625
1997	919	2,323	2,505	2,512	2,451	2,438	2,087	2,119	2,466	2,374	2,393
1998	863	1,991	2,131	2,108	2,069	2,058	1,800	1,754	2,057	1,985	2,021
1999	821	2,391	2,580	2,547	2,505	2,474	2,103	2,096	2,483	2,388	2,429
2000	656	2,388	2,566	2,621	2,730	2,505	2,121	2,059	2,502	2,435	2,472
2001	881	2,632	2,832	2,891	3,002	2,766	2,291	2,242	2,734	2,707	2,738
2002	1,454	3,049	3,339	3386	3,503	3,250	2,789	2,614	3,163	3,188	3,209
Average	*1,824*	*2,744*	*2,798*	*2,825*	*2,841*	*2,784*	*2,555*	*2,535*	*2,777*	*2,742*	*2,772*
Max (year)	*4,146*	*4,353*	*4,174*	*4,197*	*4,243*	*4,170*	*4,049*	*4105*	*4244*	*4175*	*4200*
	(1991)	*(1991)*	*(1992)*	*(1992)*	*(1992)*	*(1992)*	*(1991)*	*(1991)*	*(1992)*	*(1991)*	*(1992)*
Min (year)	*656*	*1,642*	*1,560*	*1,628*	*1,603*	*1,661*	*1,639*	*1,651*	*1,666*	*1,635*	*1,667*
	(2000)	*(1988)*	*(1988)*	*(1988)*	*(1988)*	*(1988)*	*(1988)*	*(1988)*	*(1988)*	*(1988)*	*(1988)*

Source: Farzanegan (2009). Reprinted with permission from Elsevier.

smuggling is estimated in the years 1992 and 1993 in Iran. The black market premium for the US dollar was in its high records in these two years.

5.6 Conclusion

This chapter examines illegal trade in Iran and provides the first scholarly estimates of this complex phenomenon. To estimate the economic size of smuggling, a specific form of SEM models (MIMIC) and trade discrepancy approach are used. The MIMIC estimations show that the main determinants of smuggling are the penalty rate, black market premium, trade openness, education, GDP per capita, unemployment rate, and quality of political and economic institutions.

A novel approach in this study, which is not observed in other applications of MIMIC in the shadow economy literature, is the use of interaction terms. The impact of higher incomes, education, and trade openness on the propensity to engage in illegal trade might be conditional on institutional factors. I have shown that higher education depresses illegal trade only in the case where economic institutions are of good quality.

On average, smuggling in Iran has been approximately 13 percent of total trade. The highest records of smuggling in post-revolutionary period were in 1992 and 1993. The main characteristic of these two years was a high premium in the black market of US dollar.

This study is not directly intended to analyze the welfare effects of smuggling, but the effects of smuggling on its indicators might prove interesting in this respect. A one standard deviation increase in the size of smuggling decreases import prices by about 0.96 standard deviation. The negative effect of smuggling on the general government revenues (in standard deviation terms) is smaller than its effect on import prices. There is a close and positive correlation between higher smuggling and petroleum product consumption in Iran. It would be interesting to investigate the welfare effects of smuggling in more detail in future research.

The MIMIC models and trade discrepancy method presented in this study can be applied to estimate the product of specific smuggling (e.g., cigarettes) given the availability of data. Smuggling of cigarettes is a big problem in both developed and developing countries. In summary, there are a lot of opportunities to use latent variable theory to estimate the hidden criminal behavior such as smuggling, crime, money laundering, and other types of corruption.

Appendix A

Table 5A.1
Data sources and description

Variables	Definition	Transformation/ calculation	Source
Penalty rate	Penalty amount in rial for each USD value of smuggled goods, adjusted for inflation	Inverse form of fine rate is used Logarithmic form Standardized	Madah and Pajoyan (2005)
BMP	Difference between official and black market exchange rate for USD/rial	Logarithmic form Standardized	Central Bank of Iran (CBI) (2010)
Tariff burden	Ratio of real tax on imports/ real imports	Logarithmic form Standardized	Central Bank of Iran (CBI) (2010)
RGDPPC	Real GDP per capita	Logarithmic form Standardized	Central Bank of Iran (CBI) (2010)
Openness	Non–oil exports+imports/ non–oil GDP	Logarithmic form Standardized	Central Bank of Iran (CBI) (2010)
Education	Literacy rate	Logarithmic form Standardized	Central Bank of Iran (CBI) (2010)
Polity2	Polity IV: from −10 (the lowest democracy) to +10 (the highest democracy)	Polity index/10	Marshall and Jaggers (2005) http://www .systemicpeace .org/polity/ polity4.htm
CIM	Contract intensive Money: ratio of noncurrency money to total money supply.	(M2-C)/M2, M2: money supply, C: currency held outside banks Not standardized	Based on data from Central Bank of Iran (CBI) (2010)

Table 5A.1
continued

Variables	Definition	Transformation/ calculation	Source
Van_comp	Competition variable portrays the electoral success of smaller parties, that is, the percentage of votes gained by the smaller parties in parliamentary and/ or presidential elections.	Variable is calculated by subtracting from 100 the percentage of votes won by the largest party (the party that wins most votes) in parliamentary elections or by the party of the successful candidate in presidential elections. The variable thus theoretically ranges from 0 (only one party received 100% of votes) to 100 (each voter casts a vote for a distinct party). Not standardized	Vanhanen (2000) http://www.qog .pol.gu.se
Van_index	Index combines two basic dimensions of democracy (Competition and participation).	Measured as the percentage of votes not cast for the largest party (competition) times the percentage of the population that actually voted in the election (participation). This product is divided by 100 to form an index that in principle could vary from 0 (no democracy) to 100 (full democracy). Not standardized	Vanhanen (2000) http://www.qog. pol.gu.se
Van_part	Participation in elections	Percentage of the total population that actually voted in the election. Not standardized	Vanhanen (2000) http://www.qog .pol.gu.se
IQ	Institutional quality	Score is calculated through factor analysis technique on the basis of observable variables such as van_index, van_com, CIM, and polity. Standardized	Author calculations

Table 5A.1
(continued)

Variables	Definition	Transformation/ calculation	Source
GDPPCG	Growth rate of GDP per capita	Standardized	World Bank (2008)
Import price index (IMX)	Real import price index	Logarithmic form Standardized	Central Bank of Iran (CBI) (2010)
RG	Real government revenues	Logarithmic form Standardized	Central Bank of Iran (CBI) (2010)
Gpconsum	Petroleum products consumption	Growth rate of total final consumption of petroleum products Standardized	Energy Balances of Islamic Republic of Iran http://www .iranenergy.org. ir/statistic%20 info/energy%20 balance/main840 .htm

Appendix B

Table 5A.2
Underlying data for the institutional quality (IQ) index in Iran

Year	Polity2	CIM	Van_comp	Van_index	Van_part	IQ
1970	−10	0.83	10	0.5	4.6	−1.11871
1971	−10	0.83	7	0.3	4.7	−1.22463
1972	−10	0.83	7	0.3	4.7	−1.22355
1973	−10	0.83	7	0.3	4.7	−1.22523
1974	−10	0.84	7	0.3	4.7	−1.21780
1975	−10	0.84	0	0.0	10.3	−1.24066
1976	−10	0.84	0	0.0	10.3	−1.23708
1977	−10	0.84	0	0.0	10.3	−1.23552
1978	−10	0.69	0	0.0	10.3	−1.44450
1979	0	0.74	24	6.1	26.0	1.56542
1980	−2	0.73	24	3.7	13.9	0.54495
1981	−4	0.73	24	3.7	13.9	0.42489
1982	−6	0.74	24	3.7	13.9	0.30584
1983	−6	0.75	24	3.7	13.9	0.31829
1984	−6	0.74	10	1.8	18.2	−0.20797
1985	−6	0.76	10	1.8	18.2	−0.18737

Table 5A.2
(continued)

Year	Polity2	CIM	Van_comp	Van_index	Van_part	IQ
1986	−6	0.75	10	1.8	18.2	−0.19363
1987	−6	0.76	10	1.8	18.2	−0.17891
1988	−6	0.78	10	1.6	16.1	−0.27675
1989	−6	0.81	10	1.6	16.1	−0.24290
1990	−6	0.82	10	1.6	16.1	−0.22279
1991	−6	0.84	10	1.6	16.1	−0.19686
1992	−6	0.85	13	2.0	16.1	−0.04506
1993	−6	0.86	13	2.0	16.1	−0.03503
1994	−6	0.86	13	2.0	16.1	−0.03336
1995	−6	0.87	13	2.0	16.1	−0.01297
1996	−6	0.89	28	5.7	20.2	1.21772
1997	3	0.89	28	5.7	20.2	1.78169
1998	3	0.88	28	5.7	20.2	1.77833
1999	3	0.89	28	5.7	20.2	1.78134
2000	3	0.90	12	2.9	25.2	1.08189
2001	3	0.91	12	2.9	25.2	1.09535
2002	3	0.92	12	2.9	25.2	1.10558

Note: higher values of IQ means higher quality of political and economic institutions.

Notes

1. See http://www.icgg.org/corruption.cpi_2008.html.

2. See http://epp.eurostat.ec.europa.eu/cache/ITY_OFFPUB/KS-DB-04-001/EN/KS -DB-04-001-EN.PDF.

3. Given the lack of reliable data on freight and insurance costs among Iran and its trading partners, I believe the 10 percent factor is the most appropriate adjustment. For the similar view, see Makhoul and Otterstrom (1998) and http://www.esds.ac.uk/ international/support/user_guides/imf/dots.asp.

4. Exploratory factor analysis (EFA) has been used to explore the possible underlying factor structure of a set of observed variables without imposing a preconceived structure on the outcome (Child 1990). Confirmatory factor analysis (CFA), however, allows the researcher to test the theoretical hypothesis on the relationship between observable variables and latent constructs. In this case, one would use the theory to design a path diagram and then test the hypothetical relationships.

5. Maximum likelihood (ML) methodology for SEM modeling assumes a multivariate normal distribution. Lack of normality can inflate the chi-square statistics and create upward bias for determining the significance of coefficients. Also the use of chi-square is not valid in most applications (Joreskog and Sorbom 1989). For the multivariate normality assumption it is important that each variable of the model follow univariate normality (Diamantopoulos and Siguaw 2000, p. 152). When one or more variables are

not normally distributed, transformations of variables can be used such as log transformations, square roots, or inverse transformations (for more details, see Osborne 2002). Penalty rates on smuggling had an excessive kurtosis of 5.37 with a probability of acceptance normality of zero. This makes it a candidate for the inverse transformation.

6. See http://www.lajvar.se/eghtesad/ghachage-kala.htm (access: 13.11.08, Persian Sina News Agency).

7. See http://www.mg.co.za/printformat/single/2006-06-19-oil-smuggling-costs-iran -billions-of-dollars.

8. For the multivariate normality assumption, it is important that each variable of the model follow univariate normality (Diamantopoulos and Siguaw 2000, p. 152). When one or more variables are not normally distributed, transformations of variables can be used such as log transformations, square roots, or inverse transformations (for more details, see Osborne 2002). Penalty rates on smuggling had an excessive kurtosis of 5.37 with a probability of acceptance normality of zero. This makes it a candidate for inverse transformation.

References

Ades, A., and R. Di Tella. 1999. Rents, competition, and corruption. *American Economic Review* 89: 982–92.

Agarwal, J. D., and A. Agarwal. 2006. Money laundering: New forms of crime, victimization. Presented at the National Workshop on New Forms of Crime, Victimization, with reference to Money Laundering, Indian Society of Victimology, Department of Criminology, University of Madras, India.

Agarwal, J. D., and A. Agarwal. 2004. Globalization and international capital flows. *Finance India* 19 (1): 65–99.

Alizadeh, P. 2003. Iran's quandary: Economic reforms and the "structural trap." *Brown Journal of World Affairs* 9: 267–81.

Amini, A., H. M. Neshat, and M. Eslahchi. 2007. Estimation of labor force times series in different economic activities in Iran. *Barname-va Budgeh* 102: 47–97.

Arabmazar, A. 2007. Black Economy in Iran. Tahghighat va Tosehe Olome Ensani (Research and social science development institute), Tehran.

Askari, H. 2006. *Middle East Oil Exporters: What Happened to Economic Development?* Cheltenham: Elgar.

Barnett, R. 2003. Smuggling, non-fundamental uncertainty, and parallel market exchange rate volatility. *Canadian Journal of Economics. Revue Canadienne d'Economique* 36: 701–27.

Barro, R., J. 1991. Economic growth in a cross-section of countries. *Quarterly Journal of Economics* 106: 407–44.

Barro, R., J., Lee, J.-W. 2001. International data on educational attainment: updates and implications. *Oxford Economic Papers* 3: 541–63.

Beja, E. L. 2008. Estimating trade mis-invoicing from China: 2000–2005. *China and World Economy* 16: 82–92.

Benhabib, J., and M. M. Spiegel. 1994. The role of human capital in economic development evidence from aggregate cross-country data. *Journal of Monetary Economics* 34: 143–73.

Berger, H., and V. Nitsch. 2008. Gotcha! A profile of smuggling in International trade. Working paper series 2475. CESifo, Munich.

Bhagwati, J. 1964. On the under invoicing of imports. *Bulletin of the Oxford University Institute of Statistics* 26: 389–97.

Bhagwati, J., and B. Hansen. 1973. A theoretical analysis of smuggling. *Quarterly Journal of Economics* 87: 172–87.

Braun, M., and R. Di Tella. 2004. Inflation, inflation variability, and corruption. *Economics and Politics* 16: 77–100.

Buehn, A., and S. Eichler. 2009. Smuggling illegal versus legal goods across the U.S.–Mexico border: A structural equations model approach. *Southern Economic Journal* 76: 328–50.

Buehn, A., and M. R. Farzanegan. 2011. Smuggling around the world: Evidence from a structural equation modeling. *Applied Economics*, forthcoming. Available at: http://www.tandfonline.com/doi/abs/10.1080/00036846.2011.570715.

Central Bank of Iran (CBI). 2010. The first edition of the CBI time series economic database. Available at: http://tsd.cbi.ir/IntTSD/EnDisplay/Display.aspx (accessed June 17, 2010).

Child, D. 1990. *The Essentials of Factor Analysis*. London: Cassel Educational Limited.

Clague, C., P. Keefer, S. Knack, and M. Olson. 1999. Contract-intensive money: contract enforcement, property rights, and economic performance. *Journal of Economic Growth* 4: 185–211.

De Macedo, J. B. 1987. Currency incontrovertibility, trade taxes and smuggling. *Journal of Development Economics* 27: 109–25.

Diamantopoulos, A., and J. Siguaw. 2000. *Introducing LISREL: A Guide for the Uninitiated*. London: Sage.

Dreher, A., C. Kotsogiannis, and S. McCorriston. 2007. Corruption around the world: Evidence from a structural model. *Journal of Comparative Economics* 35: 443–46.

Eilat, Y., and C. Zinnes. 2002. The shadow economy in transition countries: friend or foe? A policy perspective. *World Development* 30: 1233–54.

Farzanegan, M. R. 2009. Illegal trade in the Iranian economy: evidence from a structural equation model. *European Journal of Political Economy* 25: 489–507.

Fields, G. 1980. Education and income distribution in developing countries: A review of the literature. In T. King, ed., *Education and Income*. Washington DC: World Bank, 231–315.

Fisman, R., and E. Miguel. 2008. *Economic Gangsters: Corruption, Violence, and the Poverty of Nations*. Princeton: Princeton University Press.

Fisman, R., and E. Miguel. 2007. Corruption, norms and legal enforcement: evidence from diplomatic parking tickets. *Journal of Political Economy* 115: 1020–48.

Fisman, R., and S.-J. Wei. 2007. The smuggling of art, and the art of smuggling: Uncovering the illicit trade in cultural property and antiques. Working paper W13446. National Bureau of Economic Research, Cambridge, MA.

Fisman, R., and S.-J. Wei. 2004. Tax rates and tax evasion: evidence from "missing imports" in China. *Journal of Political Economy* 112: 471–500.

Fréchette, G. R. 2006. A panel data analysis of the time-varying determinants of corruption. Working paper 28, CIRANO, Montreal.

Frey, B. S., and H. Weck-Hannemann. 1984. The hidden economy as an "unobserved" variable. *European Economic Review* 26: 33–53.

Hsieh, C. T., and E. Moretti. 2006. Did Iraq cheat the United Nations? Underpricing, bribes, and the oil for food program. *Quarterly Journal of Economics* 121: 1211–48.

IMF. 2003. Offshore financial centers: The assessment program. A progress report and the future of the program. Washington, DC.

IMF. 2001. *Financial system abuse*: Financial Crime and Money Laundering. Washington, DC.

IMF. 1993. A guide to direction of trade statistics. Available at: http://www.esds.ac.uk/international/support/user_guides/imf/DOTGuide.pdf (accessed February 6, 2009).

International Institute for Energy Studies. 2005. Report, Iran Energy. International Institute for Energy Studies, Tehran, Iran.

Iran Customs Administration. 2010. Analysis of smuggling statistics in 2009. Available in Farsi at: http://www.irica.gov.ir/Portal/Home/Default.aspx?CategoryID=6c49f6cd-2da3-402e-9d45-d200b6f56164 (accessed June 16, 2010).

Jimenez, E. 1986. The public subsidization of education and health in developing countries: A review of equity and efficiency. *Research Observer* 1: 111–29.

Joreskog, K., and D. Sorbom. 1989. *LISREL 7: User Reference Guide*. Mooresville. Scientific Software Inc.

Kaufmann, D., and A. Kaliberda. 1996. Integrating the unofficial economy into the dynamics of post socialist economies: a framework of analyses and evidence. In B. Kaminski, ed., *Economic Transition in Russia and the New States of Eurasia*. London: M.E. Sharpe, 81–120..

Kaufmann, D., A. Kraay, and M. Mastruzzi. 2009. Governance matters. VIII: Aggregate and individual governance indicators, 1996–2008. Policy research working paper 4978. World Bank, Washington, DC.

Keshavarzian, A. 2007. *Bazaar and State in Iran: The Politics of the Tehran Market Place*. Cambridge: Cambridge University Press.

Kiguel, M., and S. A. O'Connell. 1995. Parallel exchange rates in developing countries. *World Bank Research Observer* 10: 21–52.

Loayza, N. V. 1997. The economics of the informal sector: a simple model and some empirical evidence from Latin America. Policy research working paper 1727. World Bank, Washington, DC.

Madah, M., and J. Pajoyan. 2005. Economic review of smuggling in Iran. *Pajoheshnameh Eghtesadi* 6: 43–70.

Makhoul, B., and S. M. Otterstrom. 1998. Exploring the accuracy of international trade statistics. *Applied Economics* 30: 1603–16.

Marshall, M. G., and K. Jaggers. 2005. Polity IV project: Political regime characteristics and transactions, 1800–2002. University of Maryland.

Martin, L., and A. Panagariya. 1984. Smuggling, trade and price disparity: a crime theoretic approach. *Journal of International Economics* 17: 201–17.

McDonald, D. C. 1985. Trade discrepancies and the incentives to smuggle. *IMF Staff Papers* 32: 668–92.

Morgenstern, O. 1963. *On the Accuracy of Economic Observations*, 2nd ed. Princeton: Princeton University Press.

Naya, S., and T. Morgan. 1969. The accuracy of international trade data: the case of South East Asian countries. *Journal of the American Statistical Association* 64: 452–67.

Norton, D. 1988. On the economic theory of smuggling. *Economica* 55: 107–118.

Osborne, J. 2002. Notes on the use of data transformations. Practical Assessment, Research and Evaluation 8. Available at: http://www.pareonline.net/getvn.asp?v=8&n=6 (accessed February 6, 2009).

Phylaktis, K. 1991. The black market for dollars in Chile. *Journal of Development Economics* 37: 155–72.

Pitt, M. 1981. Smuggling and price disparity. *Journal of International Economics* 11: 447–58.

Pritchett, L. 2001. Where has all the education gone? *World Bank Economic Review* 15: 367–91.

Ram, R. 1989. Can educational expansion reduce income inequality in less-developed countries? *Economics of Education Review* 8: 185–95.

Schneider, F. 2010. Money laundering and financial means of organized crime: Some preliminary empirical findings. Working paper 26. Economics of Security, Berlin.

Schneider, F. 2005. Shadow economies around the world: what do we really know? *European Journal of Political Economy* 21: 598–642.

Schneider, F., and D. Enste. 2000. Shadow economies: size, causes, and consequences. *Journal of Economic Literature* 38: 77–114.

Seif, A. M. 2008. Smuggling of Products in Iran. Majlis Research Center, Tehran. Available at: http://www.majlis.ir/book/pdf/Smuggling.pdf (in Farsi).

Sung, H.-E., and D. Chu. 2003. Does participation in the global economy reduce political corruption? An empirical inquiry. *International Journal of Comparative Criminology* 3: 94–118.

Sylwester, K. 2002. Can education expenditures reduce income inequality? *Economics of Education Review* 21: 43–52.

Tanzi, V., and K. Chu. 1998. *Income Distribution and High Quality Growth*. Cambridge: MIT Press.

Thursby, M., R. Jensen, and J. Thursby. 1991. Smuggling, camouflaging, and market structure. *Quarterly Journal of Economics* 106: 789–814.

Vanhanen, T. 2000. A new dataset for measuring democracy, 1810–1998. *Journal of Peace Research* 37: 251–65.

World Bank. 2010a. Doing business in Iran. Available at: http://www.doingbusiness.org/data/exploreeconomies/iran .

World Bank. 2010b. World development indicators online portal, Available at: http://databank.worldbank.org/ddp/home.do?Step=12&id=4&CNO=2.

World Bank, 2008. World development indicators. CD-Rom.

Yavari, K. 2000. Estimation of smuggling and over-invoicing in import section: the case of Iran. Third National Forum on Smuggling. University of Tarbiat Modarres, Tehran.

6 Modeling the Cocaine and Heroin Markets in the Era of Globalization and Drug Reduction Policies

Cláudia Costa Storti and Paul De Grauwe

6.1 Introduction

Over the last twenty years the use of cocaine and heroin in the world has remained steady. According to UNODC (2007), between 1992 and 2005, world consumption of these drugs rose by about 3.2 percent. These growth rates were 7.3 and 3.4 percent in Europe and 1.8 and 1.1 percent in the United States during the same period. Public policies to combat the drug phenomenon, namely those geared toward reducing drug supply have been extensive. In Europe, according to the existing information about six countries published by the EMCDDA (2007), the share of the overall public drug-related expenditure devoted to supply reduction policies, namely law enforcement, varied from 40 to 77 percent in 2005 (excluding Hungary where they only represented 24 percent). In the United States, according to the White House national drug control strategy (2007), the percentage of drug control funding allocated to supply reduction activities has increased from 53 percent in 2001 to 63 percent in 2007.

A further understanding of the drug supply phenomena seems urgent. Despite the public expenditure devoted to restrain drug supply, illicit production of drugs such as cocaine and heroin has continued to increase and retail prices in Europe and the United States have fallen significantly in the last twenty years. The latest available data for 2005 and 2006 show that retail prices of cocaine and heroin fell to less than half of their levels of 1990. Empirical research has showed that drug use is responsive to drug prices.[1] Thus the observed price decline may be responsible for the increased use of cocaine and heroin.

In this chapter we develop an economic model of demand and supply and of the price formation process of illicit drugs (cocaine and heroin). The model allows us to discuss the efficacy of law enforcement in influencing the price formation mechanism and drug supply. It also makes it possible to study the different ways in which globalization influences the price formation process and the demand and supply of cocaine and heroin, and how globalization interferes with the objectives pursued by the supply containment policies set up by the authorities of the drug consuming countries.

We model the cocaine and heroin markets in three steps. First, we concentrate on the retail markets of these drugs. This will lead to the demand side of the model. Second, we model the production of cocaine and heroin in the producing countries. This will lead to the supply side of the model. Third, we link the demand and supply sides by modeling the export-import business of cocaine and heroin.

We then use this model to analyze how globalization has influenced the business of producing, trafficking, and consuming drugs. Globalization is defined as a process of opening borders between countries so that movements in goods, services, and factors of production (labor and capital) face fewer obstacles. This more intense movement also facilitates the transmission of new technologies across countries. Our main argument will be that the different ways globalization affects drug phenomena contribute to explaining these empirical puzzles. Furthermore we will analyze the effects of law enforcement policies at different levels of the production and trafficking of drugs. We will suggest that these law enforcement policies risk loosing the battle against the forces of globalization.

The chapter is organized as follows. Section 6.2 presents the different empirical puzzles in the cocaine and heroin markets. Section 6.3 develops the retail side of the model, section 6.4 the supply side and section 6.5 links the two by modeling the export–import of the drugs. In section 6.6 we bring together the different effects of globalization on the markets for cocaine and heroin and in section 6.7 we present a case study about the emergence of the West Africa cocaine route.

6.2   Recent Developments in the Cocaine and Heroin Markets

During the last twenty-five years important empirical phenomena have occurred in the cocaine and heroin markets. First, retail prices of these drugs have declined significantly. We show the evolution of these prices in the US and European retail markets since 1990 in figure 6.1. We observe that both in the United States and in Europe cocaine and heroin price trends fell to less than half of their levels of 1990. (Note

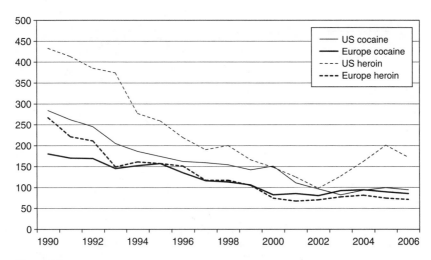

Figure 6.1
Cocaine and heroin retail prices, 1990 to 2006 (USD per gram)

that since the early 2000s a stabilization of these prices seems to have occurred and even a surge of heroin prices in the US retail market.)

Second, the producer prices of cocaine and heroin have increased or remained stable over the same period. These are the prices paid out at the farms gate in the producing countries. We show the evidence for cocaine in figure 6.2. We observe that the farm-gate prices of coca leafs have more than doubled since 1990. In Colombia both the coca paste and the cocaine HC1 have shown upward price trends. (The price data for heroin are less comprehensive but the evidence suggests that these trends have been similar for heroin; see United Nations, World Drug Report 2007).

Third, and related to the previous observations, the intermediation margins in the cocaine and heroin business have declined dramatically over the same period. We show the evidence in figures 6.3 and 6.4. Figure 6.3 shows the international intermediation margin, that is, the margin between the wholesale price in the drug importing country and the price paid to the producers in the exporting countries. This can also be called the export–import margin. Figure 6.4 shows the intermediation margin between the retail price and the wholesale price in the drug consuming countries. We see that both these margins have collapsed since 1990 for both cocaine and heroin.

Fourth, the world production of cocaine and heroin has continued to increase. We show the evidence in figure 6.5.

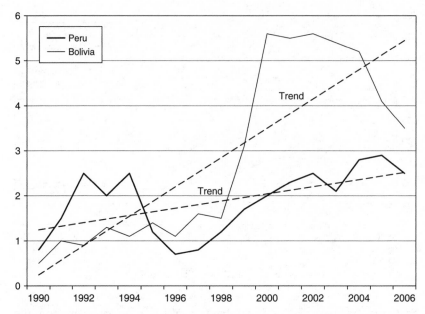

Figure 6.2
Farm-gate prices for sun-dried coca leafs, 1990 to 2006 (USD per kilo). Prices are adjusted
for inflation. Source: United Nations, *World Drug Report 2007*, Office on Drugs and Crime,
New York (pp. 223, 228)

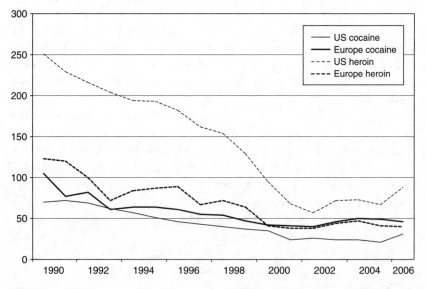

Figure 6.3
Cocaine and heroin: Margin between wholesale and producer prices, 1990 to 2006 (USD
per gram)

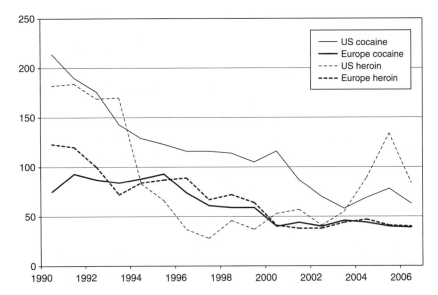

Figure 6.4
Cocaine and heroin: Margin between retail and wholesale prices 1990 to 2006 (USD per gram) Source: Costa Storti and De Grauwe (2008).

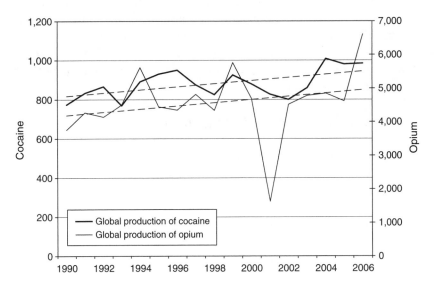

Figure 6.5
Cocaine and opium global production, 1990 to 2006 (metric tonnes). Straight lines are trend lines estimated by OLS. The estimated equations are: cocaine $Y = 815 + 7.47X$, where Y is the production and X is time; heroin $Y = 4200 + 43.0X$, where Y is the production and X is time. The US Department of State (2008) found similar trends during 2002 to 2006. Source: United Nations, *World Drug Report 2007*, Office on Drugs and Crime, New York (p. 64).

Fifth, the evidence suggests that the worldwide consumption of cocaine and heroin has remained steady. According to the Office on Drugs and Crime of the United Nations, consumption of both cocaine and heroin was 3 percent higher in 2005 as compared to 1992. These growth rates were 7.3 and 3.4 percent in Europe and 1.8 and 1.1 percent in the United States during the same period.

Finally, during the same period supply containment policies have been intense, and in some countries like the United States, these policies have been stepped up dramatically. According to Basov et al. (2001), from 1980 to 2000 the DEA budget increased by a factor of three in real terms. Drug arrests in the United States more than doubled during the same period. One could have expected that such an intensification of supply containment policies would have shown up in higher retail prices and declining consumption and production. Exactly the opposite occurred in the United States.

These are puzzling phenomena. In order to better understand them, in this chapter we propose a model of the cocaine and heroin markets. We model these markets in three steps. First, we concentrate on the retail markets of cocaine and heroin. This will lead to the demand side of the model. Second, we model the production of cocaine and heroin in the producing countries. This will lead to the supply side of the model. Third, we link the demand and supply sides by modeling the export–import business of cocaine and heroin. Finally, we discuss how globalization and law enforcement policies influence the phenomena.

6.3   The Model for the Retail Drug Market

We assume that the retail market is characterized by monopolistic competition; that is, there are many suppliers of drugs, each of whom faces a downward-sloping demand curve. The latter implies that each supplier has some limited local market power.[2] The emergence of monopolistic competitive structures at the retail level can be seen as originating from asymmetric information between the buyer and the seller of drugs; that is, the seller knows the quality of the drug while the buyer does not. This asymmetry of information leads to a market failure: the high-quality drug tends to disappear and only the low-quality drug is left over.[3] This market failure, however, can be partially overcome when buyers and sellers establish a relationship based on trust, which can be achieved by repeated transactions between the same sellers and buyers. This in turn creates a network structure in the retail market which allows the information about the quality of the drug and the reliability of the seller to be shared.[4] Once trust is achieved, the seller can charge a quality premium. These relations based on trust in a network environment have been described by economists[5] and, recently, by criminologist research.

The Matrix Knowledge Group (2007) concluded that in the United Kingdom the level of market entry is largely determined by the level of the personal contact entered through a dealer. "Most successful dealers were able to adapt to new circumstances and exploit new opportunities. These often came about through chance meetings, through ethnic ties, selling to friends who were users" (p. vi), so successful dealers are those who are better in establishing personal networks. Their success depends on the contacts they are able to establish, the trust they are able to build either from their suppliers or from their clients. A drug user will prefer to buy from his regular supplier, accepting a higher price in order to guarantee that the drug is safe and the supplier is trustworthy.

In a broader international literature review Desroches (2007) assesses the nature and structure of drug markets, focusing on "upper level drug trafficking." He concludes that upper level dealers (i.e., the local monopolists) typically operate in crews or cells made up of core and fringe members, with a dealer who oversees all the important work (where sometimes there are some partnerships with one or two upper level traffickers) with employees for non-managerial tasks. The secrecy of their activities and their structures, which are based on personal networks, prevents these drug syndicates from growing. Furthermore kinship, friendship, and ethnic bonds function as a basis for the establishment of new clients, where the capacity of each of these drug trafficking syndicates to enlarge their market share is also limited. Desroches points out that there is a certain consensus about the view that "organized crime consists of a relatively large number of small independent criminal syndicates, each of whom competes with another for a market share" (p. 831). Consequently the drug market can be seen as entrepreneurial organizations where dealers are rational actors who focus on profit, seek out economic opportunities, and attempt to minimize risk. Effectively, due to its illegal nature, drug trafficking is a high-risk activity in which traffickers manage risk with tools such as the size of their syndicate, their structure, and organization.

All this tends to create a market structure akin to monopolistic competition, in which drug dealers have a certain market power and apply a high markup initially. This markup tends to diminishes over time because new dealers are tempted to join the market. Thus a characteristic of this market structure is that there are no strong barriers deterring newcomers (see also Reuter and Haaga 1989). Consequently these markets benefit from a certain degree of competition leading to price declines.

The model to be presented in the next section is a partial equilibrium model; that is, it does not take into account general equilibrium effects. In particular, when resources are attracted into the illegal sector it is assumed that this does not affect the legal sector. Such an assumption makes sense if the illegal sector is small relative to the legal sector, or if there are unused resources (unemployment) in the legal sector.

Finally the model applies to cocaine and heroin markets that are characterized by concentration of the production in a few countries and international trade flows toward consuming countries. It does not apply to the cannabis market, which is very different in structure.

6.3.1 The Model

This local market power of the supplier is represented in our model by the assumption that each "upper level trafficker" or supplier faces a downward-sloping demand curve for the drugs he sells. We assume that there are n suppliers of drugs in the retail market. The number of suppliers is endogenously determined in the long run by imposing a long-term no-profit condition.

The profit of supplier i (π_i) is defined as follows:

$$\pi_i = p_i x_i - w l_i - p_m x_i, \tag{6.1}$$

where x_i is the quantity of the drug sold by i; p_i is the price charged; l_i is the number of "lower level dealers" employed by supplier i; we assume that the same wage, w, is paid to all "lower level dealers." Furthermore p_m is the cost of one unit of the drug at the moment of import, so that the term $p_m x_i$ is the total cost of the imported drugs for firm i (for the upper level trafficker).

We assume a very simple linear technology guiding the demand of "lower level drug dealers" or employees by firm i (the "upper level drug dealer i"):

$$l_i = \alpha + \beta x_i \tag{6.2}$$

where β_i is the number of dealers needed to sell one unit of drugs (the marginal labor input coefficient). Put differently, $1/\beta$ is the marginal productivity of a lower level dealer in selling drugs.

Efficiency improvements can lead to an increase in the marginal productivity of dealing. Conversely, stricter law enforcement can have the effect of lowering the marginal productivity of dealing in drugs. The assumption is that when the number of arrests increases, more dealers will have to be used to traffic the same amount of drugs. We assume that law enforcement has a positive marginal productivity (more law enforcement leads to the imprisoning of more drug dealers), though at a declining rate; that is, the efficacy of further law enforcement activity has diminishing returns.

Substituting (6.2) into (6.1) yields

$$\pi_i = p_i x_i - w(\alpha + \beta x_i) - p_m x_i. \tag{6.3}$$

The upper level drug dealer or firm i maximizes his profits. The first-order condition for a maximum is given by the following expression:

$$p_i = \frac{\eta}{\eta - 1}(\beta w + p_m), \tag{6.4}$$

where η is the price elasticity of the demand for drugs of supplier i (expressed in absolute value).

It is important to stress here that the price elasticity, η, measures the reaction of drug users to a change in price asked by supplier i, assuming that other suppliers do not change their price. In our model of monopolistic competition, $\eta > 1$. This price elasticity is different from the price elasticity of the total demand for cocaine. Let us call the latter the market elasticity and represent it by ε. The market elasticity, ε, measures the extent to which drug users change their demand for drugs when the price of this drug (as applied by *all* drug suppliers) changes. The market elasticity, ε, is then lower than the elasticity, η, used here.[6] It can been shown that in order for the model of monopolistic competition to have an equilibrium $\varepsilon < \eta$ (Dixit and Stiglitz 1977).

We recognize in equation (6.4) the typical markup condition of price over marginal cost. The marginal cost is $\beta w + p_m$ and consists of two components, the marginal cost of dealing drugs by the lower level trafficker (βw) and the marginal importing cost of the drug (p_m). $\eta/(\eta - 1) > 1$ is the markup.

It can be useful to express equation (6.4) in a different form, that is,

$$m_i = \frac{\eta}{\eta-1}\left(\frac{\beta w}{p_m}+1\right),$$ (6.5)

where $m_i = p_i/p_m$ is the intermediation margin in the retail market. Note that this margin includes both the wages paid to the lower level traffickers and the profits of the upper level dealer.

Equation (6.4) allows us to gauge the impact of exogenous changes on the retail price of the drug. For example, an increase in the cost of imported drugs leads to a more than proportional increase in the price of the drug, that is,

$$\frac{\partial p_i}{\partial p_m} = \frac{\eta}{\eta-1}.$$ (6.6)

It should be stressed that these effects apply to the short run. In the long run the profits of the drug suppliers are competed away by the entry of new drug suppliers. Long-run equilibrium is obtained by imposing a zero profit condition $\pi_i = 0$. We can also impose the condition that the equilibrium is symmetric, namely that prices and quantities are identical across drug suppliers. This allows us to concentrate on the representative drug supplier without subscript, namely to focus on a representative upper level drug dealer.

Thus, from (6.3) and dropping the subscript i, we obtain the long-run equilibrium condition

$$px - w(\alpha + \beta x) - p_m x = 0.$$ (6.7)

Rearranging leads to

$$p = w\left(\frac{\alpha}{x}+\beta\right) + p_m.$$ (6.8)

It can be seen that this amounts to setting price equal to average cost. We rewrite this equation to obtain the long-term equilibrium value of the intermediation margin

$$m = \frac{w}{p_m}\left(\frac{\alpha}{x}+\beta\right) + 1.$$ (6.9)

We can derive the long-run effect of a change in p_m. For example, the long-term impact of a increase in the import price of drugs, p_m, on the retail price of cocaine, p, results of the derivative of p with respect to p_m in equation (6.8). This yields

$$\frac{\partial p}{\partial p_m} = 1. \tag{6.10}$$

Comparing (6.10) with (6.6), we see that the long-term effect of a higher import price of drugs is smaller than the short-term effect. In the short run the higher import price leads to an "overshooting" of the price; that is, short-run retail price increases more than proportionally to the increase in the imported drug price, reflecting the fact that the upper level dealers maintain a markup in the short run. This result is confirmed by the Matrix Knowledge Group (2007). In this large-scale project, where interviews were made to individuals in prison convicted of serious drug-related offenses, it is concluded that "where market fluctuations did lead to increased purchase prices, dealers maintained margins by passing these increases on to customers" (p. v).

Finally, and in order to close the model, we introduce the condition that the demand for drugs is equal to the supply. Total demand is equal to the consumption[7] (c) of the representative consumer times the size of the population N (the prevalence), that is, cN. In equilibrium $cN = x$. We substitute this expression in (6.8):

$$p = w\left(\frac{\alpha}{cN} + \beta\right) + p_m. \tag{6.11}$$

The equilibrium of the model is fully described by equations (6.4) and (6.11). These two equations determine the equilibrium value of the retail price (p) and the consumption of drugs (c), in the short and long term, respectively. Note that we could also represent the equilibrium of the model in terms of the intermediation margin m, using equations (6.5) and (6.9).

We represent the short-term and long-term equilibrium expressed in equations (6.4) and (6.11) graphically in figure 6.6.

The PP line is the graphical expression of the short term showed in equation (6.4). We assume here that the retail demand curves are linear. As a result the elasticity η is declining for increasing values of c; that is, the higher the drug use the less sensitive drug demand is to price changes. This feature of the demand curve is consistent with the evidence suggesting that high drug users become addicted (dependent) so that their demand becomes less price sensitive (see Caulkins and

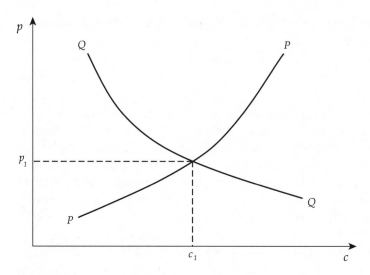

Figure 6.6
Equilibrium of the retail market

Hao 2008). This produces an upward-sloping PP line. The intuition behind the upward slope is that with a higher level of drug consumption the market power of the drug supplier is increased, allowing him to apply a higher markup. This leads to a higher retail price.

The QQ line is the graphical representation of the long-run equilibrium condition (6.11). The negative slope (which is readily seen from equation 6.11) expresses the fact that QQ is derived from the average cost curve. Thus, as consumption increases, firms' average costs decline. In the long run this leads to a declining retail price.

The equilibrium values of the price and the consumption of the representative drug user are given by the intersection point of the PP and QQ lines.

We can use this model to analyze important policy questions. The first question we analyze is how drug seizures affect the retail market. The second question is how globalization affects the market.

6.3.2 Impact of Seizures

The way we model seizures is as follows. We introduce in equation (6.1) the probability that a certain percentage of drugs sold in the retail market is seized. This leads to a new definition of the profits of supplier i:

$$\pi_i = p_i x_i (1 - s) - w l_i - p_m x_i, \tag{6.12}$$

where s is the probability that the drug supplied by i will be seized. Note that π_i now has to be interpreted as expected profits.

The supplier of drugs i maximizes his profits. The first-order condition for a maximum is now given by

$$p_i = \frac{\eta}{\eta - 1}\left(\frac{1}{1-s}\right)(\beta w + p_m). \tag{6.13}$$

This equation has the same interpretation as (6.4); that is, it describes the short-term equilibrium. We observe from (6.13) that when the probability of seizures increases, the "upper level trafficker" will raise retail price. Because of the existence of a markup, $\eta/(\eta-1)$, the price increase will be a multiple of the increase in the probability of seizures.

We can rewrite equation (6.13) so as to explain the retail margin m_i, as we did in equation (6.5):

$$m_i = \frac{\eta}{\eta - 1}\left(\frac{1}{1-s}\right)\left(\frac{\beta w}{p_m} + 1\right). \tag{6.14}$$

As before, long-run equilibrium is obtained by imposing a zero profit condition $\pi_i = 0$. This yields

$$p = \left(\frac{1}{1-s}\right)\left[w\left(\frac{\alpha}{x} + \beta\right) + p_m\right], \tag{6.15}$$

or in the form of margins

$$m = \left(\frac{1}{1-s}\right)\left[\frac{w}{p_m}\left(\frac{\alpha}{x} + \beta\right) + 1\right]. \tag{6.16}$$

Since in equilibrium $x = cN$, (6.15) becomes

$$p = \left(\frac{1}{1-s}\right)\left[w\left(\frac{\alpha}{cN} + \beta\right) + p_m\right]. \tag{6.17}$$

We can now analyze the effect of changes in the probability of seizures brought about by tighter law enforcement. We do this in figure 6.7 using the same graphical procedure as in figure 6.6. An increase in s has the effect of shifting both the PP and the QQ curves upward. However, it can be shown that the upward shift of the PP curve is higher than that of the QQ curve. This can be seen by taking the partial derivative of p with respect to s in equations (6.13) and (6.17). We obtain from equation (6.13),

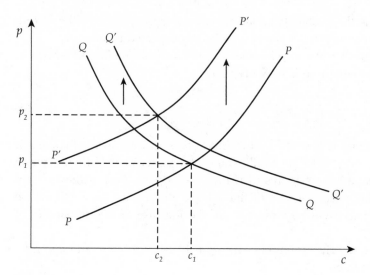

Figure 6.7
Effect of increase in probability of seizures

$$\frac{\partial p}{\partial s} = \frac{\eta}{\eta-1}\left(\frac{1}{(1-s)^2}\right)(w\beta + p_m),$$ (6.18)

and from equation (6.17),

$$\frac{\partial p}{\partial s} = \left(\frac{1}{(1-s)^2}\right)(w\beta + p_m).$$ (6.19)

It can be seen that (6.18) > (6.19) showing that the upward shift of the PP curve is higher than that of the QQ curve.

We conclude that an increase in the probability of seizures raises the retail price of drugs and reduces the amount of drug use. The latter effect follows from the fact that drug users are sensitive to a price increase. Note also that as the price increases and the drug use declines, the price elasticity, η, increases.

Finally, it can also be shown that an increase in seizures increases the intermediation margin m. This increase in the margin can be interpreted as in increase in the risk premium associated to the business of drug dealing.

There are other risks that could be analyzed in our model. One is the risk of incarceration. This risk will tend to introduce a risk premium in the wage of the low-level traffickers. In addition it leads to an increase in the risk premium that upper level dealers have to receive in order to deal the drug. This has the same qualitative effect as the risk of seizures; that is, it shifts both curves upward leading to a higher retail price. Note that in this case the increase in the retail price reflects a higher profit margin which is necessary to induce agents to engage in dealing drugs. (See Caulkins and Reuter 1998 for an in-depth analysis.) We will return to this risk in section 6.5.

6.3.3 The Effects of Globalization

The model also allows us to analyze the effects of globalization. There are several ways globalization enters the model. The first way is by reducing the import cost of drugs (p_m), which will be analyzed in section 6.5. The second way is by increasing the supply of drug dealers. We focus on the latter here. The total demand for drug dealers is

$$L_D = \sum_{i=1}^{n} l_i.$$

In equilibrium $L_D = L_S$. An increase in the supply of drug dealers leads to excess supply and thus to a decline in dealers' wage. We can now analyze the implications of this wage decline using equations (6.13) and (6.17) and their graphical representations. This is shown in figure 6.3. Both the PP and the QQ curves shift downward, producing a decline in the retail price (and in the intermediation margin). The effect on consumption however is ambiguous and depends on the parameters of the model.

The downward shift in the PP curve is obtained by taking the partial derivative of p with respect to w in equation (6.13). This yields

$$\frac{\partial p}{\partial w} = \frac{\eta}{(\eta - 1)} \left(\frac{1}{1-s} \right) \beta \tag{6.20}$$

The downward shift of the QQ curve is obtained by taking the partial derivative of p with respect to w in equation (6.11). This yields

$$\frac{\partial p}{\partial w} = \left(\frac{1}{1-s} \right) \left(\frac{\alpha}{cN} + \beta \right) \tag{6.21}$$

It is not a priori clear which expression is bigger. We know, however, that when c is high the elasticity η tends to diminish (producing a high markup). Thus for sufficiently high levels of c the downward shift in the PP line will exceed the downward shift in the QQ line, producing an increase in consumption. This is the case shown in figure 6.8.

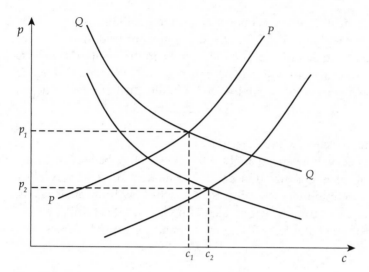

Figure 6.8
Effect of globalization in increasing supply of low-level drug dealers

From the previous analysis we note that globalization and supply containment policies have opposite effects on the retail price of drugs. This implies that as globalization proceeds, supply restrictions must increasingly become tighter to offset the price reducing forces of globalization. Thus, as globalization is an ongoing process, it forces the authorities to continuously increase the amount of resources used in supply containment policies in order to prevent the retail price from declining. Taking into account that law enforcement may be subject to diminishing returns, it is very likely that the effects of globalization do prevail.

6.3.4   Demand and Supply Policies Compared

The retail model derived in the previous sections allows us to shed some light on the relation between demand and supply policies. Demand policies (prevention, treatment, and harm reduction), if successful, reduce drug consumption (c) of the representative user. As previously shown, a decline of c has the effect of increasing the price elasticity (η) of the demand for drugs. Put differently, the success of demand policies can be gauged by their capacity of increasing the price sensitivity of the demand for drugs (which also implies that the power of the traffickers is reduced). This feature of successful demand policies in turn affects the effectiveness of supply containment policies. The reason is the following. A reduction of the supply of drugs raises the retail price. With a higher price elasticity of the demand for drugs, this supply induced price increase has a stronger negative effect on consumption. As a result supply policies become more effective in reducing drug use. Thus our model of the retail market has as an implication that when supply policies are combined with demand policies, the former become more effective in reducing drug use.

6.4 Deriving the Producers' Supply Curve

In this section we derive the producers' supply of drugs in the source countries. We assume that the supply of drugs in the producing country (e.g., cocaine in Colombia, or opium in Afghanistan) is organized in a perfectly competitive market.[8]

We start from a Cobb–Douglas production function of an individual producer i:

$$Q_{i_C} = A_C L_C^{\alpha} G_C^{\beta} (1 - p_e), \tag{6.22}$$

where Q_C is the output of the drug, L_C is the use of labor in the dug production, G_C is the use of land in the drug production, p_e is the probability of eradication, namely the share that each producer expects to be subject to the eradication policies followed by the law enforcement authority. We assume decreasing returns so that $\alpha + \beta < 1$. Finally, A_C measures total factor productivity.

The budget constraint of the individual producer is

$$C = wL_C + rG_C, \tag{6.23}$$

where C is the cost of producing drugs given the wage rate, w, and the price of land, r.

The producer minimizes his cost, C, subject to the production function. This cost minimization allows the producer to determine the optimal use of labor and land in the production process, that is,

$$\frac{G_C}{L_C} = \frac{\beta}{\alpha} \frac{w}{r}. \tag{6.24}$$

Thus, when wage costs increase relative to land costs, less labor and more land will be used in the production of drugs.

Equations (6.24) and (6.22) allow us to derive the optimal demand of labor and land in the drug sector:

$$L_C = Q^\gamma A_C^{-\gamma} \left(\frac{\alpha}{\beta} \frac{r}{w} \right)^{\beta\gamma} \left(\frac{1}{1-p_e} \right)^\gamma,$$
(6.25)

$$G_C = Q^\gamma A_C^{-\gamma} \left(\frac{\beta}{\alpha} \frac{w}{r} \right)^{\alpha\gamma} \left(\frac{1}{1-p_e} \right)^\gamma,$$
(6.26)

where

$$\gamma = \frac{1}{\alpha+\beta} > 1.$$

We note that an increase in the probability of eradication leads to a decline in the demand for labor and land in the same proportions.

Equation (6.26) allows us to analyze how much the productivity of land has to increase to offset the effects of eradication on output. We show the results in figure 6.9. This figure presents the productivity increase needed to keep output unchanged when eradication increases by 1 percentage point (from different levels of eradication). We see that this relationship is nonlinear. Consequently it means that if eradication efforts increase, the production area and/or productivity gains have to increase more than proportionally in order to keep drug production constant. For example, when eradication increases by one percentage point (starting from zero eradication) the productivity increase needed to keep output unchanged is about 0.5 percent. When the level of eradication is already 80 percent, an additional eradication of

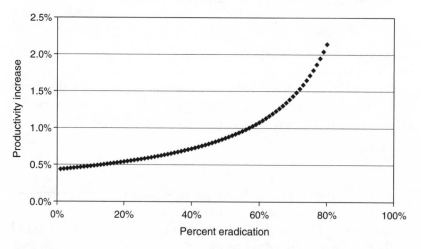

Figure 6.9
Productivity increase but output unchanged when eradication increases by 1 percent

1 percent requires a productivity effort of more than 2 percent, to keep drug production unchanged. In this sense eradication has increasing returns.[9]

The next step in the analysis is to derive the cost function. This is obtained by substituting the labor and land demand from (6.25) and (6.26) into the budget constraint (6.23). This yields

$$C = \Omega Q^{\gamma} A_C^{-\gamma} w^{\alpha\gamma} r^{\beta\gamma} \left(\frac{1}{1-p_e} \right)^{\gamma},$$ (6.27)

where

$$\Omega = \frac{\alpha^{\beta\gamma}}{\beta} + \frac{\beta^{\alpha\gamma}}{\alpha}.$$

The cost function (6.27) allows us to plot the relation between eradication effort and the cost of producing drugs. This is done in figure 6.10. We assume that $\gamma = 1.2$. (Other values lead to similar results). We have also normalized cost to be 1 when eradication is 0 percent. In addition we assume all the other variables to remain unchanged, in particular, productivity. We know from empirical evidence that eradication programs often lead to intensified efforts at increasing productivity. This effect is not taken into account in figure 6.10.

We obtain a nonlinear relationship: as the eradication effort increases, the cost of drug production increases. At low levels of eradication the

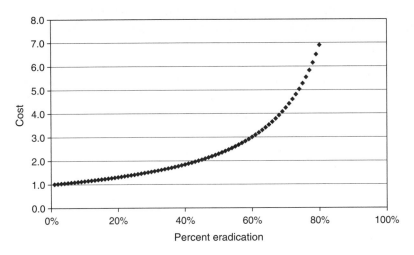

Figure 6.10
Cost of producing cocaine as a function of eradication effort

increase in cost is less than proportional to the increase in eradication. For example, when eradication increases from 10 to 20 percent (a doubling) production costs increase by only 14 percent. However, beyond a certain level of eradication (close to 60 percent), drug production costs increase exponentially. So the level of eradication has to be high in order for the nonlinear part of the cost curve to become effective.

Finally we derive the supply curve. This is obtained by setting marginal cost equal to the producer price and solving for Q_C. We then obtain

$$Q = \Omega P_C^{1/(\gamma-1)} A_C^{\gamma/(\gamma-1)} w^{-\alpha\gamma/(\gamma-1)} r^{-\beta\gamma/(\gamma-1)} \left(\frac{1}{1-p_e}\right)^{-\gamma/(\gamma-1)}. \tag{6.28}$$

Thus producers react to a price increase by raising output. The price elasticity of the supply of output is given by $1/(\gamma-1)$, which is larger than 1. It means that when price increases, producers increase drug production more than proportionally. The size of the output increase depends on the volume of capital and labor used to produce one unit of cocaine, that is, on γ.

For a given γ, the relation between price and quantities supplied is shown in figure 6.11. The relation is log-linear; that is, if we transform price and quantities supplied in logs, we obtain a linear relationship. Given that the price elasticity is higher than 1, the supply curve is relatively flat.

Eradication programs reduce the supply of output. Its impact is measured by the expression $-\gamma/(\gamma-1)$, which is negative and larger than 1 in absolute value. Graphically an increase in eradication shifts the supply curve upward as shown in figure 6.11.

An increase in productivity has the opposite effect on the supply of output. Its impact is measured by the expression $\gamma/(\gamma-1)$, which is the same as the effect of eradication except for the sign. Graphically productivity increases lead to a downward shift in the supply curve.

There is substantial evidence that the eradication efforts in Latin American countries have been offset by increased productivity leaving the supply more of less unchanged (for evidence, see Costa Storti and De Grauwe 2008). It can be argued that much of these productivity increases have been made possible by globalization. The latter has contributed to greater access of local drug farmers to new and improved production techniques. In this sense globalization has contributed to making eradication efforts relatively ineffective.

Price

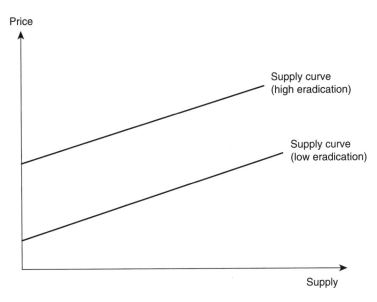

Supply

Figure 6.11
Supply curve with different levels of eradication

6.5   Linking up Demand and Supply of Drugs

In this section we link up the retail market and the producer markets. It will be remembered that the retail market determines the retail price (and the retail added value or margin, m_r) for a given import cost of the drug. The producer market in turn determines the supply of the drug for a given export price. We represent this graphically in figure 6.12. In the figure we show the retail market in the importing country, as we have developed it in section 6.3. The D_r curve represents the prices the representative drug user is willing to pay for different levels of drugs supplied at the retail level, in the importing country.

The lower D_m curve presents the different levels of the import price, p_m, that the importer is willing to pay, given the retail price he receives in the retail market. Note that we assume here that the "upper level drug trafficker" of the retail market is also the importer.[10] The vertical distance between the two curves is the retail margin, as derived in section 6.3 where we modeled the retail market.

Figure 6.13 presents the producer supply equation which was derived in section 6.4. For the sake of simplicity we represent this

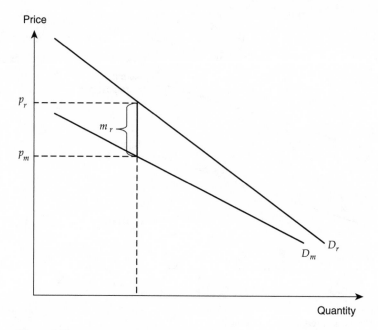

Figure 6.12
Importing country's demand side of the model

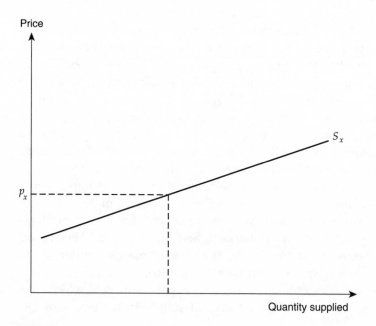

Figure 6.13
Producer country's supply side of the model

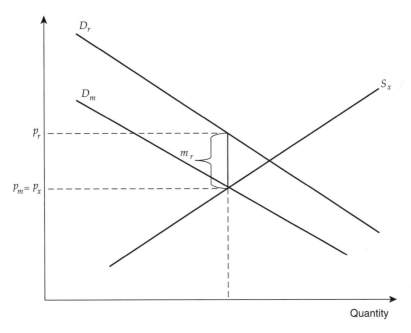

Figure 6.14
Equilibrium in the absence of import–export margin

supply curve as a linear one.[11] We assume here that the total supply is exported. Thus the price the producer is facing is the export price, p_x. An increasing export price leads producers to increase their supply.

We now bring together the demand and the supply side of the model in figure 6.14. Without intermediation costs in the export–import business the equilibrium of the model would be obtained where the supply curve S_x intersects the import demand curve, D_m, producing a retail price p_r. In this equilibrium point, the import price of the drug in the retail market, p_m, equals the producer's export price p_x. This is, however, highly unrealistic as the export/import of drugs involves transaction costs and risks, introducing a margin between the import price of the drug (CIF) and the export price (FOB) when it leaves the producing country. The difference between these two prices is the intermediation margin in the export and import business, which we will call m_t. We model this intermediation margin in the next section. This allows us to link up the retail market determining demand conditions with the main stages of cocaine supply.

6.5.1   A Theory of Intermediation in the Export–Import Business

We use the concept of intermediation as comprising all economic activities that ensure that the drugs produced by the farmers reach the final consumers. The intermediation margin is then the unit price paid for these activities.

The components of the intermediation margin, m_t, can now be analyzed as follows. First we have to take into account that the import price in the European Union (or the United States) is expressed in euros (or dollars), while the export price paid in the producing countries is expressed in local currency. Second we have to take into consideration a margin paid to the import/export activity (m_t). Thus we write the definition as

$$\frac{p_m}{p_x e} = 1 + m_t, \tag{6.29}$$

where, as before, p_m is the import price in the market of the final drug user. This price is expressed in that country's currency (e.g., euros or dollars); p_x is the export price in the producing country, expressed in that country's currency. Multiplying by the exchange rate, e, yields the export price expressed in the importing country's currency. The margin, m_t, includes all the costs incurred in the business of exporting and importing the drugs. This margin introduces a difference between the import price (CIF) and the export price (FOB) even after translating both prices in the same currency (the euro or the dollar).

The next step is to specify the variables that affect the intermediation margin m_t. We identify several cost factors that affect this margin and that therefore lead to an increase in the price, when trafficking cocaine from the producing country to the destination market.

The first cost is the "the plain vanilla" transport cost (e.g., the cost of the maritime transport from Andean countries to Europe, respectively the United States). The second cost arises from the risk of losing the trafficked drug due to being seized. The third one is the wage traffickers pay to their employees (lower level traffickers and "mules") involved in the smuggling activity. The last cost we consider is the profit earned by the upper level cocaine traffickers.

We can formalize this as

$$\frac{p_m}{p_x e} = (1 + \tau_t)(1 + \tau_s)(1 + \tau_l)(1 + r), \tag{6.30}$$

where τ_t is the "plain vanilla" transport cost, τ_s is the cost of seizure, τ_l is the labor cost, and r is the profit margin in the export-import business. We now specify the different variables that affect costs.

The Exchange Rate From equation (6.30) we see that a depreciation of the euro (an increase in the exchange rate, e) has the effect of either increasing the import price p_m or reducing the export price p_x, or a combination of these two changes. This is because the variables on the right-hand side of (6.30) are independent from the changes of the exchange rate. As a result the ratio between the two prices on the left-hand side of (6.30) must remain unchanged. To achieve this, the import price must increase and/or the export price must decline in such a way as to keep the ratio unchanged.

"Plain Vanilla" Transport Costs The transport cost, τ_t, is a function of the number of hours the trip from the exporting country to the importing country last (h) and its price, p_t (e.g., the introduction of low costs transatlantic flights or faster boats influence transport costs). We have

$$\tau_T = \tau_T(h, p_t), \tag{6.31}$$

where

$$\frac{\partial \tau_T}{\partial h} > 0 \quad \text{and} \quad \frac{\partial \tau_T}{\partial p_t} > 0.$$

Seizures Seizures add to import price in the following way. Call ρ the probability of a unit of cocaine being seized. Then shipping one dollar of the drug will lead to an expected value at arrival of $1 - \rho$. Thus, to ensure that one dollar value of drugs reaches destination, $1/(1-\rho)$ should be exported. The transport cost can then be said to have increased by a factor of $1/(1-\rho)$. We write this as

$$1 + \tau_S = \frac{1}{1-\rho}. \tag{6.32}$$

The probability of seizure, ρ, is a function of the supply reduction policies of the countries involved and the associated resources invested in supply reduction policies

$$\rho = \rho(SR), \tag{6.33}$$

where SR are the resources invested in supply reduction policies.

Labor Costs   The third cost component is labor cost. Let us write the wage cost per dollar of drug transported, w. We assume that the wage rate is determined by the reservation wage of the drug carriers (i.e., the wage they can earn in other employments) plus a risk premium. The latter arises because drug trafficking involves the risk of incarceration.[12] People will only engage in a risky activity if they are compensated by a higher wage. The higher wage above the shadow wage is the risk premium. We write

$$w = \bar{w} + \pi_w, \tag{6.34}$$

where $\bar{w}$ is the shadow wage; that is, the wage this worker would receive in a job he would manage to get as alternative. Then π_w is the risk premium component of the wage, that is, the payment the drug dealer requires for accepting the risk of trafficking. The latter is determined by a number of factors. First, the resources invested in supply reduction policies increase the risk of incarceration, and thus the risk premium required by this trafficker.

Second, globalization increases the pool of agents who are capable and willing to enter trafficking at a lower shadow wage. Furthermore globalization can also supply lower level traffickers willing to accept high risks for small reward (less risk adverse labor force Z). This tends to reduce the risk premium. Note that we implicitly assume that the newcomers in the trafficking have a lower degree of risk aversion than those already employed in trafficking (e.g., see section 6.7).

Formally we have

$$\pi_w = \pi_w(SR, Z), \tag{6.35}$$

with

$$\frac{\partial \pi_w}{\partial SR} > 0 \quad \text{and} \quad \frac{\partial \pi_w}{\partial Z} < 0$$

Profit Margins   The final component in equation (6.30) is the profit margin in the export–import business. Resources invested in the export–import business should earn a rate of return that reflects the return of alternative activities plus a risk premium. Thus we write

$$r = \bar{r} + \pi_r. \tag{6.36}$$

As in the case of the wage rate, the risk premium π_r is influenced by the risk of incarceration (SR) and by the supply of new entrants in the

exporting/importing business (Z). The risk of incarceration has a positive influence on the risk premium while the supply of new entrants
tends to reduce the risk premium, and thus the rate of return in the
exporting and importing business:

$$\pi_r = \pi_r(SR, Z) \tag{6.37}$$

with

$$\frac{\partial \pi_r}{\partial SR} > 0 \quad \text{and} \quad \frac{\partial \pi_r}{\partial Z} < 0.$$

Note that in a similar way as in the retail market, we implicitly assume
two types of agents in the trafficking business. There are the "higher
level traffickers." These are the entrepreneurs who organize the traffic
and who earn the residual profits, r. Then there are the "lower level
traffickers." They are hired by the higher level traffickers and earn the
wage rate, w. Both are affected by the same factors, the resources
invested in supply reduction policies and globalization which affects
the entry of newcomers in the business.

**Simultaneous Equilibrium: Retailers, Producers, and Import–
Export Markets**   The equilibrium in the model is described graphically in figure 6.15. S_x is, as before, the producer supply curve in the
exporting country. S_m is the supply curve at the point of import in
the retail market. The vertical distance between the two lines is given
by the intermediation margin of export/import activity, m_t. These
curves are influenced by those variables discussed in the previous
paragraphs.

Equilibrium is obtained where supply of imported drugs (S_m) and
demand for exported drugs (D_m) intersect. This intersection point
determines the import price in the retail market (p_m).

The retail price p_r is then obtained by adding the retail margin m_r
(derived in section 6.3). We then obtain an equilibrium in the retail
market, where the upper level drug dealer operates in a monopolistic
competition framework. The intermediation margin m_r includes costs
such as the lower level dealer wage, productivity and markup. The
latter is a function of the demand elasticity of the representative drug
user. The higher the level of drug use (higher addiction), the smaller
the elasticity is. Conversely, a recreational drug user, in a relatively
early stage of his drug use, to whom treatment is supplied, will reduce

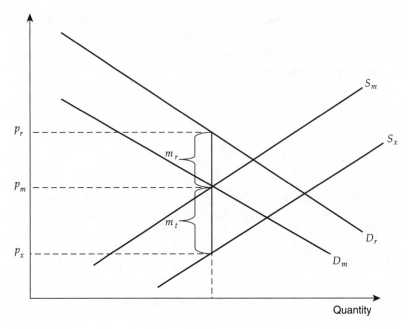

Figure 6.15
Equilibrium with import–export margin

his drug use more strongly, when prices rise. Therefore, in this frame-work, demand reduction polices that successfully represent an alterna-tive to drug use may diminish the demand elasticity. As specified in the model, the price elasticity of drug use will determine the markup: the higher the price elasticity, the smaller the upper level trafficker markup.

Finally, the producer price (export price) p_x is obtained by subtract-ing the export–import margin, m_t, derived in this section.

6.5.2 Effects of Globalization

Globalization affects the labor market structure and the risk involved in the export and import business. It does this in the following way. First, it increases the pool of low-level traffickers available in the import–export smuggling. The opening up of countries since the 1980s has added millions of low-skilled workers who have little to loose and are willing to take risks (see Freeman 2005). The increase in the com-petition in the market of low-level traffickers leads to a decline in the shadow wage $\bar{w}$. It also tends to reduce π_w, the risk premium

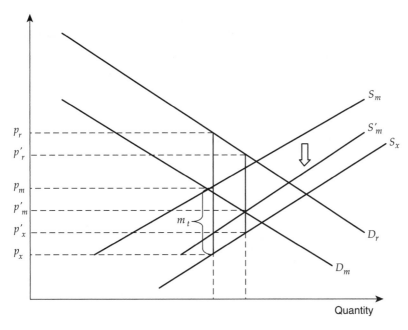

Figure 6.16
Effects of globalization

component of the wage of the lower level traffickers in (6.34). Second, globalization also leads to entry of higher level traffickers in the export–import business, which in turn leads to a lower return of these activities (equation 6.35). The combined effect is to reduce the margin m_t. We show the effect in figure 6.16. The reduction of the margin, m_t, shifts the import supply curve downward to the position S'_m compared to its initial position, S_m. In the new equilibrium the import price declines to p'_m and so does the retail price (to p'_r). This is exactly what has been observed in the price data since 1980.

It is also interesting to note that the reduction of the margin m_t brought about by globalization also increases the producer price. This shown in figure 6.16 by the increase of the producer price increases from p_x to p'_x. As was shown in section 6.2, producer prices have been increasing significantly in the last twenty years. Thus our model is capable of explaining the opposite movements in retail and producer prices of cocaine and heroin. The major driving force is the reduction of the margins in the export–import business as was made possible by the massive influx of low- and high-level traffickers.

These forces of globalization appear to have overwhelmed the attempts of the authorities of the different countries to disrupt the supply of drugs. As we argued earlier, the resources spent in these supply policies have increased significantly. Our model predicts that these policies increase the intermediation margin m_t mainly because they increase the risk of trafficking. However, this effect has been more than compensated by the effects of globalization. In this sense supply policies have been waging a loosing battle against the forces of globalization.

6.6   Globalization Once Again

In the previous sections we analyzed the different channels through which globalization affects the markets of cocaine and heroin. In this section we put the pieces together. The purpose of this section is not to provide rigorous empirical evidence of the main propositions of our theoretical model. Rather, it is an attempt at synthetically describing the different mechanisms globalization has set in motion in the markets of cocaine and heroin.

We distinguish three broad effects of globalization: a market structure effect, a risk premium effect, and an efficiency effect.[13] We discuss these consecutively and indicate where these effects enter into the model.

6.6.1   The Market Structure Effect
In a very general way globalization tends to open markets, thereby changing the market structure away from monopolistic toward more competitive structures. As a result competition is enhanced and the markup, namely the difference between the retail price and the marginal cost, is reduced. The drug market has been subject to the same forces of globalization that have changed the market structure in the drug-consuming countries, increasing competition. As a result the retail margins (markups) are being squeezed, contributing to a lowering of the retail prices of drugs. We analyzed this effect extensively in section 6.3 (the retail market).

6.2   The Risk Premium Effect
Globalization has opened the borders of many countries with a surplus of poor and low-skilled workers. Richard Freeman has estimated that the opening up of China, India, and Russia since the 1980s

has doubled the world supply of cheap and unskilled workers (Freeman 2005). Coupled with the increased possibility of international travel, this has increased the pool of individuals who have little to lose and who want to profit from the large intermediation margins in the drug business.

We introduced this effect into our model in several ways. In the retail market and in the export–import business, it has led to an influx of high-level and low-level traffickers. As a result the risk premium component of the wage of low-level traffickers has declined and the risk premium component of the return of the high-level traffickers has been pushed down. The joint effect of these declining risk premia has been to reduce the intermediation margins in the cocaine and heroin markets.

6.6.3 The Efficiency Effect

Lower transport, communication, and information costs have increased the efficiency of intermediation in the drug business. In addition lower transport costs have increased international trade in general, allowing to better conceal drug trade. Finally, by opening up borders, globalization has also made it possible to transfer scientific and technological knowhow.

Our model captures some of these effects. In particular, we have seen how the lowering of transport costs reduces the intermediation margin in the international trafficking of drugs. In addition we have shown how increased productivity in the production of cocaine and heroin increases the supply, even in an environment of tight policies of supply interdiction and eradication.

6.6.4 Globalization and Supply Containment Policies

Globalization has had forceful effects in the drug market. The force of these effects can be gauged by the fact that as globalization unfolded, governments of major drug-consuming countries significantly tightened policies aimed at reducing supply. These policies in isolation should have increased retail prices, reduced consumption and production. We observe that exactly the opposite occurred: retail prices declined significantly, and consumption and production continued to increase. This suggests that the forces of globalization more than offset the effects of supply containment policies. In this sense it can be concluded that these policies are waging a loosing battle against the forces of globalization.

Our model of the retail market, however, also shows that the effectiveness of supply containment can be enhanced by combining it with demand policies. The latter, if successful, tend to increase the price sensitivity of drug users. As a result policies that reduce the supply of drugs in the retail market, and thus increase drug prices, become more effective in reducing the consumption of drugs.

6.7 A Case Study: The Development of the West African Cocaine Route toward Europe

Since 2005 the role of West Africa as transit, storage, and repacking place for the traffic of cocaine from South America to Europe has been sharply reinforced. According to UNODC (2007b) almost 30 percent of the drugs used in Europe in the last few years has been trafficked via the West Africa.

UNODC (2007b) estimates that in 2000, total seizures in West Africa only amounted to 97 kg, whereas in 2007, preliminary estimates point to 6,458 kg. Despite the fact that this indicator is insufficient to accurately assess traffic, as it is influenced by other factors such as the level and effectiveness of police activity, it is certainly indicative of the dimension of the problem. In any case, all the available sources that report on drug trafficking stress that cocaine that enters Europe is increasingly passing by West Africa.[14]

The model developed in this chapter supplies us the tools to better understand the growing importance of the Western African route in contributing to the decline of cocaine prices in Europe.

6.7.1 Short Description of the West African Cocaine Route toward Europe

There are two traditional cocaine routes that supply Europe.[15] The Northern Route, which transports cocaine produced in the Andean region toward the Caribbean and then to Europe. The second one, the Central Route traffics cocaine from South America via Cape Verde or Madeira and Canary Islands to Europe. These routes have been used for years, and they are well known by the law enforcement authorities. Furthermore, as they partially coincide with the routes used to smuggle cocaine into the United States, they have been closely monitored by law enforcement authorities for a long time.

According to Europol (2007) and UNODC (2007a), the Western Africa route of cocaine is organized in two main stages. From South

America to Africa, cocaine is in the hands of either South American or European traffickers. It is transported either by sea or by air. Maritime shipments occur in large commercial fishing or freight "mother ships," often specially modified for cocaine storage. These ships discharge their cargo at sea to smaller fishing vessels. Air shipments use relatively small aircraft modified for trans-Atlantic voyages. Then traffickers use vulnerable African territory for storage, repackaging, and re-routing cocaine. From Africa to Europe, two parallel systems are in place. The first one involving large quantities of cocaine is organized by South American upper level traffickers and uses a maritime route. The second one, done mostly by air, deals with smaller quantities, being mainly organized by West Africans, both at the upper and lower level of the trafficking. These traffickers sometimes benefit from the knowledge and expertise of preexisting cannabis routes. This second route involves a large number of air couriers sent on commercial flights in a "shotgun approach," namely with a large number of couriers placed on a single flight, knowing that customs officers have a limited capacity to arrest and process a large number of passengers. Upper traffickers explore the new aerial liaisons made available by low cost air companies. In addition they profit from a great availability and low cost of African body packers or body couriers. For instance, the latter are willing to ingest larger loads of drugs, and thereby taking more risks than their counterparts trafficking on alternative routes.

Since West Africa includes some of the poorest countries of the world, local governments are not prepared nor have the economic and technical means to combat this source of criminality. Their judicial and law enforcement systems are very poorly developed. Recently some international and especially European action has already been taken, such as the creation of MAOC–N (a European Law Enforcement unit with military support aiming at responding to the threat posed by the transatlantic cocaine traffic). Nevertheless, on the whole, the control of this route falls short of the one applied on alternative routes.

6.7.2 Applying the Model to the West African Route

This short description of the West African route illustrates some of the points we made in our analysis of how globalization affects the drug business and how it tends to interfere with supply containment policies. We find the three effects of globalization indentified in the previous section.

The Market Structure Effect   The entry of newcomers has affected international trafficking. The emergence of a new route has introduced more competition in the business of international trafficking, undermining the market power of the older participants. The market structure has become more competitive and less cartelized, thereby lowering markups.

The Risk Premium Effect   The abject poverty of West African countries has released a large number of cheap workers who are willing to take large risks in drug trafficking. This has reduced the risk premium to be paid to lower level trafficking and, in so doing, has lowered the intermediation margin in the export–import business.

The reduction of the risk premium is also related to the relatively low level of enforcement observed in West Africa as compared to alternative routes. In this sense globalization is a mechanism searching for the route of least resistance. As a result law enforcement tends to lag new developments.

The Efficiency Effect   The emergence of low-cost air carriers has made it possible to organize the drug traffic in small quantities carried by cheap African traffickers. This together with the exponential growth of air traffic has complicated detection. In addition the openness of the international trading system has allowed the spillover of existing knowledge and experience of the older cannabis routes to be used in the new ones. All these effects have lowered the cost of international trafficking, contributing to the decline in the retail price of cocaine in Europe.

These different effects have no doubt been stimulated by the increased tightness of supply containment policies. The West African route can be seen as a mechanism aimed at escaping law enforcement policies. Globalization has greatly facilitated the organization of such an escape mechanism.

6.8   Conclusion

Retail prices of cocaine and heroin have declined significantly during the last decades while at the same time producer prices have tended to increase. As a result intermediation margins in the business of transporting and dealing these drugs have declined spectacularly. In addition consumption and production of cocaine and heroin have continued to increase. These are puzzling developments because at the same time efforts to limit the supply of drugs by law enforcement methods (seizures, incarceration) have intensified. These supply containments policies should have increased retail prices, increased intermediation margins, and reduced consumption and production. The opposite occurred. We argued in this chapter that this has happened because the forces of globalization have overwhelmed the supply containment policies.

To understand these developments better, we developed a theoretical model of the cocaine and heroin markets. The model consists of three parts, a retail market determining the demand side, a producer supply process, and an international part describing the export–import business.

The main novelty of the analysis is to model the retail market as a market characterized by monopolistic competition. This is a market form often analyzed in economics. We consider the upper level dealers to have some market power, allowing them to charge a markup and thus to earn extra profits. This is the "monopolistic" part. At the same time this extra profit attracts newcomers in the business so that these profits tend to disappear. This is the "competition" part in the model. There is a lot of research sustaining this way of modeling the retail market. This research suggests that upper level dealers seek local market power by developing networks but that this market power is continuously being eroded by the entry of newcomers.

We used this model to analyze how supply containment policies affect the retail market, the producer market and the export–import business. For example, in the retail market law enforcement in the form of seizures tends to increase the retail price and the retail margin (i.e., the difference between the retail price and import cost of the drug). In general, law enforcement measures (e.g., incarceration) increase the risk premia that have to be obtained by both the lower and higher level traffickers in order to engage in drug dealing.

Much of our analysis was focused on modeling the different ways globalization affects the drug markets. We distinguished between a market structure effect, a risk premium effect, and an efficiency effect of globalization.

We found that in general, globalization has the opposite effects of supply containment policies. It lowers intermediation margins and as a result tends to lower retail prices, thereby stimulating consumption. At the same time it increases the prices obtained by the producers, tending to increase production. In so doing, globalization offsets the effects of supply containment policies. Since retail prices have declined, producer prices have increased, and production and consumption have increased, one should conclude that globalization has overwhelmed the effects of supply policies.

Finally, using the model of the retail market, we showed that the effectiveness of supply containment policies can be enhanced by combining them with demand policies. The latter, if successful, tend to increase the price sensitivity of drug users. This is so because demand policies create alternatives for drug users in the form of treatment. As a result policies that reduce the supply of drugs in the retail market become more effective in reducing the consumption of drugs because they operate in an environment in which consumers react more strongly to price increases.

Notes

1. Different studies point to a price elasticity faced by aggregate demand for cocaine relatively small but different from zero. See Caulkins et al. (1995), Caulkins (2001), Bretteville-Jensen and Biorn (2004), Abt Associates (2000), Dave (2004), and Grossman (2004).

2. This is the standard definition of monopolistic competition. The model presented in this section is an extension of the Krugman (1979) model. See also Feenstra (2006). It has its origin in work on monopolistic competition by Chamberlin (1936) and Robinson (1933).

3. The classic analysis of this "lemon problem" was first made by Akerlof (1970).

4. In other markets this lemon problem is often dealt with by the use of brand names. The illicit character of drugs makes this solution to be based on personal networks, where the trust on a seller's reputation is crucial.

5. See Reuter and Caulkins (2004).

6. Caulkins and Hao (2008), have an interesting discussion about the European and the US demand elasticities for cocaine and heroin. They put the market elasticity for the United States within a range of 0.5 to 1 (absolute values). See Abt Associates (2000), Bretteville-Jensen and Biorn (2004), Caulkins et al. (1998), Caulkins (2001), Dave (2004), and Grossman (2004). The estimates of the price elasticity ε obtained in these studies typically are below 1 (but larger than 0).

7. Consumption of a representative drug user should be identical to the product of the amount of cocaine per dose, purity, and the number of doses a day, taking into account that this pattern varies over the year (Singleton et al. 2006).

8. See also Kennedy et al. (1993).

9. Several reports point to the fact that the current eradication efforts implemented in the Andean region have been more than compensated by productivity gains (UNODC 2007a, b).

10. This assumption could be relaxed without affecting the results. Caulkins and Hao (2008) analyze the different distribution layers between the importer and the retailer.

11. In section 6.4 this is derived to be log-linear.

12. See Caulkins and MaccCoun (2003) for a further discussion on how this risk may affect drug dealers wage.

13. See Costa Storti and De Grauwe (2008).

14. See Europol (2007), INCB (2008), UNODC (2007a), or USDS (2008).

15. Europol (2007).

References

Abt Associates. 2000. Illicit drugs: Price elasticity of demand and supply. Report Prepared for the National Institute of Justice, Cambridge, MA.

Akerlof, G. 1970. The market for "lemons": Quality uncertainty and the market mechanism. *Quarterly Journal of Economics* 84 (3): 488–500.

Basov, S., M. Jacobson, and J. Miron. 2001. Prohibition and the market for illegal drugs: An overview of recent history. *World Economy* 2 (4): 133–57.

Bretteville-Jensen A. L., and E. Biorns. 2004. Do prices count? A micro-econometric study of illicit drug consumption base on self-reported data. *Empirical Economics* 29: 673–95.

Bretteville-Jensen, A. 2006. Unresolved issues associated with current economic models of substance abuse. *Substance Use and Misuse* 41: 601–6.

Caulkins, J., and R. Padma. 1993. Quantity discounts and quality premia for illicit drugs. *Journal of the American Statistical Association* 88 (423): 748–57.

Caulkins, J. P. 1996. Estimating elasticities of demand for cocaine and heroin with DUF data. Working paper. Heinz School of Public Policy, Carnegie Mellon University.

Caulkins, J., and P. Reuter. 1998. What price data tell us about drug markets. *Journal of Drug Issues (National Council of State Boards of Nursing (USA)* 28 (3): 593–613.

Caulkins, J. 2001. Drug prices and emergency department mentions for cocaine and heroin. *American Journal of Public Health* 91 (9): 1446–48.

Caulkins, J., and R. MacCoun. 2003. Limited rationality and the limits of supply reduction. JSP/Center for the Study of Law and Society Faculty. University of California, Berkeley.

Caulkins, J. 2005. Price and purity analysis for illicit drug: Data and conceptual issues. RAND Drug Policy Research Center.

Caulkins, J., P. Reuter, M. Y. Iguchi, and J. Chiesa. 2005. How goes "war on drugs"? An assessment of the U.S. drug problems and policy. RAND Drug Policy Reseach Center.

Caulkins P., Reuter P., Taylor L. (2006. Contributions to economic analysis and policy. *Berkeley Electronic Press* 5 (1): art. 3.

Caulkins, J., and H. Hao. 2008. Modeling drug market supply disruptions: Where do all the drugs not go? *Journal of Policy Modeling* 30: 251–70.

Chaloupka, F., and H. Saffer. 1995. The demand for illicit drugs. *Economic Inquiry* 37 (3): 401–11.

Chamberlin, E. 1936. *The Theory of Monopolistic Competition: A Reorientation of the Theory of Value.* Cambridge: Harvard University Press.

Costa Storti, C., and P. De Grauwe. 2008. Globalization and the price decline of illicit drugs. *International Journal of Drug Policy* (accessed online, February 12, 2008).

Dave, D. 2004. The effects of cocaine and heroin prices on drug-related emergency department visits. Working paper 10619. NBER.

Deroches F. 2007. Research on upper level drug trafficking: A review. *Journal of Drug Issues* 4 (37): 827–44.

Dixit, A., and J. Stiglitz. 1977. Monopolistic competition and optimum product diversity. *American Economic Review* 67 (3): 297–308.

Europol. 2007. Project Cola: European Union Cocaine Situation Report.

Feenstra, R. 2004. *Advanced International Trade: Theory and Evidence.* Princeton: Princeton University Press.

Ferguson, B. 2006. Economic modeling of the rational consumption of addictive substances. *Substance Use and Misuse* 41: 573–603.

Freeman, D. 2005. What really ails Europe (and America): The doubling of the global workforce. *Globalist Paper*, June 3.

Grossman, M. 2004. Individual behaviors and substance abuse: The role of price. Working paper 10948. NBER.

Grossman, M., F. Chaloupka, and K. Shim. 2002. Illegal drug use and public policy. *Health Affairs* 21 (2): 134–45.

Helpman, E., and P. Krugman. 1985. *Market Structure and Foreign Trade.* Cambridge: MIT Press.

INCB. 2008. *Annual Report 2007.*

Kennedy, M., P. Reuter, and K. J. Riley. 1993. A single economic model of cocaine production. *Mathematical and Computer Modelling* 17 (2): 19–36.

Krugman, P. 1979. Increasing returns, monopolistic competition, and international trade. *Journal of International Economics* 9: 469–79.

Matrix Knowledge Group. 2007. The illicit drug trade in the United Kingdom. Home Office Report 20/7.

Pearson G., and D. Hobbs. 2001. Middle market drug distribution. Home Office Research Study 227.

Reuter, P., and M. Kleiman. 1986. Risks and prices: An economic analysis of drug enforcement. *Crime and Justice* 7: 289–340.

Reuter, P., and J. Haaga. 1989. The organization of high-level drug markets: An explanatory study. RAND note N-2830-NIJ.

Reuter, P. 2001. The limits of supply-side drug control. *The Milken Institute Review* 1 (1): 14–23.

Reuter, P., and V. Greenfield. 2001. Measuring global drug markets: How good are the numbers and why should we care about them? *World Economy* 2: 4.

Reuter, P., and J. Caulkins. 2004. Illegal "lemons": Price dispersion in cocaine and heroin markets. *UNODC, Bulletin on Narcotics: Illicit Drug Markets* 56 (1–2): 141–65.

Ritter, A. 2005. *A Review of Approaches to Studying the Illicit Drug Markets*. DPMP monograph 8. Fitzroy: Turning Point Alcohol and Drug Centre.

Robinson, J. 1933. *The Economics of Imperfect Competition*. London: Macmillan.

Saffer, H., and F. Chaloupka. 1999. The demand for illicit drugs. *Economic Inquiry* 37 (3): 401–11.

Singleton N., R. Murray, and L. Tinsley. 2006. Measuring different aspects of problem drug use: Methodological developments. Home Office Online Report 16/06.

UNODC. 2007a. *Cocaine Trafficking in West Africa: The Threat to Stability and Development*. Vienna.

UNODC. 2007b. *2007 World Drug Report*. Vienna.

US Department of State. 2008. *International Narcotics Control Strategy Report*, vol. 1. Washington, DC: Government Printing Office.

World Bank. 2007. *World Development Indicators Database*. Washington, DC.

7 The Impact of Globalization on the UK Market for Illicit Drugs: Evidence from Interviews with Convicted Drug Traffickers

Kevin Marsh, Laura Wilson, and Rachel Kenehan

7.1 Introduction

In the United Kingdom the heroin, cocaine, and crack market is estimated to have a value in excess of £4 billion per annum (Pudney et al. 2006). Such drugs have a substantial social cost beyond this market valuation. It is estimated that crack and heroin users commit £16 billion worth of crime each year to fund their drug use and cost a further £8 billion each year in their impact on health and social services (Pudney et al. 2006). To address the drug problem, the UK government developed the National Drug Strategy (Home Office 2002), whose mission (identified as four pillars) is to prevent young people from becoming drug misusers, increase the number of individuals accessing effective drug treatment, reduce drug-related crime, and reduce the supply of illegal drugs. A recent update (Home Office 2008) emphasized the following work program: protecting communities by blocking drug supply, drug-related crime, and antisocial behavior; preventing harm to children, young people, and families affected by a member's drug misuse; delivering new drug treatment approaches to drug addicts and social re-integration of addicts; and public information campaigns, through communications networks and community engagement.

The impact of globalization on the illicit drugs market may hold important lessons for the effectiveness of the National Drug Strategy. Just as globalization has improved the efficiency of markets for licit goods, it is argued that it has also improved the efficiency of markets for illicit goods, undermining the effectiveness of supply policies (Costa Storti and De Grauwe 2008b).

Costa Storti and De Grauwe (2008a, b) identify a number of phenomena in the cocaine and heroin markets that they argue can be attributed to the forces of globalization deterring efforts of policies to constrain drug supply, even though attempts at limiting their supply through law enforcement measures (seizures, incarceration) have intensified. While a lowered supply would be expected to have increased retail prices and intermediation margins as well as reducing consumption and production, exactly the opposite is happening: consumption and production of cocaine and heroin have increased, retail prices are declining, producer prices have increased, and margins in the business of dealing drug have declined. Costa Storti and De Grauwe argue that "this suggests that the forces of globalization more than offset the effects of supply containment policies" (2008a, p. 36).

Similar trends are observed in the United Kingdom. Pudney et al.'s (2006) analysis of street drug prices from the National Criminal Intelligence Service demonstrates consistent price falls across all drugs between December 2000 and December 2004, with the exception of amphetamines.

Costa Storti and De Grauwe (2008a, b) consider three effects of globalization that can account for these phenomena:

1. The market structure effect, arising from the increased level of competition due to the opening up of markets, which reduces retail prices and the profit margins earned by dealers.

2. The risk premium effect, arising from the influx of both high-level and low-level traffickers into the market, which reduces the risk premium component of wages and in turn reduces the margins earned in the market.

3. The efficiency effect, arising from the reduced cost of operating in the market for illicit drugs associated with the lower transport, communication, information, and financial costs, and the increased ability to conceal trafficking activities as a result of the increased international trade, travel, migration, and capital flows.

The evidence for these effects is limited. There are few data on the organization of markets for illicit drugs. Caulkins and Reuter (1998) suggest that the market is characterized by monopoly power but point out that the evidence is inconclusive. The evidence on the organization of the illicit drug market in the United Kingdom is similarly limited. The evidence that is available is derived from locally specific case studies. Cragg Ross Dawson (2003) describes the UK crack market as comprising many street and middle-level dealers, Hales and

Silverstone (2005) describe the increased competition in the cocaine markets with the arrival of Jamaican dealers in the 1980s, and Pitts (2007) describes how four crime families in a London borough came together to force the Jamaican "Yardies" out of the market.

INCB (2001) uses intelligence data to support the notion that traffickers exploit new technologies to improve the efficiency of their operations. Communications technology, such as prepaid telephone cards, restricted-access Internet chat rooms, and "cloned" cellular phones (employing the identity codes of legitimate customers), allow traffickers to communicate safely and to launder money by electronic transfer. Encryption technology allows traffickers to securely store information on shipments of illicit drugs, bank accounts, and associates.

Paoli and Reuter (2008) describe the role played by immigrants in drug dealing and trafficking in Europe. They point out that while the overrepresentation of immigrants in criminal justice statistics may be a manifestation of the "priorities and biases" of law enforcement agencies, there is empirical research that demonstrates that the open drug markets in most large western European cities are dominated by ethnic minorities. In support of the efficiency effect hypothesized by Costa Storti and De Grauwe (2008a, b), Paoli, and Reuter (2008) argue that one reason for the predominance of such minorities in the drug trade is that they are part of diasporas, which allow dealers to effectively hide their illegal operations. However, it is important to note that Paoli and Reuter point to a number of other reasons why ethnic minorities are overrepresented in drug trafficking, including: their low social and economic position, which reduces their options for alternative employment; the strength of their family ties making their operations impermeable to law enforcement activities; and their proximity to source countries and major trafficking routes.

There is also evidence that ethnic minority groups play a role in the UK market for illicit drugs. Turkish groups dominate the supply of heroin (Pearson and Hobbs 2001; SOCA 2007), while Columbian and West Indian traffickers dominate the supply of cocaine (Pearson and Hobbs 2001; SOCA 2007). Hales and Silverstone (2005) describe how groups with links to Jamaica became key players in the UK crack market. The criminal groups responsible for the spread of crack cocaine in the United Kingdom had links with both Jamaican and UK-based Caribbean communities that were first established in the 1950s.

7.2 Superterritoriality: Illicit Drug Markets as Flexible Social Networks

The account of the effect of globalization on illicit drug markets described in the previous section presumes what Scholte (2007, p. 8) refers to as a "continuity in the underlying character of social geography." That is, this description of globalization is based on an increased rate of exchange between preexisting social and territorial spaces, or "a shrinking world occur[ing] *within* territorial geography" (Scholte 2007, p. 11). This description of globalization, Scholte argues, can be captured within existing concepts such as "internationalization" (a growth of transactions and interdependence among countries), "liberalization" (a removal of officially imposed restrictions on the movement of resources between countries), and "universalization" (a process of dispersing various objects and experiences to people at all inhabited parts of the earth).

Scholte (2007) proposes a different conception of globalization, the spread of "transplanetary" or "supraterritorial" connections among people. That is, globalization cannot be explained simply by blending the existing notions of internationalization, liberalization, and universalization. An explanation of globalization requires a break from the territorialist geography implicit in these notions. It is the reduction of "barriers to transworld social contacts [and the] shift in the nature of social space" (Scholte 2007, p. 8) that is the novel characteristic of globalization.

The manifestations of Scholte's notion of globalization include those described above—the increased exchange of information, the movement of people, global production by multinational corporations, global consumption of similar products, and increased international capital flows. However, the difference with the "superterritorial" notion of globalization is that it "takes social relationship substantially *beyond* territorial space" (Scholte 2007, p. 11). That is, this conception of globalization incorporates the changing nature of the social space in explaining the effects of globalization.

The implications of the "superterriorial" notion of globalization for the illicit drug market is described by Hobbs (1998) in this study of English drug dealers. Hobbs argues that "unlike previous eras, contemporary organised crime . . . simultaneously occupies both the local and global. . . . [C]riminal career trajectories no longer are limited to specific, often stereotyped geographic locations of some urban 'underworld.'

Drug networks in particular constitute: '. . . continuous paths that lead from the local to the global, from the circumstantial to the universal, from the contingent to the necessary'" (Hobbs 1998, p. 419).

Hobbs describes how the process of the fragmentation of traditional working-class neighborhoods and local labor markets has made it difficult for family-based units to "establish the parochial dominance previously enjoyed by the feudal warlords of the 1950s and 1960s" (1998, p. 409). In turn, this has led to the "dissolution of those traditional forms of organised crime that were so reliant upon this milieu" (1998, p. 409) along with their traditional criminal territories.

In place of this traditional, territorially specific, family-based organized crime have arisen new networks of criminal *entrepreneurs*. These networks are comprised of small flexible firms that do not limit themselves to specific neighborhoods or "pledge allegiance to some permanent structure" (Hobbs 1998, p. 412). Hobbs describes one such network: "there are no key players in this network, no ring leaders, bosses or godfathers. It is a co-operative, a series of temporary social arrangements that enables a constantly changing group of actors to make money from predominantly criminal opportunities" (p. 413).

Hobbs rejects explanations of the global nature of organized crime "that rely heavily upon transnationality, cross border, international or other metaphors of globalisation at one end of a spectrum and local street gangs at the other. Such a model fails to embrace the complexity of 'local contextualities.' [That is] it makes no good sense to define the global as if the global excludes the local . . . defining the global in such a way suggests that the global lies beyond all localities, as having systematic properties over and beyond the attributes of units within a global system" (Hobbs 1998, pp. 418–19).

Na'im (2005) also describes how the illicit drug trade follows many of the same rules as the licit goods trade. Just as trade in licit goods has taken advantage of the global economy, so has the illicit drug trade. Mirroring Hobb's description of the impact of globalization on drug markets, Na'im describes an illicit drug trade being carried out through decentralized networks that change with every transaction.

Just as Scholte's notion of globalization as "superterritoriality" was defined as taking social relationships *beyond* territorial space, so the new networks "are the media through which individuals and groups move between the local and the global" (Hobbs 1998, p. 419). The relations that make up these networks will vary with "differentiation in demographic dispersion, familial composition, ethnic distribution and integration, commercial practice, trading patterns, the economic back-cloth of the legitimate culture and the particular use of space" (Hobbs 1998, 419). For instance, the role of traditional social bonds in criminal networks may be greater for dealers from ethnic minorities, as noted in the work of Paoli and Reuter (2008).

The flexible social networks described by Hobbs can be observed in a number of recent studies of the UK market for illicit drugs. NCIS (2003, 2006) describe how white British crime groups have developed contacts that have enabled them to bypass British-based Turkish organized crime groups and purchase heroin closer to the source. Pearson and Hobbs (2001) interviewed convicted drug traffickers who were involved in the "middle market." They describe how "much of this traditional middle ground—between importers and retailers—is increasingly now played out in mainland Europe. Middle market drug brokers, regionally based and operating in the UK, liaise with systems of drug brokerage and warehousing in the Netherlands and elsewhere [including the Iberian Peninsula], and are directly involved in importation" (Pearson and Hobbs 2001, p. 17).

The fragmentation of traditional social bonds with globalization also influences the demand for drugs. Yi-Mak and Harrison (2001) argue that through the weakening of traditional society in Hong Kong, globalization has created both a collective crisis of identity and the means by which this crisis might be resolved—participation in an internationalized consumer culture that was oriented toward, among other things, drug use. This argument is mirrored in Fransico Thoumi's analysis of drug use in the United States. Thoumi (2005) argues that a lack of social capital—"bridges between different social groups and generates solidarity, trust, and reciprocity within the community in a broader sense" (p. 192)—is the reason why certain groups in the United States have a tendency to take drugs. Further lack of social capital is related to the breakup of the traditional nuclear family.

7.3 Summary

A number of authors have suggested mechanisms by which globalization may explain the changes in prices in the market for illicit drugs and undermine the efforts of supply containment policies. However, there is little direct evidence to support their hypotheses. This chapter attempts to add to the evidence in this area by analyzing interviews with convicted drug traffickers to identify evidence for the following effects of globalization:

• The market structure effect of increased competition in reducing retail prices and the profit margins earned by traffickers.
• The risk premium effect of an influx of traffickers into the market in reducing the risk premium component of wages, and in turn reducing the margins earned by traffickers.
• The efficiency effect of (1) reduced transport, communication, information, and financial costs and (2) the ability of traffickers to conceal their activities as a result of the increased international trade, travel, migration, and capital flows.
• Superterritoriality from (1) the break down of traditional social groups, creating international networks of entrepreneurial, flexible traffickers, and (2) the break down of traditional social groups, increasing the demand for drugs.

7.4   Method

7.4.1   Data Collection Process

Interviews with convicted drug traffickers and dealers were conducted by The Matrix Knowledge Group as part of the study *The Illicit Drug Trade in the United Kingdom*, performed for the UK Home Office.[1] The final report (Matrix Knowledge Group 2007) contains a complete description of the data collection, but the key attributes are reported here.

Twenty-two UK prisons with most inmates serving seven years or more for drug-related offenses agreed to participate in the research. All inmates sentenced to seven years or more for drug offenses in these prisons were invited to take part in the project. A total of 1,390 were invited to take part, 263 volunteered to be interviewed. The research team successfully interviewed 222 of these volunteers between 2005 and 2007. Not all volunteers were successfully interviewed as a small number of them changed their mind on the day of the interview, and some had been moved to different prisons or released before the interviews could be conducted.

An informed consent approach was adopted, and a letter was sent to each respondent in advance outlining the project and its confidentiality protocols. The interviews were conducted in private rooms, and data were documented in a manner that maintained anonymity. The only incentive offered participants was a letter documenting this participants. It was suggested that this letter would benefit the participants should they become eligible for parole.

The prisoners were asked a range of questions relating to their experiences of operating in the drug market, including their entry into the market, the drugs they bought and sold, their role and methods of working, the people they worked with, whether they had ever exited the industry, the costs of operating in the market; their customers, their competition, what they did with their money, the risks they faced, their knowledge and perception of law enforcement activities, and how they came to be arrested.

While the resulting dataset represents a large number of detailed and consistently conducted interviews, with an emphasis on business and organizational aspects of drug dealing, there are four key limitations with the data (Matrix Knowledge Group 2007):

1. Sample selection bias: There is the possibility of sample selection bias as respondents had to volunteer to be interviewed.
2. Sample size: The 222 interviews cover a range of drugs, time periods, and market levels. When grouped by these characteristics, the sample sizes are small.
3. Gaps in the data: As the interview protocol was semi-structured, and as participants had varying levels of knowledge of the trafficking industry, the same questions were not always asked of every interviewee. Further none of the questions asked interviewees directly for their views on globalization.
4. False reporting: It is possible that some information provided by the interviewees is not genuine. False reporting could result from either exaggeration or because subjects were still maintaining their innocence.

These limitations mean that it is difficult to assess the extent to which observations made in the interviews are representative of the UK drug market as a whole.

7.4.2   Analysis
The 222 interview transcripts were reviewed for examples of drug transactions, so that they could be coded by drug type, market level, and date. All interviews that could not be coded this way, as well as those that related to the trafficking of drugs other than cocaine, heroin,

or cannabis were excluded from the analysis. Once this process was complete, 105 interviews remainder for analysis.

The interviews were coded by the following market levels: importers, national level traffickers who would buy and sell in different locations in the United Kingdom, wholesalers who bought and sold in the same location but who did not deal directly to the street; and retailers who dealt directly to the street.

The contents of the remaining 105 interviews were coded by the following categories: profit margins, level of competition, labor supply, wages, the use of technology, access to information, the role of ethnic networks in trafficking, the use of trade and travel to conceal trafficking, the demand for drugs, and international financial investments. The data identified in each of these categories were analyzed and key themes identified.

7.5 Results

7.5.1 The Market Structure Effect: Increasing Competition, Reducing Prices and Margin

Most of the interviewees who discussed profit margins averred that they made a consistent return on their trafficking activities during the period they operated. Interviewees were aware of a number of factors that could influence price, including temporary "droughts," and location (prices in London and Liverpool were identified as relatively low, those in Glasgow and Guernsey were relatively high), but few individual traffickers reported variations in margins. This may be partly the result of margins being so high that slight variations go unnoticed. However, there was evidence that some traffickers compete on price and that increases in the level of competition had caused prices to reduce.

A number of interviewees, representing a range of drug types and market levels, indicated that they competed on price. CF_04, who operated in the heroin wholesale market in 2003 and 2004, described the market as "just like a supermarket, some customers are loyal but others would sniff out drugs anywhere if they cost less." FZ_25 was a retail dealer of heroin and cocaine between 1990 and 2002. He was aware of numerous other dealers in the areas, and would do special deals to beat the competition, keeping the price constant but making his bags a little bigger. Price competition was also described by importers of both heroin and cocaine. FZ_02 was importing cocaine from Europe in 2005.

He identified ten other traffickers selling in similar quantities. Customers would claim they could get cocaine cheaper from his competitors, thus forcing down prices. SL_02 imported heroin from Europe between 1997 and 2003. He talked about a "price war" with his competitors, though he noted that this was unusual.

Those traffickers who identified increases in the numbers of competitors causing reductions in drug prices all operated at the wholesale level. VR_04, a heroin dealer, said that gangs targeting the market post-1990 had caused the price to fall from £21,000 in 1994 to £15,000 in 2000. This reduction in price meant that VR_04's profits declined over this period. RT_09 described how cocaine was difficult to get hold of in Leicester in the 1990s, as there were only a couple of dealers. Identifying this gap in the market, he started dealing in 1994, at which time he knew three other people operating at the same level as him. By 1996 there were more than twenty people in the market, causing prices to drop toward the end of the 1990s. KG_08 was a wholesale cannabis dealer between 1988 and 2000. He described how there were few competitors in the market until a local car plant closed down and some of those who had been laid off entered the drug trade. The resulting fall in prices meant that he was "making no profits at this stage."

These descriptions of a competitive market for drugs populated by many dealers support the accounts of Cragg Ross Dawson (2003) and Hales and Silverstone (2005). However, the interviews also revealed that in some markets dealers have more control, in agreement with the accounts of Caulkins and Reuter (1998) and Pitts (2007). A number of traffickers did not think they faced much competition, and there was evidence that a number of factors limited the level of competition in the market. First, dealers used violence in an attempt to control the market. While a number of interviewees thought that violence was confined to the retail level, the interviews contained examples of traffickers at all levels, dealing all drug types, who had experienced violence. Furthermore there was evidence that the level of violence increased. CU_08 dealt cocaine and cannabis across the United Kingdom in the 1980s and 1990s, and she described how the trade became more violent in the 1990s:

[It was] different when I used to do it, in the 1970s and 1980s, you know, well different. Like, we used to—we're looking at parties, put drinks on the table and they'd stay there, just help yourself. Right? Now, it would go, pulling out guns and, you know, robbing you. Wasn't like that in them days, you know.

But nowadays, I know it is, people get shot, don't they? God knows. They'd be gangsters now, do you know what I mean? They'd be going for God knows what. You know, you could be one minute sitting in this chair and they can take you off and there's no more—no more me, you know? Disappeared. You know? Concrete coat or blooming, like, what was it? Davy thingies' locket, you know, gangsters with his feet tied up. You know?

Second, traffickers cooperate to reduce the impact of competition. A number of interviewees who dealt at different market levels revealed how they shared information on law enforcement activities with their competitors, and would even lend them drugs, transportation, or money when they were short. However, there was variation in whether traffickers were willing to share information on suppliers, though there was not obvious relationship between their willingness to do so and drug types, date, or market level.

Third, information asymmetries mean that customers remained loyal to dealers as they trusted them to supply good quality drugs. QG_08, a national-level heroin dealer between 1991 and 2000, described how competitors would try to poach his customers, but his customers remained loyal as "they knew what to expect." KF_01, a wholesale-level dealer of cannabis, cocaine, and heroin in 2002 to 2004, described how he did not follow competitors when they cut their prices as he was confident he would not lose customers because of the quality of his drugs.

7.5.2   The Risk Premium Effect: Increased Labor Supply Reducing Wages

The money to be made in trafficking meant that there was always a steady supply of labor. VD_01 described how dealers could easily be replaced as it was a lucrative trade and many young men wanted to make good money. KF_11 described how he took few precautions, as his "footsoldiers" were easily replaced. The motivations of a number of dealers for entering the market support this notion. For instance, KF_13 described how he decided to become a dealer after comparing his own subsistence wage against that of his dealer friends who wore designer clothes, drove new cars, and ate out at expensive restaurants.

Only one interviewee provided an example of how globalization opens up the pool of labor available to the drug markets. CF_10 described how he preferred to hire Croatian drivers, as they were reliable and cheap. They were reliable as they were desensitized to the illegality of the trade, and they had less fear as "their lives are quite poor so they've less to lose."

However, the entry of labor into the market is limited by the requirement for trust. A number of interviewees indicated that the importance of trust meant that they only recruited employees largely through their existing social networks (VD_09, VK_03) and limited the number of people they worked with at one time to small groups (ER_01). Other techniques employed to verify the trustworthiness of potential recruits included checking whether they were known to existing contacts (KG_09), and the use of "probationary periods" within which the levels of responsibility given to new recruits were gradually increased (ER_01).

7.5.3   The Efficiency Effect 1: Lower Information Costs

The few interviewees who discussed accessing information suggested that traffickers rely on three sources for information on the market: their own observations, other traffickers, and law enforcement insiders. There is some evidence that mobile phones are improving access to these sources. Mobile phones were described as "crucial, everyone uses them and the business cannot operate without them" (SL_01). They ensure that traffickers do not have to meet face to face when organizing a deal. FZ_15 received text messages from other traffickers warning him of police presence in the area.

7.5.4   The Efficiency Effect 2: Concealing Trafficking Activities in Flows of Goods, People, and Capital

The interviews provided a number of examples the involvement of ethnic minorities in the drug trade, in particular members of the Turkish community (supporting the observations of Pearson and Hobbs 2001 and SOCA 2007). CF_01 describes how someone from Turkey controlled the heroin trade in London and trafficked heroin all round the country. LZ_12, a member of the Turkish community in London, describes his introduction to the trade by other members of the community, and how there were many other people in the Turkish community involved in the trade. However, it is important to note that this predominance of Turkish dealers in the responses of the interviewees may well be the result of bias introduced into the sample by the priorities of law enforcement activities—to the extent that law enforcement activity focuses on dealers in the Turkish community instead of at other dealers, they will be overrepresented in the sample.

The interviewees also provided a number of examples of the advantages that people from ethnic minority groups had in the market for illicit drugs. In particular, in support of the observations of Paoli and Reuter (2008), the fact that some ethnic minorities have contacts both in the United Kingdom and in producing countries facilitated their entry into the market. VR_04 arrived in the England in 1992 from Turkey as an asylum seeker. He was employed in a Turkish social club in North London. He described how the traffickers who frequented the social club were always on the lookout for people to work for them who had not previously had a run-in with the police. L-15 was from Ghana. In 2000 he was approached by a Ghanaian friend to manage his drug business in the United Kingdom. He was trusted by the dealers he had to manage because they knew his family in Ghana.

Transportation of licit goods was seen as crucial to the drugs trade. KZS_06's family owned a transport company through which he met people involved in drug trafficking. This provided him with access to heroin from Pakistan or Turkey, which he sold out of his newsstands. He described how "transport is the key" to trafficking drugs. The heroin would arrive in special compartments in trucks in Liverpool or Dover. The drivers would bring in a load of 100 kilograms every three months, for which they would receive £20,000 to £25,000. K_02 owned a large haulage company in Liverpool that would send 15 to 20 vehicles to Spain each day. He described how reducing border controls was a mistake, as it meant that drivers no longer needed permits and could drive through customs unhindered, and his vehicles could come from Morocco without being checked.

The increase in travel and tourism was also thought to mask drug importation. QG_08 imported cannabis from Morocco in the 1970s. He would find a family willing to complete a drug run, provide them with a camper van, and send the family off on holiday to Tunisia. The family would then stay in Tunisia for two weeks and then travel back through Algeria and Morocco where the van was taken from them for a day and loaded with drugs. They would then get the ferry to Spain and drive up through Spain and France to get back to England. The family would be paid £10, 000 and they could keep the camper van.

KZS_04 described how he would use British couples to import cocaine. The couple would be sent on holiday to the Caribbean and were preferred to local mules as they had a "higher chance of getting through." CU_06's reason for flying cocaine out of the Dominican Republic rather than other Caribbean locations was because it was a tourist destination. CU_02 used the cover of having a cheap breast implant operation to make multiple trips to Brazil to smuggle drugs.

The interviews also provided examples of traffickers investing their earnings abroad, including banks in the Cayman Islands and in France. J_02 had offshore bank accounts, and used his solicitor to buy warehouse properties in Austria, Belgium, Prague, and Spain. The warehouses were owned by his company, which he registered each country. He described how "now we are a free trade area you can invest anywhere, as long as you can prove it is legitimate."

7.5.5   "Superterritoriality" 1: International Networks of Entrepreneurial Traffickers

The Matrix Knowledge Group (2007) has already analyzed the interviews for their insight into the networks formed by traffickers and the nature of the business operations adopted by traffickers. In support of Hobbs's (1998) description of contemporary UK drug market, they conclude that most of the traffickers operated "within small and medium sized enterprises or collaborative networks" (2007, p. 32). Furthermore the study concludes that a number of interviewees were "entrepreneurial" (2007, p. 51) in the way they exploited their connections, and that:

The most successful dealers were able to quickly adapt to new circumstances and exploit new opportunities. These opportunities often came about through chance meetings with others involved in the drug market although ethnic ties, selling to friends who were users, having contacts within legitimate businesses that could facilitate dealing operations, and meeting contacts in prison were also identified a key factors that enabled business growth. (2007, p. 50)

Therefore the analysis undertaken in this paper focused on the nature of the "social space" occupied by traffickers. In correspondence with the observations of Pearson and Hobbs (2001), the interviews provided a number of examples of the expansion of the social space occupied by traffickers allowing them access to drugs closer to source and to foreign investment opportunities. A number of interviewees described how work or travel abroad had provided them with contacts who later facilitated their involvement in trafficking. FZ_18 had worked in the oil industry in Holland in the late 1980s. The contacts he made in his time there facilitated his purchase and transport of 200 kilograms of cannabis in 1991, as "you need to know someone with influence." KF_06 had also lived in Holland, where he worked in a factory. During this time he got to know the locals who dealt drugs, which allowed him to access the drugs much cheaper than he could in the United Kingdom. Similar stories were told by interviewees who had worked in Germany and traveled to Spain on holiday.

The change in British traffickers' social space is not only facilitated by greater travel and work opportunities abroad. A number of interviewees described how the multicultural nature of contemporary life, especially in London, facilitated their entry into the drug trade. KZS_04 described how it is important for dealers to know someone in the West Indies. However, "this is not difficult to do. Because London is multicultural, you can meet a contact." CU_02 was originally from Tanzania. Her Nigerian friends, who she had met in a bar in London, had Nigerian contacts in Brazil who imported cocaine. It was this contact that allowed CU_02 to enter the trade.

Prison also provides the opportunities for contacts with other ethnic groups. While in prison QG_8 met a number of Turkish dealers. He described how prison was "the best place in the world to meet good contacts." After he was released, he moved to Liverpool where he was asked if he could get hold of heroin. Around the same time he "bumped into one of the Turkish guys" he had met in prison, who introduced him to a Kurdish man who had half a kilo of heroin that he wanted to get rid of.

7.5.6   "Superterritoriality" 2: Increase in the Demand for Drugs

Interviewees invariably described the level of demand as high. The only variation in demand identified in the interviews was the increase in demand at weekends and during festive periods, such as at Christmas (and one interviewees also mentioned high demand during Ramadan), and on "Giro day" when their customers collected their benefit cheques. There was also evidence that the source of this demand was not confined to problem users. A number of traffickers reported selling to professionals, among them, doctors, stockbrokers, and solicitors (GO_08) and journalists, bank managers, and lawyers (LZ_18).

7.6   Discussion

It has been hypothesized that globalization undermines the efforts of supply containment in the market for illicit drugs through a number of mechanisms—including increased levels of competition; increased the supply of labor; reduced transportation, information, communication, and finance costs—enabling trafficking activities to be concealed in greater flows of people and goods and producing networks of entrepreneurial, flexible traffickers to meet an increased demand for drugs.

This chapter analyzes interviews with convicted traffickers to determine whether there is evidence for any of these mechanisms in the UK markets for cocaine, heroin, and cannabis. The evidence in support of these mechanisms is varied, and there is no obvious relationship between drug type or market level and the nature of the market.

There is no evidence to support the idea that levels of demand had increased, or that more labor is entering the drug market. Drug demand is still invariably reported as high, and the only variation in demand described by traffickers were increases at weekends and at the Christmas and Ramadan festivals. Similarly traffickers reported a consistently high supply of labor to the market. However, these observations may partly be a function of traffickers' inability to perceive changes in the market, either because they limit their customer base to those who are trusted or because a number of them only operated in the market for limited periods of time.

There is good evidence that the use of mobile phones is common among traffickers, and has increased access to information on law enforcement activities, as well as reducing the time traffickers had to spend dealing with each other face to face. However, there is no evidence on transport costs or financial costs.

The evidence is mixed on whether drug markets are becoming more competitive. There is evidence that some traffickers compete on price, and that increases in the level of competition has caused prices in some markets to drop. Furthermore the interviews suggest that the more successful traffickers operated in small groups, and were entrepreneurial in their exploitation of opportunities in the market. However, this trend is not supported by all traffickers. A number of traffickers described consistent profit margins and limited competition. Further the use of violence, cooperation among traffickers, and issues of trust and loyalty among dealers and customers, are identified as limiting the level of competition in the market.

There is more evidence for the benefits derived by traffickers from the increased movement of people, goods, and capital. There is evidence of the role of ethnic minorities in the UK market for illicit drugs, as well as the advantages conferred on ethnic minorities due to their contacts in both producing and consuming countries. A number of traffickers emphasized the importance of their connections with transportation companies, the tactic of using holiday travelers as a cover for smuggling drugs, and their ability to invest abroad. There is also evidence that greater opportunities for travel and working abroad, the multicultural nature of contemporary UK society, and traffickers' ability to network with foreign traffickers in prison have expanded the social space in which British traffickers operate, allowing them to operate more efficiently.

It is important to emphasize the limitations of the data used in this study. First, the observations are drawn from a small, and possibly biased, sample of traffickers. Second, the varying level of market knowledge among the traffickers interviewed, as well as the semi-structured nature of the interview employed mean that there are likely to be gaps in the data collected. These two limitations mean that it is difficult to assess the extent to which observations made are representative of the UK drug market as a whole. Furthermore, as the interviews did not address the issue of globalization directly, the interviews cannot be used to attribute observations to globalization.

Despite these limitations, this study improves our understanding of the nature of illicit drug markets in the United Kingdom, and provides support for the existence of some mechanisms through which globalization is thought to impact this market. Further research is required before the impact of globalization on the market for illicit drugs can be demonstrated unequivocally.

Acknowledgments

The authors would like to thank the research team at The Matrix Knowledge Group who helped design and undertake the offender interviews, including Jonathan Caulkins, Jamie Drysdale, Sophie Gurr, Dick Hobbs, Vanessa Jones, Monika Kalyan, Trudy Lowe, Kerry McCarthy, Sarah Morton, Prinny Patel, Geoff Pearson, Peter Reuter, Andrew Richman, Colin Roberts, Miguel Sanchez Garcia, Edward Semple, and Jenny Ward.

Note

1. "Trafficker" tends to be used to refer to those who move drugs between locations—generally those at the higher end of the market—and "dealer" is used to refer to those who operate at the lower end of the market. Because some observations are relevant to all market levels, these two terms are used interchangeably in this text.

References

Caulkins, J. P., and P. Reuter. 1998. What price data tell us about illicit drug markets. *Journal of Drug Issues* 28: 593–612.

Costa Storti, C., and P. De Grauwe. 2008a. Modelling the cocaine and heroin markets in the era of globalization and drug reduction policies. International Society for the Study of Drug Policy Conference, Lisbon, April.

Costa Storti, C., and P. De Grauwe. 2008b. Globalisation and the price decline of illicit drugs. *International Journal on Drug Policy* 20 (1):48–61.

Cragg Ross Dawson. 2003. *Crack Cocaine in London: Qualitative Research Focussing on Brent, Camden, Lambeth and Westminster.* London: Cragg Ross Dawson.

Hales, G., and D. Silverstone. (2005) Interviews with 15 convicted offenders. In G. Hales, ed., *Gun Crime in Brent.* Portsmouth: University of Portsmouth Press, ch. 3. http://www.port.ac.uk/departments/academic/icjs/staff/documentation/filetodownload,58106,en.pdf.

Hobbs, D. 1998. Going down the Glocal: The Local Context of Organised Crime. *Howard League Journal* 37: 4.

Home Office. 2002. *Updated Drug Strategy.* London: Home Office.

Home Office. 2008. *Drugs: Protecting Families and Communities.* London: Home Office.

INCB. 2001. *Report of the International Narcotics Control Board.* http://www.incb.org/incb/en/annual_report_2001.html (accessed June 24, 2008).

Matrix Knowledge Group. 2007. *The Illicit Drug Trade in the United Kingdom.* London: Home Office.

Na'ım, M. 2005. *Illicit: How Smugglers, Traffickers, and Copycats Are Hijacking the Global Economy.* New York: Doubleday.

National Criminal Intelligence Service (NCIS). 2003. *United Kingdom Threat Assessment of Serious and Organised Crime, 2003.* London: NCIS.

National Criminal Intelligence Service (NCIS). 2006. *UK Threat Assessment: The Threat from Serious and Organised Crime, 2004/5–2005/6.* London: NCIS.

Paoli, L., and P. Reuter. 2008. Drug trafficking and ethnic minorities in western Europe. *European Journal of Criminology* 5: 13.

Pearson, G., and D. Hobbs. 2001. *Middle Market Drug Distribution. Home Office Research Study,* 227. London: Home Office.

Pitts, J. 2007. *Reluctant Gangsters: Youth Gangs in Waltham Forest.* Luton: University of Bedfordshire. http://www.walthamforest.gov.uk/reluctant-gangsters.pdf.

Pudney, S., C. Badillo, M. Bryan, J. Burton, G. Conti, and M. Iacovou. 2006. Estimating the size of the UK illicit drug market. In N. Singleton, R. Murray, and L. Tinsley, eds., *Measuring Different Aspects of Problem Drug Use: Methodological Developments.* Home Office Online Report 16/06. London: Home Office.

Scholte, J. A. 2007. Defining globalisation. *World Economy* 31 (11):1471–1502.

SOCA 2007. *The United Kingdom Threat Assessment of Serious Organised Crime: 2006/7.* http://www.soca.gov.uk/assessPublications/downloads/threat_assess_unclass_250706 .pdf (accessed September 4, 2007).

Thoumi, F. 2005. Drug policies, reforms, and Columbo-American relations. *Proceedings from the International Seminar Drug Trafficking: the Relations between Europe, Latin America and the United States.* Bogotá, Colombia October 24–26, 2005. http://www.drugpolicy .org/docUploads/Drug_Trafficking_Europe_Latin_America_United_States.pdf.

Yi-Mak, K., and L. Harrison. 2001. Globalisation, cultural change and the modern drug epidemics: The case of Hong Kong. *Health Risk and Society* 3: 1.

8 Khat, and the Informal Globalization of a Psychoactive Commodity

Axel Klein

8.1 Introduction

Globalization is often proffered as a cause for the seemingly ineluctable spread of illicit drugs. Yet without a clear definition of what is meant by the multiple processes of globalization, this can become a circular argument, listing the very thing one wishes to analyze as causal factor in its appearance. By looking at the spread of khat, a psychoactive stimulant plant that is a class 1 drug in the United States but imported legally as a vegetable in the United Kingdom, in this chapter I seek to contribute to the exploration of the analysis of both "drug trade" and "globalization." I draw on first-hand research findings in the khat production/distribution field, and concepts from different academic and policy constituencies, and I argue that the resolution to policy dilemmas begins with the re-framing of the issue. This is particularly pertinent for khat producers in East Africa for whom cultivation is a question of livelihood, and distribution a development strategy. The long-term feasibility of this issue raises important questions over the shaded meanings of globalization and the question of governance within an intergovernmental context.

8.2 The Global Spread of Drug Use

It has become an untested assumption that the flow of drugs is an unintended consequence of "globalization," a negative by-product of an otherwise constructive process, comparable to the spread of infectious diseases with intensified human contact. Although the term "epidemic" is often used to describe the spread of illicit drug use, it is usually as a metaphor, not an analytic term. Drug use is essentially an aspect of human behavior, and the comments on its stipulated proliferation in the twentieth century resemble the way in which nine-teenth-century rationalists took to the study of psychiatric disorders, noting "insanity as the price we pay for evolution."

There is no further probing to uncover why substance use has such cross-cultural appeal. The phenomenon is instead resignedly accepted: "Globalisation also carries risks such as the adoption of aberrant behaviour, involvement in crime and copying problems that may be prevalent in other communities" (Ghodse 2008, p. 1). For the drug control community, globalization is therefore both a remote and proximate cause in the spread of drug use, while at the same time drug use is one of the key manifestation of that process, neces-sitating the international coordination of control efforts. To support the effectiveness of such collaboration, control advocates tend to point at the shrinking number of opiate and coca producer countries, and historic achievements like the fall in global opium production in the course of the twentieth century (UNODC 2008). It is then argued that eventually, with further sustained efforts, the commit-ment of national governments, and well-funded international agen-cies, drug use will be eliminated. Returning to the opening metaphor, drug abuse will be wiped out with the right policy interventions just like the transmission of measles and other infectious diseases have been successfully controlled through medical intervention. In the meantime the community struggles with the seeming paradox of rising drug consumption and falling prices despite sharply rising control efforts.

I argue that the assumption that drug use spreads like an epidemic is a spurious claim to bolster a vast, but ineffective drug control indus-try that imposes steeply rising social costs. The inherent flaws in the drug control system become apparent when looking at the response by international agencies to khat, and the way in which the definition of the substance as drug predetermines the issue. What this framing of the discussion achieves is to marginalize other arguments—such as development economics or rural livelihood—and to disenfranchise some of the main stakeholders: khat farmers and consumers. The term "globalization" equally needs to be unpacked, in order to reach a better understanding of how power relations, vested interests, and cultures of consumption interact in the exchange of commodities and lifestyles. The spread of khat and the responses by national and international agencies to it are significant in pointing at the chronic inequities in a global system.

8.3   Globalization as a Conceptual Tool in the Analysis of Drug Markets

The mechanical inevitability of globalization in reducing prices has been used by Corsti and de Grauwe (2008) to explain the continuous fall in drug prices in the main Western retail markets despite sharply increasing drug control efforts. Drawing on textbook explanations of the function of markets, it is argued that "globalization affects the labor market structure and the risk involved in the export and import business." A straightforward process of market expansion has eroded monopolistic structures of drug importers by allowing for greater competition among traffickers willing to work for a much lower markup. The influx of the low-level courier has reduced the wage component in drug importation, with a knock-on effect on the risk premiums collected further up the chain. Additionally there have been overall efficiency gains in the fall in transport, communications, and information costs. The general economic benefits of globalization—greater competition, cheaper production and distribution cost, and lower profit margins—are providing cheaper drugs for all. Working within the classic drug control paradigm that repressive activities—seizures, arrests, and confiscations—will raise the drug price beyond the reach of consumers, they ignore the importance of cultural disposition and lifestyle.

Their relevance for understanding global drug markets has long been advocated by sociologists, historians, and anthropologists engaged in so-called qualitative research. In policy terms they are often marginalized because of a tendency to undermine the prohibition model (Buxton 2006; Rhodes and Moore 2001) by critically examining the impact of interventions on the phenomenon in question. Concerned with the exploration of concepts, the starting point is the term globalization, which we take as "process which embodies a transformation in the spatial organisation of social relations and transaction—assessed in terms of their extensity, intensity, velocity and impact—generating transcontinental or interregional networks of activity, interaction, and the exercise of power" (Held et al. 1999, p. 16).

It has since been argued that this is not a natural or self-sustained process but is critically fashioned by "chance, contingency, and agency" (Nuetzenadel and Trentmann 2008). The notion of chance in the guise of the "unintended consequence" theory is also often heard in the drugs field, and allegedly further exemplified by the spread of khat, a plant-based psychoactive substance popular in parts of eastern Africa and now sold all over the world. But a closer look will show that the trade has been contingent on a number of structural changes achieved in the course of the last one hundred years, and finally that it is driven by particular groups and individuals who as producers, traders, and consumers have been the creative agents of the khat nexus.

Nutzenagel and Trentmann go on to claim that the process is not deterministic or teleological in necessarily producing Western hegemony or imperialism, while impacting differently on different parts of the world. In light of much recent African scholarship this a highly contentious assertion. While the actual pattern of exchanges may not be predetermined, there is no denying the flow of power and the way it is allocated and distributed. Globalization may be a useful term to refer to the acceleration of flow in capital, goods, and people, but the process of connection and linkage is accompanied by one of exclusion and segregation. If some parts of the world are becoming closer interconnected and integrated others are excluded, with Africans particularly excluded from the benefits of trade and travel. "It is global but not [in the sense] of planetary communion, but of disconnection, segmentation, and segregation—not a seamless world without borders, but a patchwork of discontinuous and hierarchically ranked spaces, whose edges are carefully delimited, guarded and reinforced" (Ferguson 2006, p. 49). The story of khat illustrates how the different forces at play in globalization impact on the producers of a commodity that arrives in global market so to speak from below.

A number of psychoactive commodities are traded globally. Most prominent are tobacco products and alcohol, whereas tea, coffee, and cocoa also fall into the category of mild stimulants consumed for taste and effect, rather than nutrition or medical purpose. While domesticated and still mainly produced in the Americas, Africa, and Asia, the trade in all these products is dominated by Euro-American companies. Indeed it can be argued that the production and trade in these products was critical in the formation of the current global trade system. But as historians have pointed out, though these psychoactive substances were first discovered and domesticated in different cultures, they only became "global" after they had been adapted to European consumption patterns, rebranded, and repackaged (Courtwright 2001; Goodman 2002; Schivelbusch 1992). Khat, however, has arrived on global markets straight from African farms, without having been culturally processed.

8.4   Khat—Cultivation and Use

Khat (*Catha edulis*) is a shrub of the *celastraceae* family found in many parts of Africa and Asia. Its domestication is believed to have occurred in Ethiopia, though Yemen is also a strong contender, some thousand years ago or so (Kennedy 1987; Weir 1985). With regard to both story of origin and in its stimulating pharmacological effect, khat therefore resembles coffee. There is another tradition of khat cultivation and use in the mountain regions of Kenya, though it is not known if this was an independent discovery or a cultural import (Carrier 2005).

The shrub grows up to fifteen feet, and grows ideally within an altitude range of 300 to 1,500 meters. The leafs and shoots contain a mix of psychoactive alkaloids that remains potent for a mere 72 hours after harvest. While many of humanity's psychoactive substances depend on complex preparations, as in the case of alcohol, opium, or ayuasca, khat is consumed fresh. The leaves of the plant are rolled into bundles, packed into tight wads inserted into the side of the mouth and masticated over the course of 30 minutes to two hours. The need for freshness has historically circumscribed the spread of khat use to the environing region of the production zone. It is in eastern Ethiopia, Yemen, and the Meru mountains that we find cultures of khat consumption, with patterns of use prescribed by custom. The earliest accounts by Arabic and Turkish travelers, and early European explorers provide insights into the use of khat in rituals, such as weddings and festivals, or how it is used to punctuate the daily rhythms of work and play (Burton 1987).

Changes to the distribution system began to be felt in the midtwentieth century, when road and rail links were driven into the hitherto remote production areas. The impact on rural producers across the region was dramatic, with a sharp rise in urbanization, and the creation of new communities no longer regulated by tradition. As people moved from agricultural work, performed in small communities governed by face-to-face relationships, into the formal and informal sectors of growing cities, marked by anonymity and ready contact between different tribes or clans, they freed themselves from many culturally established control mechanisms. Urbanization then created, first, the disposition for migrants for engaging in new forms of behavior, including consumerism, and, second, provided income opportunities to fund these new habits (Donham 1999; Cassanelli 1986).

Colonial governments in Djibouti, Kenya, Aden (South Yemen), and Somaliland tended to view the spread of khat with dismay. To some administrators, the image of the once proud and self-reliant nomads, reduced to idleness and habitual khat chewing was an image of modern degeneration (Brooke 1960; Klein et al. 2008). More important, khat was seen as dissipating the productive energies of colonial subjects, or as a drain on foreign exchange. The commoditization of khat during the early to mid-twentieth century was accompanied by albeit short-lived efforts at suppression—Aden 1957 and 1958, Djibouti 1956 and 1957, Kenya 1945 to 1956, and Somaliland 1921 to 1957. The difficulty in effectively controlling such a popular habit is graphically illustrated by the quixotic attempts of Sir Gerald Reece, one of the most passionate advocates of khat prohibition and the governor of British Somaliland, 1948 to 1954. He finally gave up after realizing that his driver had built up a busy distribution network, using the back of the governor's official vehicle for transporting his leafy cargo. More effective than outright bans, all of which were eventually lifted, proved regulatory schemes such as those introduced in Aden, where khat sales were restricted to Fridays. Building on existing customs of regulating access to khat across the working week, the weekend window remained in force until the unification of North and South Yemen in 1990.

8.5   State Decline and the Growth of the Informal Sector in Africa

The governing principles of the early twentieth-century colonial administrations were to generate benefits for the "motherland" while providing for the welfare of subject populations. With independence sweeping across the African continent in the 1960s, the successor regimes maintained these paternalistic concerns while allegedly dropping the exploitative intent. African governments had to balance the legitimacy gained from representative government with the potential instability of competitive election processes in a multi-ethnic society. The emerging regimes further justified their authoritarianism by emphasizing the development role of the state and the necessary leadership of technocratic elites in underdeveloped societies. Supported by rising commodity prices and advantageous terms of trade, this allowed for the rapid expansion of the government apparatus and the formal functions of the state in much of sub-Saharan Africa during the 1960s. After the first ten years of independence, however, the main export markets in Europe and North America went into recession and reducing their commodity imports—with the exception of oil. African states were left with a hangover of financial commitments that they could only meet by taking on debt from private lenders, and a rising set of demands they met increasingly by a resort to force.

In the 1970s and 1980s many African governments were losing both reputation for responsible stewardship and legitimacy, when civil war, famine, and underdevelopment visited large sections of the continent. Ethiopia was involved in a border war with Somalia in 1977, and subsequently became mired in civil war that only ended with the ousting of the communist regime in 1991. In many countries, state officials, often army officers, had given up all pretense at responsible government and were instead exploiting offices for private gain. The state was no longer the agent of development but, as in the case of Kenya ruled by Daniel arap Moi, 1978 to 2002, had become a byword for incompetence at best and corruption at worst. As many services, including statistical data gathering, simply ceased to exist, official explanations and definitions could no longer be relied upon. In a study of a neighborhood of Accra, Ghana, the anthropologist Keith Hart noted that officially "these people should all be dead" (Hart 1973) yet formed part of a thriving community. Coining a term that was taken up by the ILO, he described the areas of activity as the informal sector. While "informality" was originally applied to urban economies, it was always a residual category, describing economic activity outside of the formal sector, defined in turn by being regulated and accounted for. Coinciding with the retreat of the state from rural areas, it has therefore come to cover agricultural activities outside the plantation complex (Klein 1999).

The dynamic energy of the informal sector and the obstructive, stifling role of the state was not confined to Africa; it found the most coherent expression in the work of Peruvian economist Hernado de Soto (1989). Unlocking the creative power of the private sector became the driving principle of the International Financial Institutions that emerged as the principle sources of discretional lending to sovereign African states in the 1980s. Loans and aid packages came with strict conditions, including a comprehensive downsizing of the state, in a wave of programs rolling across the continent under the rubric of "structural adjustment." The withdrawal of the state, while opening spaces for entrepreneurial activity, also left a need for service provision, which could only be met with the assistance of external agencies. Often bypassing the state, setting up parallel systems of administration, and self-contained projects, these were run by both intergovernmental and nongovernmental agencies. This remarkable interference in aspects of sovereignty gathered pace in the 1990s and to the present, and has taken place in an era of growing interconnectivity between diverse global production and consumption centers. These multiple processes, bundled under the term "globalization," have often been referenced as a justification for the tightening of transnational systems of governance and regulations (Andreas and Nadelmann 2006).

The elision of boundaries, it was argued, would require codes of conduct that transcended the discrete realms of national sovereignty, with harmonized rules, such as enforceable rights of contract and property. While globalization was undermining the absolute assertions of states over their national territory, it was met by a strengthening and extending governmentality—via multilateral agreements and the pooling of sovereignty into international accords and multinational groupings. This was particularly pertinent in Africa where international agencies held not only a supervisory or advisory function but were operational on the ground, providing services that domestic agencies could not deliver.

8.6   African States and International Agencies

The ongoing engagement of intergovernmental and nongovernmental organizations in Africa remain critical because the hoped-for inflow of foreign direct investment has been falling short of expectations, with concomitant reduction in economic activity and functionality of the state. After two decades of structural adjustment and economic stagnation, the state in most African countries has withdrawn from many activities and regions and remains geographically confined to capital cities and economic enclaves. There has been an increase in FDI from 2 billion USD in 1986 to around 14 billion USD in 2004 (UNCTAD), but this has not fed into domestic consumer industries and has produced very debatable trickle-down benefits. The large investments are targeted at extractive industries, mining and oil, often offshore, or in exclusive economic zones. Such investment has done little to bring peace or stability; indeed some of the largest recipients of FDI have been countries in the throes of civil war such as Democratic Republic of Congo, Sudan, and Angola. Economic activity instigated by external investment has sparked off unrest in Nigeria and Gabon. Yet the most vulnerable states have collapsed altogether in Somalia and Sierra Leone.

The restricted capacity of the African state has important ramifications for the reconfiguration of governing elites, particularly in countries that are resource poor. Two decades of structural adjustment have not eliminated the rent-seeking behavior of the political class, though fewer African countries are ruled by the military. Instead, they are more dependent on bilateral and international aid flows and more compliant to donor pressure. International agencies in turn derive their greatest sense of justification and enjoy the greatest degree of operational independence working in Africa. Often programs are identified and projects are defined by remit and requirements of each particular agency with little strategic coordination.[1]

The significance of these organizations is not merely in terms of programming and resource transfer. International agencies are a key element of the formal sector; they are a visible part of the regulatory framework, upholding standards, abiding by the law, and demonstrating good practice. In their close working relationship with host country counterparts, they furthermore give support and legitimacy to these institutions. In Foucauldian terms, then, bi- and multilateral development cooperation partners are not, strictly speaking, a part of government, they are essential elements of governmentality.[2] They advocate for sheer obviousness of government to citizens who accept it and its demands without question, target particular population groups, and seek to exert control over negligent conduct and behavior. This is significant when international agencies become involved in the discussions over khat.

8.7   Khat as an Economic Success Story

Given the difficulties of globally low and export-oriented FDI flows, African economies depend on endogenous growth. Governments, as we have seen, have contracted many functions to development agencies, leaving an even more important role of economic growth to the private sector. With low levels of industrialization, it is the agriculture and extractive industries on which the hopes for African development are usually based, as recognized in Ethiopia's economic strategy (Anderson et al. 2007). There is a burgeoning domestic demand, prompted by the steady pace of urbanization, and several niche markets in the rich European and North American markets not protected by tariff walls. Neglected for many years (Bates 1981), African agriculture has received favorable attention from international agencies and national extension services over the last decade. In both Kenya and Ethiopia there have been concerted efforts to encourage export-oriented production by providing extension services, credit facilities, marketing, and land leases to foreign investors, particularly producers of flowers, fruit, and vegetables. These efforts have depended to a large extent on the direct involvement of multinational trading partners, who bulk either at national auctions or from exporters (coffee) and may become involved in the management of production (flowers, fruit, and vegetables). Benefits accruing to coffee farmers are limited by the fluctuations of the world market price for coffee (Oxfam 2002). Purchases are made in Ethiopia, where control of the crop, and the benefits from add-on value are taken over by the multinational partner. In the case of flower, fruit, and vegetable cultivation, the main benefit is the wages paid to the rural worker on the quasi-plantation complex. These wages have to be offset by the often considerable demands in water, farmland, and rural support services.

Similar opportunity costs are also borne by khat production in Ethiopia (Anderson et al. 2007) and Yemen (Kennedy 1987), but the distribution of benefits is different. First, khat production caters to an expanding domestic and regional market. Restricted historically to a band around the production zones in the Kenyan Meru mountains and the Hararghe region of Ethiopia today, khat consumption has, within fifty years, become a national phenomenon in both Ethiopia and Kenya. This has not occurred without protest. In Addis Ababa, for example, organizations have been formed to campaign against the use of khat, warning of dependence and the diversion of precious resources. Traditionally khat was associated with the Islamic population of the eastern part of the Abyssinian empire, whereas the Christian highlands preferred alcohol. In the holy city of Lalibela khat remains prohibited by the Ethiopian Orthodox church. But all across Addis Ababa, the capital of Ethiopia and cultural nerve center of the Christian highlands, khat chewing is endemic. It has been argued that the habit was introduced by students returning from literacy campaigns in rural areas during the years of the Mengistou regime (Gebissa 2004). Khat's stimulating effect made it a popular study aid, spreading through universities and schools. Popular use, for recreational and functional purpose, therefore has overcome barriers of custom and tradition. By the mid-1990s khat was traded at the Merkado, the largest market in Addis Ababa and was consumed across the ethnic and religious spectrum of this highly diverse country. A regular supply is guaranteed by the Addis Ababa–Djibouti railway passing through Dire Dewa near the cradle of production in Hararghe. Over recent years production has spread all over the country however, with Gurage and Sidama in the South, and Bahir Dar in the northern Amhara region, all reporting sharp increases in production (Anderson et al. 2007; Gebissa 2004).

In Kenya the best *miraa* (khat) is allegedly still grown in Meru, but other areas like the Chyulu and the Taita Hills are catching up fast. A fleet of lorries and pickup trucks known nationally for their "need for speed" (Carrier 2005) distribute the leafy matter to the farthest reaches of the country, including the Swahili coast. The arrival of new groups of strangers involved in selling the stimulant, and the impact on local youth culture, are giving rise to concern (Klein and Beckerleg 2007). Much of this relates to the emerging youth cultures in societies that were once stratified by age groups, and the tensions arising from inter-ethnic contact. Suffice at this point is that both Kenya and Ethiopia have thriving local cultures of khat use supporting and supplied by a dynamic production base.

8.8   The Significance of Khat in Exports, Tax Revenue, and Foreign Exchange Earnings

Besides driving the growth of domestic markets, khat is being shipped to neighboring countries, principally Djibouti, Somalia, Somaliland, and to a lesser extent Tanzania. Also there has been a sharply increasing intercontinental export trade from Addis Ababa and Nairobi to London and Amsterdam. In London alone it is estimated that just under eight tons of khat were being imported weekly in the mid-2000s. According to Her Majesty's Customs and Excise, the bulk 5,000 to 7,000 kilograms came from Kenya, 500 kilograms from Ethiopia, and under 200 kilograms from Yemen (ACMD 2005); see tables 8.1 and 8.2.

In both Ethiopia and Kenya the international khat trade has delivered substantial economic benefits. In 2003 and 2004, khat exports constituted some 15 percent of Ethiopia's export earnings. Between 1990 and 2004, Ethiopia earned 413 million USD from exporting 86,625 metric tons of khat (Anderson et al. 2007). Over the same period income from coffee, once the mainstay of the country's export economy, fell to

Table 8.1
Khat imports to Heathrow in 2005

Country of origin	Weight (in kg)	Number of flights	Trade name of bundle	Price
Kenya	5,000–7,000	Four times a week	Mirra or *Murungi*	£3–4
Ethiopia	500	Two times a week	Hereri	£5
Yemen	175	Two times a week	Taizi	£7–10

Source: ACMD (2006).

Table 8.2
Value of the five major exports of Ethiopia and volume of exported khat

	Value (in thousands of birr)					Volume (in metric tons)
Period	Coffee	Khat	Oil seeds	Hides and skins	Pulses	Khat
1984–85	466,269	15,903	15,640	95,408	16,875	1,380
1985–86	664,790	8,477	7,686	119,459	12,635	711
1986–87	524,348	28,677	9,793	108,291	8,481	2,931
1987–88	439,181	21,323	22,015	133,004	16,093	3,363
1988–89	626,448	7,906	11,029	123,528	16,317	537
1989–90	405,103	21,024	8,387	134,049	35,961	1,816
1990–91	268,451	20,422	3,633	92,206	15,716	1,469
1991–92	168,324	5,073	383	58,645	386	251
1992–93	536,982	65,727	1,186	134,515	4,050	1,936
1993–94	718,019	107,932	44,187	203,610	27,704	2,808
1994–95	1,799,034	172,339	50,130	373,549	103,287	4,073
1995–96	1,724,008	174,444	41,938	309,701	77,224	3,698
1996–97	2,307,394	199,533	74,239	372,253	87,854	5,031
1997–98	2,889,531	272,355	314,660	347,699	102,953	5,981
1998–99	2,112,713	444,988	271,462	243,052	101,658	9,702
1999–00	2,133,646	618,772	255,329	286,459	80,021	15,684
2000–01	1,520,101	510,506	269,598	633,752	72,800	11,982
2001–02	1,393,809	418,674	278,738	474,426	281,409	9,377
2002–03	1,418,324	497,866	395,565	448,003	171,244	6,106
2003–04	1,926,679	758,878	712,738	375,844	194,679	7,825

Source: *National Bank of Ethiopia Quarterly Bulletin* (various issues), as quoted in Anderson et al. (2007).

1.9 billion birr, down from 2.1 billion birr in 1999, as a result of decreasing coffee prices.

Farmers who had also to contend with rising costs for fertilizer and pesticides therefore switched to khat because of the dramatic fluctuation in the price for coffee, the traditional cash export crop of Ethiopia, "coffee farmers made a conscious decision to increase their khat plantations rather than continue to plant a cash crop that got diseased, fetched low prices and whose marketing was monopolised by the government" (Gebissa 2004, pp. 153–54).

The development of the Ethiopian khat industry owes much to the improvements in transport and the fragmentation of rural land holdings resulting from feudalism, post-revolutionary land reform, demographic pressures, and the sedentarization of pastoralists. Government policies have been at best indifferent to khat. Under the Derg government khat plants were uprooted in eastern Ethiopia and replaced with high-value food crops and coffee. Since the change of regime in 1991, khat has been notably excluded from the government's agricultural strategy. Farmers receive none of the benefits, such as access to credit, seedlings, subsidized fertilizer, and pesticide. If Christian Orthodox morality accounts for the hostility of the imperial government, and communist orthodoxy for the objections by the communist Derg, the current ambivalence owes much to the regime's sensitivity to international attitudes toward khat.

International aid agencies, including Irish Aid in Gurage, the German Gesellschaft für Technische Zusammenarbeit (GTZ), and Swedish International Development (SIDA), have funded schemes to woo farmers away from khat. Inputs such as pesticides, fertilizers, farming tools, as well as credit, training, and infrastructure, have been provided on the condition that farmers grow other crops. The Ethiopian government, which is highly dependent on foreign aid flows, has to balance its diplomatic position on khat with a the need for internally generated revenue. Over the period 1980 to 2001 tax earnings from khat composed an average of 12.63 percent of revenue, and constituted an average of 1.7 percent of GDP. Public health expenditure during the 1990s accounted for some 1.2 percent of GDP, implying that "khat revenues more than finance national expenditure on health" (Anderson et al. 2007).

Local authorities, such as the municipality of Dire Dewa, and state governments in eastern Ethiopia are even more indebted to khat earnings.

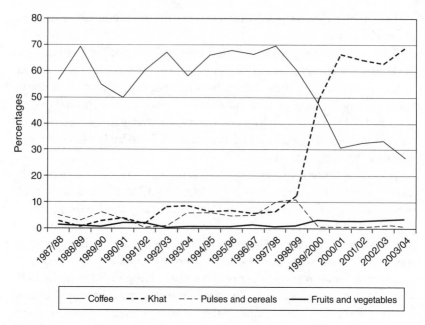

Figure 8.1
Exports Earnings from Eastern Ethiopia, 1987 to 1999. Source: Dire Dawa, Ethiopia, Foreign Trade Office, 2004 (in Anderson et al. 2007).

The khat crop moreover is popular among farmers for its hardiness, minimal labor input, and some multiple benefits:

The wood of the plant is commonly used for fuel and due to its resistance to termites is used in the construction of houses and fencing. It is also used for making rafters, handles of farm tools (hammers and chisels), and handles of household articles such as pots and pans, rolling pins, and to make forks, combs, spoons and for rulers. . . . Processed leaves and roots are used to treat influenza, cough, gonorrhea, asthma, and other chest problems. The root is used for stomach aches and an infusion is taken orally to treat boils. (Lemessa 2001)

The crop can be planted year-round and in different soils; it is usually grown on marginal land where it does not compete with food crops. For many smallholders:

Khat cultivation is also part of risk spreading and diversification strategy. Net return per acre from khat is greater than that from coffee. It only takes 13 percent of cultivated land, and it accounts for 30–50 percent of the total cash income per year or 40–60 percent of the total value of home-produced food used by the farm household. (Anderson et al. 2007, p. 24)

Most important, neither in Ethiopia nor in Kenya has khat produced a plantation complex. In Ethiopia, it is mainly a smallholder crop, grown in conjunction with food crops, to provide a source of income to the farmer. In Kenya, larger farms have been reported from the Meru mountains, but control remains in the hands of established communal structures (Anderson et al. 2007; Carrier 2005).

Both countries also enjoy the benefits of processing and marketing. Khat sales in Kenya provide a source of income for thousands of market women across the country. In Nairobi several thousand people are employed in the washing, sorting, and packaging of khat for export.

8.9   The Anti-khat Campaign

It is important against this extensive list of benefits to look at the reasons for the sustained international assault on khat. At face value, it may be argued that in countries with uncertain food security, precious agricultural land should be reserved for food production. There is certainly such a debate in Yemen, where khat has displaced a wide range of different produce and is consuming a large proportion of water resources. This has to be measured against the viability of rural households. Studies of famine in Ethiopia (de Waal 1997) and India (Sen 1981) have demonstrated that famines that kill do not occur because of national food scarcity, but because famine victims lack the means to make up local shortfalls through imports (due to so-called market failure) and have no political entitlement to assistance from the political authorities. What development aid agencies are advocating is not autarky but sustainable livelihoods. Many farmers simply do not have the land or the inputs for self-sufficiency to be a realistic option, and therefore they aim for higher value crops that can earn an income. International aid agencies seek to divert farmer from khat and encourage coffee, flower, or fruit cultivation instead.

The objection then is not to the cultivation of a non-food crop but to khat as a psychoactive substance. This is significant, as khat use in Yemen and large parts of Ethiopia and Kenya is culturally embedded as is, for instance, beer and wine in Europe. International development agents are therefore making a cultural judgment that needs to be squared with claims to cultural sensitivity and appropriateness. The situation is made even more complicated by the persistent lack in evidence for the adverse health consequences of moderate khat use (ACMD 2005; Warfa et al. 2007). There are certain associations between khat use and a number of mental health conditions, but these are confounded by other variables such as post-traumatic stress disorder and excessive khat consumption (WHO 2006). Traditional patterns of use found in the heartland of khat cultivation, however, have resulted in little by way of medical complications. It seems that in its established form, khat is a benign substance, facilitating conviviality with minimal debilitating consequences.

Colonial prohibitions were motivated largely by economic and moral considerations. Where khat was imported, it proved to be a drain on foreign exchange reserves, and the chewing of khat was seen to promote idleness. The sudden appearance of bars serving khat, coffee, and tea was seen as a threat to the moral order—enabling men and women and members of different tribes to mix freely—and as potentially subversive. This response to the social reality of urban life noted in other parts of the continent in relation to alcohol (Akyeampong 1996) was echoed by the Somali government, which banned khat in 1983 and ended in its ill-fated eradication campaign of khat fields in the north of the country (Elmi et al. 1987).

In African countries with a tradition of khat cultivation, like Ethiopia and Kenya, the thought of banning khat is officially eschewed by governments that happily reap the economic benefits it provides. As supply and cultivation spread into new areas, such as Uganda (Klein and Beckerleg 2007), South Africa, and Rwanda, a public discussion emerged in which khat is defined not as a traditional plant-based stimulant but a dangerous drug, with much of the language, argumentation, and symbolism imputed from drug control discourses held overseas.

8.10 Propping up the Lame Leviathan—The Role of International Agencies

The ban of the three plant-based psychoactive substances, opium, cocaine, and cannabis in the years after the First World War set a precedent for international agencies. The Opium Control Board set up under the auspices of the League of Nations, considered the case of khat in the mid-1930s. The issue was subsequently taken up by the Commission of Narcotic Drugs in the United Nations, which authorized the World Health Organization to set up an expert committee on khat. Once the psychoactive ingredients of khat were identified, cathine and cathinone became controlled substances, slotted into schedules of the Convention of Psychotropic Substances (Pantelis et al. 1989).

After the funding of the United Nations Office of Drugs and Crime was formed in 1989, officers were set up in Nairobi, Lagos, Dakar, and Johannesburg. Without much domestic production of hard drugs, and only a limited role played by African countries like that which Nigeria and Guinea Bissau have in the transit of drugs, the role of the UNODC was mainly to prevent domestic consumption. Khat was identified in a scoping study (UNDCP 1998) as a target for control. UNODC officers have since been calling for controls of khat, with the backing of the International Narcotic Control Board (INCB 2006). International organizations are also actively involved in the anti-khat campaigns at the civil society level, such as in faith-based organizations with affiliations to Western and especially US-based churches, which have likened khat to cannabis and are calling for government action (Klein et al. 2008).

The role of international organizations is, as was argued above, of critical importance in the African context, where they can act with far greater degree of moral authority and operational freedom, be these the regional offices of UN agencies, bilateral development cooperation partners, or NGO/faith-based organizations. As guardians of international standards of governance and professionalism, their role is to transfer expertise and benefits from the advanced to less developed countries for the benefit of ultimately both, but primarily the latter. The ostensible long-term objective is to assist recipient countries toward self-sustaining economic growth and social development. Development theory has long abandoned the idea of resource transfer as an end in itself for a more strategic role in effecting and assisting policy development that yields multiplier benefits and encourages countries to realize comparative advantage.

It is therefore surprising that khat production has not become a cause célèbre in development circles, as it is after all a bottom-up initiative, driven entirely by indigenous producers and entrepreneurs in one of the poorest and most aid-dependent regions of the world. It provides tens of thousands of rural households with a livelihood, has generated processing industries and a complex transport network, and allows for the formation of capital. The khat trade links regions within countries and is the single most important commodity exported from Ethiopia to Somaliland and Djibouti. It provides income opportunities for urban traders and a ready source of entertainment for the burgeoning and poorly served African cities. It is remarkable then that this opportunity has not been seized as the engine for development.

For a closer look at the processes involved, we have to return to the informality debate of the 1970s and 1980s, and the depiction of the state as a destructive parasite. Two decades of restructuring have reduced the powers of African states, and therefore the attention of researchers who had recognized the often destructive role played by international agencies that have stepped in and displaced the role of the state (Ferguson 2006; Escobar 1995). What the conduct of drug control agencies demonstrates is that institutional self-interest overrides all development principles, as agencies seek to carve out ever greater areas of control and to lobby for funding streams. Agencies dominated by expatriate professionals are furthermore importing cultural mores at the expense of local patterns of consumption and values, which, when considering psychoactive substances, are critical. The UNODC Agency staff in Nairobi refrains from chewing khat but do not uphold a ban on smoking cigarettes or drinking alcohol.

8.11   Swimming against the Stream

If globalization is a set or interlocking processes in which agency and chance are critical factors, the future of khat is in the balance. There is a strong likelihood that khat will follow coca, cannabis, and opium onto the list of internationally controlled substances. Countries with powerful drug control bureaucracies such as the UNDCP and DEA in the United States, and countries with a strong prohibitionist ethos, like Sweden, have already imposed national bans. The fact that a substance with only a mild psychoactive effect, no incidence of addiction—in the medical sense of withdrawal and tolerance—has been controlled in countries where use has been restricted to immigrant groups is suggestive of the persuasive force of the drug control template and the lobbying power of the drug control industry. For the moment khat, while widely and legally available in the United Kingdom and the Netherlands, has not moved beyond the circles of East African immigrants. It has only been the arrival of large numbers of Somali refugees in the wake of state collapse and ongoing civil war that has created a large European and North American khat market. While this has brought khat to the attention of Western governments, and thereby energized the control efforts of international agencies, a quieter process of expansion has been taking place within Africa. Already khat has become established in Uganda (Klein et al. 2008) and has been reported in Rwanda, South Africa, and Israel. As long as governments refrain from intervention, both the exchequer and local economies stand to gain considerable benefits that may come to outweigh the institutional interests of the control campaigners. A sober assessment of the benign pharmacological properties and enormous development benefits of East African khat production could even trigger a re-examination of existing control mechanisms at international level, not just for khat but for other plant-based psychoactives. That would prove to be a truly remarkable unintended consequence of globalization and the international drug trade.

It is therefore suggested that the costs and benefits of khat production, trade, and consumption be put to a multisectoral assessment, taking into account health and mental risks, social costs, and opportunity costs of production and trade on one side. On the other are the economic benefits for producers, the processing industry, transporters and traders, and the entertainment value for users. The cost of establishing a regulative framework has to be deducted from savings made by eliminating khat crime (trafficking and crop eradication) and the criminalization of khat users. Khat provides a ready opportunity as the harmful effects of prohibition, already factored into the harms index of controlled substances, do not distort the calculus (Nutt et al. 2007).

8.12 Conclusion

Global financial crises are set to impact resource allocation for governmental and intergovernmental agencies alike, and may well prompt a review of drug control provisions. Already initiatives on medical marijuana in many US states are driven primarily by fiscal considerations owing to the high costs of penalizing drug offenses. These may set a trend for other countries and lead to a revision of the prevailing restrictions on the trade in plant-based psychoactives. While global regimes obtain for cannabis, coca, and opium, khat remains at the margins of global governance. Given that it has a hybrid status, banned in some in some countries, openly traded in other countries, it has the potential to spearhead a regime shift from prohibition to regulation.

While details of such a change fall outside the scope of this chapter, it is possible to speculate on the potential consequence for khat producers. At present around 300 tons of khat enter the United Kingdom annually, much of which is then re-exported clandestinely to markets in North America and Scandinavia where khat is currently banned. If the demand for khat in these countries were to reach the same as in the

United Kingdom, we could expect a significant increase in exports. This rests on the assumption that demand is equivalent, and that the regulative regime would be equally lax. We should also have to deduct the considerable quantities of khat that are being seized by the authorities, at 106.9, 97.5, and 101.4 tonnes in 2004, 2005, and 2006, respectively (UNODC 2009), and also khat that because of holdup occasioned by controls has become spoiled. Because of the criminalization of two social processes—the consumption of psychoactives and cross-border migration—it is not possible to present realistic figures on either the import of the commodity or the number of consumers. What we are left with are extrapolations from social research for the mapping of future trends.

Although there is an uptake of khat use among some UK-born Somalis, the majority of their peers opt for more conventional drugs, cannabis, MDMA, and amphetamine. Khat in the diaspora is an old man's drug, chewed by those who picked up the habit before entering the United Kingdom (Klein 2008). Notwithstanding the demand for stimulants across the mainstream of the population, the awkward mode of administration—chewing large wads of vegetable matter—stands in the way of khat's popularity outside the East African community. The prediction is therefore that the export demand for khat is driven by a cohort of aging men who are constrained by limited purchasing power and restricted social mobility. Their habit is not going to be taken up by new groups of consumers, and their numbers will not be replenished because of the ever-tightening restrictions on immigration in North America and Europe. While khat exports will therefore experience a sharp rise following the lifting of restrictions, they will start falling off by the end of the decade. Moreover any rise in volume will be tempered by efficiency gains in marketing and distribution following legalization.

For resource-poor economies like Ethiopia and Kenya the increase in khat exports may yield considerable benefits in the short term. It could raise foreign exchange incomes and lead to an expansion of income opportunities in the processing industries in Addis Ababa and Nairobi. There will also be benefits for producers as exports provide an element of price stabilization. But there are potential risks to agricultural producers as the opportunity costs for khat consumption impact the management of finite resources, particularly land and water. There is already a disconcerting development in Yemen, where water from underground aquifers is extracted at unsustainable rates for agriculture, 40 percent of which is for the irrigation of khat fields (Ahmed and Scholz 2006).

Given the overall size of the diaspora communities, linked with the projected decline in the pattern of khat consumtion, exports, however, play a minor role in the overall volume of khat production in core countries, even though they earn valuable foreign exchange and have engendered a labor-intensive processing industry. While the environmental impact is limited, the economic stimulus is considerable. Criminal organizations, potentially with link to terrorist groups, will furthermore be displaced by licit traders. The main beneficiaries of a globally constituted framework of khat regulation will be farmers across eastern and central Africa where khat consumption is currently expanding at pace. Farmers and petty traders are currently driven underground by prohibitionist regimes that fail to eliminate either the demand or the supply for khat, while negating the development benefits from this cash crop.

Instead of driving khat underground and fueling the informal economy, corrupt practices, and eroding governance in weak states, a legal regulative framework would allow governments to work with farmers, to derive revenue through taxation, and to invest in public awareness and, where necessary, health care provisions. As African farmers find it difficult to gain voice at international forums, there is a ready opportunity for the drug control agencies like the UNODC and INCB to broaden their remit from prohibitionist to regulatory interventions.

Notes

1. See Chin (2007) on the reluctance by WHO field offices in Africa and African public health agencies to engage with AIDS in the early 1980s. In 1985, with some 1 to 2 million people living with AIDS on the continent, African health researchers and epidemiologists were arguing vigorously that AIDS was a Western disease of homosexuals and drug addicts and not a problem in Africa.

2. See the discussion of governmentality by Michel Foucault in Mitchell (1999) and Foucault (1991 [1978]).

References

Advisory Council on the Misuse of Drugs (ACMD). 2005. *Quat: Assessment of Risk to Individual and Communities in the UK*. London: British Home Office.

Ahmed, A., and M. Scholz. 2006. Agriculture and water resources crisis in Yemen: Need for sustainable agriculture. *Journal of Sustainable Agriculture* 28 (3): 55–75.

Akyeampong, E. 1996. *Drink, Power and Cultural Change: A Social History of Alcohol in Ghana, c.1800 to Recent Times*. Portsmouth, NH: Heinemann.

Anderson, D. M., S. Beckerleg, D. Hailu, and A. Klein. 2007. *The Khat Controversy: Stimulating the Drugs Debate*. Oxford: Berg.

Andreas, P., and E. Nadelmann. 2006. *Policing the Globe. Criminalization and Crime Control in International Relations*. Oxford: Oxford University Press.

Bates, R. 1981. *Markets and States in Tropical Africa*. Berkeley: University of California Press.

Beckerleg, S. 2006. What harm? East African perspectives on khat. *African Affairs* 104 (418):219–241.

Brooke, C. 1960. Khat (*Catha edulis*): Its production and trade in the Middle East. *Geographical Journal* 126.

Burton, R. F. 1966 [1856]. *First Footsteps in East Africa or, An Exploration of Harrar*. New York: Schuster.

Buxton, J. 2006. *The Political Economy of Narcotics: Production, Consumption and Global Markets*. London: Zed.

Carrier, N. 2005. The need for speed: Contrasting timeframes in the social life of Kenyan miraa. *Africa* 75 (4): 539–58.

Cassanelli, L. V. 1986. Quat: Changes in the production and consumption of a quasi-legal commodity. In A. Appadurai, ed., *The Social Life of Things: Commodities in Cultural Perspective* Cambridge: Cambridge University Press.

Chin, J. 2007. *The AIDS Pandemic: The Collision of Epidemiology with Political Correctness*. Oxford: Radcliffe Publishing.

Costa Storti, C., and P. De Grauwe. 2008. The cocaine and heroin markets in the era of globalisation and drug reduction policies. *International Journal on Drug Policy* 20:488–496.

Courtwright, D. 2001. *Forces of Habit. Drugs and the Making of the Modern World*. Cambridge: Harvard University Press.

de Soto, H. 1989. *The Other Path: The Invisible Revolution in the Third World*. New York: Harper and Row.

de Waal, A. 1997. *Famine Crimes: Politics and Disaster Relief Industry in Africa*. Oxford: James Currey.

Donham, D. 1999. *Marxist Modern: An Ethnographic History of the Ethiopian Revolution*. Berkeley: University of California Press.

Elmi, A. S., Y. H. Ahmed, and M. S. Samatar. 1987. Experience in the control of khat-chewing in Somalia. *Bulletin on Narcotics* 39 (2): 51–57.

Escobar, A. 1995. *Encountering Development: The Making and Unmaking of the Third World*. Princeton: Princeton University Press.

Foucault, M. [1978] 1991. Governmentality. In *The Foucault Effect: Studies in Governmentality*, ed. G. Burchell, C. Gordon, and P. Miller. Chicago: University of Chicago Press.

Ferguson, J. 2006. *Global Shadows: Africa in the Neoliberal World Order*. Durham: Duke University Press.

Gebissa, E. 2004. *Leaf of Allah: Khat and Agricultural Transformation in Hararge, Ethiopia 1875–1991*. Oxford: James Currey.

Ghodse, H. 2008. *International Drug Control in the 21st Century*. London: Ashgate.

Goodman, J. 2002. *Tobacco in History*. London: Routledge.

Hart, K. 1973. Informal Income Opportunities and urban employment in Ghana. *Journal of Modern African Studies* 11: 61–89.

Held, D., D. Goldblatt, A. McGrew, and J. Perraton. 1999. *Global Transformations: Politics*. Stanford, CA: Economics and Culture.

International Narcotic Control Board. 2006. *Annual Report*. Vienna: United Nations.

Kennedy, J. G. 1987. *The Flower of Paradise: The Institutionalized Use of the Drug Qat in North Yemen*. Dordrecht: Reidel.

Klein, A. 1999. The barracuda's tale: Fishing trawlers, the informal sector and a state of classificatory disorder off the Nigerian coast. *Africa, Journal of the International African Institute* 69 (4).

Klein, A. 2007. Khat and the creation of tradition in the Somali diaspora. In J. Fountain, D. J. Korf D. and J. Fountain, eds., *Drugs in Society: A European Perspective*. Oxford: Radcliffe Publishing.

Klein, A. 2008. Khat in the neighbourhood: Local government responses to khat use in a London community. *Substance Use and Misuse* 43 (6): 819–31.

Klein, A., S. Beckerleg, and D. Hailu. 2008. Regulating khat: Dilemmas and opportunities. Presented at the 2nd conference of the International Society for the Study of Drug Policy, Lisbon, April 3, 2008.

Klein, A., and S. Beckerleg. 2007. Building castles of spit: The role of khat chewing in worship, work and leisure. In J. Goodman, P. Lovejoy, and A. Sherrat, eds., *Consuming Habits*. London: Routledge, pp. 238–54.

Lemessa, D. 2001. *Khat: Botany, Distribution, Cultivation, Usage and Economics in Ethiopia*. Emergencies Unit for Ethiopia. Vienna: United Nations Development Programme.

Mitchell, D. 1999. *Governmentality: Power and Rule in Modern Society*. London: Sage.

Nadel, A., and F. Trentmann. 2008. Mapping food and globalization. In A. Nutzenadel and F. Trentmann, eds., *Food and Globalization: Consumption, Markets and Politics in the Modern World*. Oxford: Berg.

Nutt, D., L. King, W. Saulsbury, and C. Blakemore. 2007. Development of a rational scale to assess the harm of drugs of potential misuse. *Lancet* 369: 1047–53.

Nuetzenadel, A., and F. Trentmann. 2008. *Food and Globalization: Consumption, Markets and Politics in the Modern World*. Oxford: Berg.

Oxfam. 2002. *Mugged: Poverty in Your Coffee Cup*. Oxford: Oxfam.

Pantelis, C., C. G. Hindler, and J. C. Taylor. 1989. Use and abuse of khat (*Catha-Edulis*): A review of the distribution, pharmacology, side-effects and a description of psychosis attributed to khat chewing. *Psychological Medicine* 19 (3): 657–68.

Rhodes, T., and D. Moore, eds. 2001. Addiction: On the qualitative in drug research: Part 1. *Addiction Research and Theory* 9 (4): 279–402

Schivelbusch, W. 1992. *Tastes of Paradise: A Social History of Spices, Stimulants and Intoxicants.* New York: Pantheon.

Sen, A. 1981. *Poverty and Famines, An Essay on Entitlement and Deprivation.* Oxford: Clarendon Press.

Storti Costa, C., and P. De Grauwe. 2008. Money laundering and financial means of organized crime: Some preliminary modelling of the cocaine and heroin markets in the era of globalization and drug reduction policies. Presented at Ces-Info Venice Summer Institute Workshop on Illicit Trade and Globalization.

UNDCP. 1998. *The Drug Nexus in Africa United Nations Office of Drug Control and Crime Prevention Studies on Drugs and Crime.* New York: United Nations.

UNODC. 2008. *World Drug Report.* Vienna: United Nations Drug Control Programme.

Warfa, N., A. Klein, K. Bhui, G. Leavey, T. Craig, and S. Stansfeld. 2007. Association between khat use and mental disorders: An emerging paradigm. *Social Science and Medicine* 65 (2): 309–18.

Weir, S. 1985. *Qat in Yemen: Consumption and Social Change.* London: British Museum Publications.

World Health Organization. 1964. Expert report on addiction-producing drugs: Khat (*Catha edulis*). *Bulletin on Narcotics* 16 (2).

World Health Organization Expert Committee on Drug. 2003. WHO Expert Committee on Drug Dependence. *World Health Organization Technical Report Series* 915: i–v, 1–26.

9 Organized Crime and Foreign Direct Investment: The Italian Case

Vittorio Daniele and Ugo Marani

9.1 Introduction

In the geographical distribution of foreign direct investment (FDI) inflows into Italy, the eight less developed regions of the south (the Italian *Mezzogiorno*), receive a very modest share of FDI. For instance, in the period 2005 to 2007, these regions received less than 1 percent of total inflows; in Campania, the southern region with the best performance, FDI amounted to only 0.2 percent of all those inflows into Italy.

The low share of FDI in the southern regions is also evinced by the "geography" of multinational firms located in Italy. In 2006 the firms with foreign participation in these regions amounted to less than 5 percent of the Italian total. For the sake of comparison, in Lombardy alone there were ten times as many firms with foreign capital as in the entire area of the Mezzogiorno.

Despite this dismal performance, in southern Italy there are several factors that, at least potentially, could attract foreign investors. First, this area represents a major share of the domestic market: its population is of almost 21 million people, that is, 35 percent of the national total. Second, in the Mezzogiorno there is a considerable skilled workforce, and the labor cost is lower than the Italian average. Furthermore, in many southern regions there are extensive uncongested industrial areas able to offer business location benefits for investors (IPI 2005). Finally, firms that invest in the south—especially in the less developed regions—may benefit from a series of financial incentives provided by European and national programs.

However, against such potential benefits, southern Italy has several comparative disadvantages that negatively affect its attractiveness (Basile 2004). One of these disadvantages is the historically rooted presence of several criminal organizations of the Mafia type: *Camorra, Cosa* nostra, 'Ndrangheta, and Sacra Corona Unita.[1] The incidence of these "Mafia" is particularly high in certain regions: notably Calabria, Campania, Sicily, and, to a lesser extent, Apulia. From an economic point of view, crime may be considered an additional risk (or cost) for business activities (Krkoska and Robeck 2006). Crime, especially if of the Mafia type, tends to damage business in various ways: racketeering, retailing market limitations, and forcing firms to take on suppliers of raw materials or being pressurized to employ workers, creating local monopolies and distortions to the markets (Gambetta 1996; Centorrino and Signorino 2003; Arlacchi 2007). All in all, the presence of crime can be considered as contributing to a somewhat unfavorable business climate, and as a disincentive for foreign and national investments.

Besides having been pointed out many times by scholars, economic operators, and politicians, the deterrent effect of crime on foreign investment has been amply confirmed in surveys conducted among national and foreign investors (Marini and Turato 2002; GPF-ISPO 2005). Additionally the detrimental effects of crime on regional economic development in Italy have been examined by sociologists and economists (Peri 2004; La Spina 2008; Centorrino and Ofria 2008; Daniele 2009). Yet surprisingly, little attention has been paid to estimating the effects on foreign investment. By using data for different kinds of crime, this study analyses the geography of organized crime in Italy and estimates its impact on the distribution of FDI inflows at the provincial level. The results show how the correlation between organized crime and FDI inflows into the Italian provinces is both negative and significant. The correlation results have proved to be robust even when an indicator for financial incentives for investments is included in the regressions.

The conclusions reached in this study suggest that the quality of the "local business environment" influences the location of foreign companies and also diminishes the effectiveness of financial incentives for investments. While our analysis shows that organized crime is indeed a disincentive for investment, certain levels of crime may be perceived as a signal of an unfavorable socioinstitutional system for foreign investors.

The chapter is organized as follows. Section 9.2 illustrates the regional distributions of FDI inflows in Italy and its determinants. Section 9.3 contains a brief review of the economic effects of crime. Section 9.4 describes the data and the results of the empirical analysis. Section 9.5 offers some conclusive remarks.

9.2   The Location of FDI in Italy

9.2.1   Regional Distribution

In all countries there are clear regional differences in the locations of multinational firms. In Spain, for example, Madrid and Cataluña are the main destinations of FDI; in France, Greece, and in the United Kingdom, it is also possible to find distinctive regional differences.[2] In Italy FDI inflows are concentrated in a few regions only. As shown in table 9.1, which reports the share of FDI inflows into the twenty Italian regions, Lombardy receives the largest amount (69 percent), followed by Piedmont (13 percent) and Lazio (7 percent). The shares of the other regions are far less. Overall, the central-northern area receives almost all the FDI inflows into the country; consequently the share of the southern regions is residual, amounting to less than 1.0 percent of the national total. Equally high regional differences are encountered if we consider the ratio of FDI to GDP. In the period 2000 to 2006, net FDI inflows on average represented about 1.6 percent of GDP in the northwest, 0.6 in the central regions, and just 0.1 percent in those of the south.

At the provincial level the concentration of FDI is even greater. Table 9.2 reports the first and last ten provinces in the ranking of FDI inflows in the period 2004 to 2006. Notably the province of Milan absorbs over

Table 9.1

FDI inflows in the Italian regions in percentage of Italy, 2005 and 2006

Regions	2005	2006	Regions	2005	2006
Abruzzo	0.1	0.1	Piedmont	15.5	11.4
Apulia	0.1	0.2	Molise	0.1	0.0
Basilicata	0.2	0.2	Sardinia	0.0	0.1
Calabria	0.0	0.0	Sicily	0.0	0.0
Campania	0.3	0.2	Tuscany	3.6	1.9
Emilia Romagna	2.5	3.7	Trentino Alto Adige	0.2	0.5
Friuli	0.1	0.1	Umbria	1.0	0.8
Lazio	6.2	7.8	Valle d'Aosta	0.0	0.0
Liguria	0.5	0.7	Veneto	4.3	4.2
Lombardy	69.7	68.2	North central	99.2	99.3
Marche	0.1	0.0	Mezzogiorno	0.8	0.7

Source: Italian Exchange Office (UIC).
Note: Data refer to FDI gross flows IDE and do not include trade credits and transactions in the banking sector.

Table 9.2
Top and bottom provinces ranked for FDI inflows in the years 2004 to 2006, in percent

Rank	Provinces	FDI	Rank	Provinces	FDI
1	Milan	66.46	94	Foggia	0.001
2	Turin	9.25	95	Ragusa	0.001
3	Rome	6.33	96	Reggio Calabria	0.001
4	Florence	3.06	97	Gorizia	0.001
5	Verona	2.86	98	Agrigento	0.001
6	Bologna	2.63	99	Catanzaro	0.001
7	Cuneo	2.03	100	Caltanissetta	0.001
8	Terni	0.99	101	Enna	0.000
9	Alessandria	0.75	102	Vibo Valentia	0.000
10	Vicenza	0.56	103	Oristano	0.000

Source: Calculations on Italian Exchange Office data.

Table 9.3
Number, employees and sales of foreign-participated Italian firms

	Firms		Employees		Sales	
Years	North central	South	North central	South	North central	South
2001	6,359	329	850,698	62,136	315,290	18,611
2004	6,739	347	867,294	60,071	346,353	18,031
2006	6,776	318	811,144	46,895	378,597	15,481

Source: Elaborations of the Reprint data base, ICE—Milan Polytechnic.
Note: For the region where the firm is headquartered; data refer to January 1st in each of the years considered.

66 percent of total flows among all the Italian provinces. Moreover the data show that nine of the last ten places are held by provinces in the Mezzogiorno area.

The presence of foreign firms in the Italian regions may be examined more closely through data on the number of firms with foreign participation located in Italy (table 9.3). Overall, among the over 7,100 firms with foreign participation operating in Italy in 2006, only 318 had their headquarters in southern regions, creating only 3 percent of the total number of jobs generated by foreign enterprises located in Italy. The case of Lombardy is striking: the region hosts half of the all Italian firms with foreign capital, and generates over 45 percent of employment and sales of all such firms. As observed for FDI inflows, Lombardy is followed by Piedmont, Lazio, and Emilia.

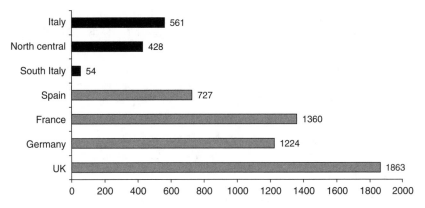

Figure 9.1
Number of "greenfield" investments, 2000 to 2007. Source: OCO Monitor.

Figure 9.1 reports the number of greenfield investments in the two Italian macro regions and in other European countries. First, it easy to see how the attractiveness of Italy is relatively low in comparison with other European countries with analogous levels of development (Committeri 2004; Basile et al. 2009). Second, the number of investment projects located in the south is very low, less than 10 percent of the total. In addition these investments comprise, almost entirely, small-scale projects in low-skill sectors such as tourism or retail trade.

Overall, these data confirm how the geography of foreign investment in Italy is characterized by profound regional differences and how the south is completely marginal with respect to the dynamics of the internationalization of Italian firms.

9.2.2 Determinants of FDI Inflows

The location choices of multinational firms are influenced by several factors. At the national level, empirical studies show how a large share of FDI involves countries with large market dimensions and geographical proximity; other factors, such as common borders and a common language, tend also to influence the investment flows (Barba Navaretti and Venables 2004). Studies referring to the European Union show how the location of foreign firms is guided mainly by the firms' specific characteristics and, to a lesser extent, by observable national or regional factors. Broadly speaking, the determinants of FDI location can be classified in four groups: expected market demand, factor costs, the presence of agglomeration economies, and public policies capable of influencing the firms' activities (Devereux and Griffith 2003; Crozet et al. 2004; Pelegrìn and Bolancé 2008).

At the subnational level, the location decisions of foreign investors are influenced by several factors and regional-specific factors (Artige and Nicolini 2005; Alegría 2006; Devereux et al. 2007; Basile et al. 2009). For example, a study on the location factors conducted by the European Commission (2006), on a sample of approximately 100,000 foreign companies, showed how, in the context of the European Union, FDIs tend to locate in regions with:

• a large presence of previous foreign investors;
• good infrastructure and accessibility;
• a highly educated workforce and a high level of R&D expenditure; and
• the presence of agglomeration economies, determined by a large presence of competitors, clients, and suppliers within the firm's industry.

Studies on Italy suggest how the relative level of development, the labor costs, the efficiency of the bureaucratic system, and the quality of human capital significantly influence the regional location choices of foreign firms. The low competitiveness of the south is, in large part, explained by these variables, even if some factors (e.g., red tape) are common throughout Italy (Barba Navaretti et al. 2009).

Foreign investments can be a propulsive factor in regional development, contributing toward raising employment and income levels, transferring technologies, and producing spill-over effects that increase industrial productivity (Konings 2004; Devereux et al. 2007). For these reasons many countries, besides Italy, offer incentives or subsidies to foreign companies that invest in their less developed areas.

Empirical studies offer mixed evidence on the effects of financial incentives in attracting FDI. For example, a study of the Irish case shows that regional policies, despite promoting foreign business location in disadvantaged areas of the country, have acted almost "selectively" on firms with a low technological content (Barrios et al. 2003). In Italy, as in France, Spain, or the United Kingdom, research shows that financial incentives for investments (e.g., grants or easy-term loans), tax relief, and EU structural policies do not have a significant effect in attracting foreign investment in underdeveloped regions

(Mayer 2004; Devereux et al. 2007). Rather, a study conducted by Basile et al. (2009), using data for 5,509 foreign subsidiaries established in 50 European regions, found that structural and cohesion funds allocated by the European Union to laggard regions have contributed to attracting multinationals.

A recent strand of literature has been devoted to the investigation of how FDI is influenced by cross-country differences in the political, institutional, and legal systems. There are several reasons for which the quality of institutions may be important for FDI. The first reason is that—according to the studies on long-term growth determinants—efficient institutions improve productivity prospects and in turn attract investors. The second reason is that a poor institutional environment can bring about additional costs for firms, as may be the case with crime and corruption (Broadman and Recanatini 2000; Wei 2000). A further reason is that—due to high sunk costs—FDIs face high uncertainty, mostly stemming from government inefficiencies, graft, or the weak enforcement of property rights (Bénassy-Quéré et al. 2007).

Studies generally confirm that a "good" institutional environment is an important determinant of FDI inflows. This institutional environment includes ease of creating company startups, government efficiency, secure property rights, effective judicial systems, and low corruption levels (Globerman and Shapiro 2002; Habib and Zurawicki 2001). The World Bank (2001) has emphasized how the attraction of investments is greater in areas where the public institutions are perceived as being more credible by the community of investors. This means that governments are considered capable, and that they put into practice the policies undertaken, as well as ensuring predictable and consistent administrative and judicial practices, guaranteeing low levels of crime and corruption. Some case studies, such as those concerning Central American countries (United Nations 2007) and Russia (Broadman and Recanatini 2001), further indicate that violence and crime deter foreign investors.

From the international literature clear evidence emerges on how the quality of the institutional system and the business climate influence decisions regarding the location of foreign firms. These factors also appear relevant at a regional level where, as in the Italian case, notable differences exist in the quality of the local socioinstitutional environments.

9.3   Crime and the Economy

9.3.1   The Economic Effects of Crime

Crime inflicts considerable costs on society. There are costs of protection and prevention, costs sustained by victims as a consequence of crime, and costs relative to prosecuting and incarcerating those responsible for the crime. These costs are monetary disbursements sustained by private individuals and the community as a whole. Estimating these costs is a complex but useful operation, both for designing strategies to fight crime and for evaluating the effectiveness of the measures applied (Brand and Price 2000; Czabanski 2008).

Not always, however, does the social cost of crime correspond to a monetary disbursement. Since a high incidence of crime is detrimental to legal economic activities, it implies a loss in employment and investments, negatively affecting economic development (Peri 2004; Bonaccorsi di Patti 2009). For instance, in analyzing the relationship between crime and the enterprise sector in a range of countries with different levels of development, Krkoska and Robeck (2006) show how organized crime has a deterrent effect on businesses, particularly their entry and expansion, while the perception of crime results as a serious disincentive for foreign investors.

In the Italian case the effects of organized crime on economic outcomes have been widely examined from sociological and historical points of view but far less from the economic point of view. Often economists have analyzed the determinants of criminality, rather than the effects that it produces on the economy (Marselli and Vannini 2003; Buonanno 2006).

Some studies have nevertheless shown how organized crime produces detrimental effects on economic growth and local institutional systems. For instance, Centorrino and Ofria (2008) demonstrate the negative effect of crime on the growth rate of labor productivity, in particular in the southern regions. Peri (2004), in examining the economic performance of the Italian provinces over the period 1951 to 1993, found a strong and negative correlation between the incidence of organized crime (measured as a high murder rate) and economic development. More recently Bonaccorsi di Patti (2009) has analyzed the relationship between the terms of bank loans and crime rates, using a survey of over 300,000 bank–firm relationships. The results are striking: where the crime rate is higher, borrowers pay higher interest rates and pledge more collateral than in low-crime areas; furthermore access to bank credit is negatively influenced by crime. Since less credit implies lower investment, the economic growth of the less developed Italian regions is negatively affected.

There are many ways in which crime encroaches on the legal economy. The most obvious is the racket of extortion. Extortion activity is typical of the criminal organizations of the Mafia type. It has two main aims: to ensure a sufficiently steady income, generally directed at financing other illegal activities, and to permit the criminal clans to exercise a widespread control over the territory. Extortion—"pizzo" in the slang of the *mafiosi*—is a crime typical of the Italian Mafia. The reason is that "pizzo" is paid by businesses, for "protection" offered by the criminal families in a certain area (Catanzaro 1991). As pointed out by Gambetta (1996), "providing" protection to legitimate industries has been, for a long time, the *distinctive* activity of the Sicilian Mafia. The extortion racket, thus, allows the Mafia to take control of a territory.

Criminal organizations of the Mafia type also practice other forms of control over the local economy. Often the clans force legal firms to purchase raw materials from specific suppliers, to hire personnel that are linked to the same organizations, or to impose limitations on sales markets. The activity of extortion and the control over a part of the legal economy has been well documented in judiciary inquests and remains a subject of much research (La Spina and Lo Forte 2007; CPI 2008).[3] Numerous inquests testify how organized crime manages to condition the activities even of large companies involved in programs of public works for the southern regions (Confesercenti 2007).

In general, crime increases the risks for (and the costs of) investment, and therefore has a depressive effect on the economy. In particular, crime discourages investment by raising the economic risks to companies, deriving from possible attacks, the destruction of property, and intimidation. Insurance against such risks implies financial expense, both in acquiescence (the payment of bribes, being obliged to purchase raw materials from firms with criminal connections) and in self-defense (private police and security measures).

A further negative effect on the economy derives from the operations of the same "entrepreneurs of crime." Through the use of violence or corruption to impose monopolies, the "criminal 'firms" condition the functioning of the markets and local institutions, distorting the allocation of resources and capturing a part of public expenditure, including European funds for regional development (CPI 2008).The result is that the functional capabilities of local market and institutional systems are compromised and consequently the development of the economy (Centorrino and Signorino 1993; Zamagni 1993).

The notable economic and social costs imposed by the presence of organized crime in many areas of southern Italy that discourage both domestic and foreign investment are confirmed by surveys. One such survey, by Marini and Turato (2002) conducted on a panel of businessmen from the northeast of Italy involved in a process of internationalization, showed how almost all of those interviewed (93 percent) believed the presence of criminality to be the principal block to investment in the Mezzogiorno area. Another survey, conducted in eleven countries on behalf of the Italian Ministry of the Economy, showed how, in the perception of businessmen, the Mezzogiorno is a region seriously deficient in security (GPF-ISPO 2005).[4] Such deterrents for foreign investors have been highlighted by economists for years. For example, Sylos-Labini (1985) observed how the presence of organized crime in the south forces companies to choose to locate elsewhere, and discourages investment. Olson (1984) pointed out how, as a result of organized crime, southern Italy has accumulated, over time, a number of extra-governmental institutions that have eroded the economic opportunities and increased the risks for investment. For this reason Olson argued that whoever thinks of starting a new business in such an environment will confront a great many risks that could be avoided by starting the business in a less "risky" area.

Although rich with implications for research, the problems raised by Sylos-Labini and Olson over twenty years ago have received little attention in the economic literature. Only recently has some research on the determinants of FDI considered the crime rate among the explicative variables included in the regressions, showing how, in Italy, high crime rates tend to be negatively correlated with the regional attractiveness for foreign investors (Basile 2001; Daniele 2005).

Our analysis, however, differs from these studies both in method and in content. We used panel data for a disaggregated level of territory (103 provinces) and different estimate procedures. Furthermore we considered different kinds of crime, in particular some typical of the Mafia. As far as we are aware, our research constitutes the first attempt explicitly aimed at estimating the impact of crime on FDI in the case of Italy.

9.3.2 Measuring Organized Crime

The Italian Penal Code defines organized crime, making a clear distinction between "criminal association" (article 416) and "Mafia type association" (article 416-bis), defining the latter as follows: "the association is of the Mafia type when its components use intimidation, subjection and, consequentially, silence (*omertà*), to commit crimes in order to directly or indirectly acquire the management or the control of businesses, concessions, authorizations, public contracts and public services, to obtain either unjust profits or advantages for themselves or others . . . ." Despite this clear definition, measurement of the actual extent of criminal organizations, in particular the Mafia, is very difficult: crime networks are in fact complex and an elusive phenomenon (Lampe 2004; Paoli 2004).

In this study, in order to estimate the incidence of criminal organizations, we refer to official data relative to different crimes that are *symptomatic* of the presence of the Mafia. Even if is not always possible to disentangle crimes committed by the Mafia from crimes committed by *other* criminals, some offenses are not typical of organized crime: for example, theft, fraud, and sexual violence are not, in general, committed by the Mafia. From existing studies of the subject (La Spina and Lo Forte 2006) we have therefore constructed an index of organized crime based only on certain crimes: extortion, bomb attacks, arson, and criminal association.

Extortion represents a crime typical of the Mafia organizations. As judiciary inquests testify, all Mafia families exercise their power over a territory through the racket of extortion. However, official data notably underreport the number of cases of extortion committed, particularly in the southern regions. Whenever extortion is imposed by the *mafiosi*, only a small fraction of those victimized will dare to denounce the crime. Estimates and inquiries suggest that the spread of the extortion is much greater than noted in official data. According to some estimates, the "racket of kickbacks" would affect 70 percent of Sicilian businessmen, 50 percent of those in Calabria, 40 percent of those in Campania, and 30 percent of those in Apulia, for a total of over 120,000 businessmen in these four regions (Confesercenti 2007). Even if these estimates were considered prudently, in some regions the cost of extortion would be notable. In the case of Sicily, extortion has been estimated as representing a cost equal to 1.3 percent of the regional GDP (Asmundo and Lisciandra 2008).

Since the number of complaints significantly underreport the effective extent of the extortion racket, our analysis considers other crimes that are symptomatic indicators of the activities of organized crime. These are bomb attacks and arson, which are carried out to threaten and intimidate the economic operators or politicians and which, because of their characteristics, cannot be concealed by the victims, as often happens in cases of extortion. In particular, bomb attacks and arson are often used to compel reluctant businessmen to pay extortion. Finally, we considered the crime of criminal association as covered by the articles 416 and 416-bis of the Italian Penal Code. This crime is measured by the number of people denounced to the Judicial Authorities.

In summary, the incidence of organized crime is given by the sum of these four crimes (extortion, bomb attacks, arson, criminal association) per 10,000 inhabitants. In the period 2001 to 2005 these crimes represented approximately 1 percent of the cumulate total of crimes denounced in Italy.

As figure 9.2 shows, in the south the number of crimes for every 10,000 inhabitants is far higher than in the rest of the country.

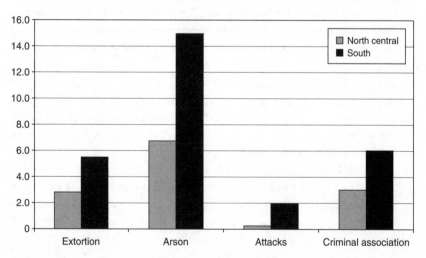

Figure 9.2
Crime rates per 10,000 inhabitants, 2000 to 2005. Data refer to crimes denounced to judicial authorities. Source: Calculations on ISTAT data.

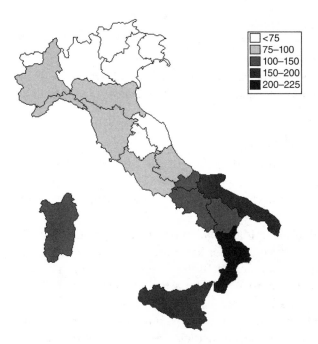

Figure 9.3
Organized crime index, 2001 to 2005. Cumulative values per 10,000 inhabitants (Italy = 100). Source: Elaborated from ISTAT data, "Territorial information system on justice."

Significant differences further exist in the incidence of crime within the Mezzogiorno area. The crime figures are extremely high in Calabria, Campania, Sicily, and Apulia, or rather in those regions where the Mafia organizations, *Cosa nostra*, *'Ndrangheta*, *Camorra*, and the *Sacra Corona Unita*, are historically rooted (Paoli 2004).

The "geography of crime" resulting from the index of organized crime we calculated is illustrated in figure 9.3. Besides indicating the existence of significant differences between the north and south, the criminal geography seems to adhere fairly faithfully to the "map" of the Mafia families that emerged from judicial enquiries, and from reports compiled by the institutions that deal with criminal phenomena (CPI 2008). On the basis of this index, in the following paragraph we will examine the impact of crime on FDI, and seek to verify whether, as the entrepreneurs interviewed in the surveys and numerous economic analysts and politicians claimed, crime is an effective block to potential foreign investors.

9.4   The Empirical Analysis

9.4.1   Data Description

To examine the effect of organized crime on FDI inflows, we use data for 103 Italian provinces for the period 2002 to 2006, estimating different specifications as

$$FDI_{i,t} = \alpha + \beta_1 X_{i,t-1} + \beta_2 Crime_{i,t-1} + w_{it}, \tag{9.1}$$

where i represents province, t time and $w_{i,t} = e_i + u_{i,t}$ is the error term. The dependent variable is the log of FDI inflow in the provinces, $X_{i,t-1}$ is a set of lagged control variables, while *Crime* is a measure of the incidence of crime.

The data on FDI inflow into the Italian provinces is gathered by UIC (the Italian Exchange Office) in order to compile a balance of payments. In conformity with international definitions, the FDI establish a long-term interest between a company headquartered abroad and one head-quartered in Italy.[5] Because of the way that the data are collected, the information on FDIs has some limitations; the most important is the fact that when investment flows transit via one or more intermediaries, the methods of reception (immediate beneficiary) do not permit control over the final geographical destination (Mariotti and Mutinelli 2005). For these reasons, great care must be taken when making a comparison between data on FDI flows and data on the number of multinational companies. Notwithstanding the limitations, the regional distribution of foreign firms that results from data on FDIs, and data based on the number of plants, present many similarities; furthermore empirical research on FDI determinants, conducted using the two data sources, generally leads to analogous results. The FDI data have the advantage of provincial disaggregation and of a wide temporal coverage, permitting comparison to analogous data furnished by international institutions. Furthermore these data are used both in empirical analyses on the determinants of FDI (Bronzini 2004) and in descriptive research to quantify Italy's attractiveness to investors.

The incidence of organized crime is measured by the index described in the previous section, calculated as the sum of extortions, bomb attacks, arsons, and criminal associations per 10,000 inhabitants. Other kinds of crimes have been considered as control variables: the number of crimes against property (with the exception of that included in the "organized crime index") and thefts and robberies per 10,000 inhabitants. All data on crime was collected by the Italian National

Institute of Statistics (Istat) in the "Informative System on Italian Justice."

On the basis of studies on FDI determinants, the control variables included in the regression are related both to the dimension and to the economic structure of the provinces. Market size, one of the main determinants of FDI, is proxied by the log of the resident population (*Population*) in each province, and by the share of provincial GDP of that of the region (*Size*). Considering the profound regional development imbalances that characterize Italy, the GDP per capita (in log) is included among the regressors. We also included a measure of the degree of openness of the provincial economy, given by the share of exports on GDP (*Export*), and a proxy of R&D activities, given by the number of patents presented to the European Patent Office (*Patents*). Furthermore some variables related to the economic and productive structure have also been considered. These were the share of medium and large firms (with more than 50 employees) of the total number of firms (*Big firms*), and the number of firms in nonagricultural sectors per 1,000 people (*Firms*). Since the location of companies also tends to be influenced by an area's accessibility, we considered an index of total infrastructural endowment (*Infrastructure*). We then inserted, among the regressors, a proxy of the financial incentives to companies conceded under the Law 488/92 (*Incentives*) which, in the period under examination, was the principal instrument of incentives for investment in Italy. This variable was considered in order to evaluate whether financial incentives and subsidies, conceded particularly to companies investing in southern Italy, also influenced the location of foreign companies in areas where disincentives related to the social and institutional context exist. Table A9.1 in the appendix describes the data and their sources.

9.4.2 Estimation Results

To choose the most appropriate estimator, we first tested for the presence of heteroskedasticity, running a basic specification of equation (9.1) with GDP per capita, population and crime index as control variables. The standard assumption of homoskedasticity disturbances can in fact be too restrictive when, as in this case, the cross-sectional units present different sizes and, consequently, different variations (Baltagi 2008). Table 9.4 reports the results of the diagnostic for panel data—F statistic, Breusch–Pagan's test, and Hausman's test—that suggest that the fixed effect model is not adequate for the nature of the data. Based

Table 9.4
Diagnostic for the basic model

Test	Results
White	LM = 40.48 – p-value = P (chi^2 (9) > 40.48) = 0.000
Wald[a]	chi^2 103 8049.87 – p-value = 0
Joint significance F	F (102.4) = 4.40 – p-value 0.000
Breusch-Pagan[b]	LM = 160.7; p-value = P (chi^2 (1) > 160.7) = 0.000
Hausman test[c]	H = 5.34 p-value = P (chi^2 (3) > 5.34) = 0.14

Note: FDI is regressed on GDP per capita, population and organized crime index.
a. Based on FGLS residuals.
b. A low p-value counts against the null hypothesis that the pooled OLS model is adequate, in favor of the fixed effect alternative;
c. A low p-value counts against the null hypothesis that the random effects model is consistent, in favor of the fixed effects model.

on this, in our analysis we used a groupwise weighted least square (WLS) estimator for panel data, a specific case of feasible GLS estimators. The FGLS estimator is consistent under the basic random effects assumptions; consequently it is generally used when dealing with simple forms of autocorrelation or groupwise heteroskedasticity (Wooldridge 2002, pp. 257–64) and appears appropriate to our data.

Table 9.5 reports the results of estimations. The model has a high explicative power. The results confirm how the provincial distribution of FDI inflows is primarily influenced by the level of development and by the dimension of the local market, as measured by resident population. Nevertheless, the number of firms, the proxy of R&D activities (*patents*), and the share of large firms result among the determinants of FDI. In all specifications the organized crime index is significant, and negatively correlated with FDI. Furthermore it is possible to observe how financial incentives to investment do not seem to influence the distribution of FDI, probably because such incentives are granted in greater measure to those firms that invest in the less developed areas of the country, and therefore this variable also tends to reflect some regional characteristics. To analyze the effects of crime more in depth, we have considered other specifications that included the incidence of theft and robberies and the rate of crimes against property (*Property crime*) as control variables. Table 9.6 reports the results of estimations. There is a negative, but not significant, correlation between these crimes and FDI, while the other explanatory variables maintain their significance and coefficient signs. This is not a surprising result: research

Table 9.5
Organized crime and FDI inflows

	(1)	(2)	(3)	(4)	(5)	(6)
Constant	−72.37**	−62.00**	−61.71**	−61.65**	−62.75**	−61.54**
	(−35.74)	(−22.18)	(−19.67)	(−19.57)	(−19.26)	(−17.88)
Organized crime	−0.039**	−0.046**	−0.046**	−0.047**	−0.047**	−0.042**
	(−2.39)	(−2.71)	(−2.69)	(−2.69)	(−2.75)	(−2.41)
GDP pc	5.831**	4.918**	4.901**	4.902**	5.029**	4.954**
	(29.87)	(19.12)	(18.20)	(18.17)	(17.56)	(15.38)
Population	1.952**	1.757**	1.745**	1.741**	1.757**	1.706**
	(33.97)	(24.55)	(18.94)	(18.81)	(18.86)	(16.67)
Big firms		0.463*	0.4845*	0.457	0.359	0.552
		(1.95)	(1.95)	(1.32)	(1.01)	(1.52)
Firms		0.0082**	0.0082**	0.0081**	0.0064**	0.0068**
		(3.08)	(3.07)	(3.00)	(2.13)	(2.26)
Patents		0.0029**	0.0029**	0.0029**	0.0030**	0.0031**
		(4.85)	(4.80)	(4.76)	(4.89)	(4.85)
Size			0.0006	0.0008	0.0003	0.0011
			(0.21)	(0.26)	(0.11)	(0.34)
Export				0.052	0.053	−0.102
				(0.11)	(0.11)	(−0.22)
Infrastructure					−0.001	−0.001
					(−1.29)	(−1.09)
Incentives						0.0001
						(0.103)
N	515	515	515	515	515	492
R^2 adjusted	0.86	0.87	0.87	0.87	0.87	0.88
ln L	−728.3	−724.6	−724.3	−724.3	−723.8	−690.5

Method: Groupwise WLS; t-statistics in parentheses. * indicates significance at the 10 percent level; ** indicates significance at the 5 percent level

Table 9.6
Crimes and FDI inflows

	(1)	(2)	(3)
Constant	−67.67**	−66.50**	−64.88**
	(−24.37)	(−24.81)	(−22.66)
GDP pc	5.369**	5.189**	5.033**
	(19.77)	(19.29)	(17.68)
Population	1.856**	1.891**	1.856**
	(24.82)	(20.91)	(24.42)
Big firms	0.4386*	0.5667**	0.7801**
	(1.72)	(2.36)	(2.86)
Firms	0.0089**	0.0088**	0.0115**
	(3.09)	(3.04)	(3.65)
Patents	0.0026**	0.0024**	0.0023**
	(4.50)	(4.02)	(3.73)
Infrastructure	−0.0011	−0.0010	−0.0011
	(−1.06)	(−0.97)	(−0.99)
Theft	−0.0007		
	(−1.57)		
Robberies		−0.0091	
		(−1.23)	
Property crime			−0.0002
			(−0.70)
n	515	515	442
R^2 adjusted	0.87	0.87	0.87
ln L	−725.5	−726.8	−622.3

Method: Groupwise WLS; t-statistics in parentheses. *indicates significance at the 10 percent level; **indicates significance at the 5 percent level

shows that the incidence of crime (excluding Mafia type) is generally higher in those areas with greater economic activity (Cracolici and Uberti 2009). In our analysis this suggests that not all crimes, only some crimes linked to the presence of a Mafia-type organization, tend to discourage potential investors.

9.5   Conclusion

Organized crime affects the legal economy in various ways: through extortion, by direct or indirect control of business, or simply by increasing the risks and the costs of business. This chapter studies the effects of organized crime on foreign investment, focusing on the case of Italy. The case of Italy is interesting for diverse reasons. First, in Italy there is a historical presence of organized crime of the Mafia type, rooted particularly in the southern regions. Second, Italy is characterized by profound regional disparities, and the presence of the Mafia is unanimously considered one of the main constraints to economic development in the less developed areas. Third, the south of Italy receives a very low share of FDI inflows.

Our analysis shows how, ceteris paribus, a higher presence of crime, especially of the Mafia type, significantly reduces foreign investment inflows. Such a correlation is significant, even when the regressions include a proxy of the financial incentives granted to firms that invest in the less developed areas. This result suggests that the presence of crime, a strong disincentive related to the socioeconomic environment, tends to reduce the effectiveness of development policies. Our analysis does not indicate the presence of crime as the main or the sole reason for the low attractiveness of the southern regions. FDI inflows are, of course, influenced by different economic and institutional determinants. The presence of the Mafia can be, however, considered a specific "comparative disadvantage" of the less developed regions.

Our results are consistent with some surveys that contain the opinions of potential foreign investors about opportunities for investing in southern Italy. Said surveys indicate in fact how the presence of organized crime is perceived by businessmen as a powerful block to investments in the Mezzogiorno. It is possible to observe how, in some areas, crime is only one aspect—certainly the most evident and dramatic—of a social and institutional context characterized by other forms of illegality that include corruption and, even more widespread, the violation of regulations necessary for the good functioning of the market (La Spina and Lo Forte 2006).

Our analysis does not exclude that a high incidence of crime, other than discouraging investment, can also be perceived as a signal of a socioinstitutional system unfavorable for business activities. This "signal effect" can be particularly important to potential foreign investors, who are generally less informed in respect to national investors. The magnitude of the effect of crime on firms' location decisions is probably amplified by investors' perceptions about the business climate quality in regions with a comparatively higher incidence of crime.

Although our analysis refers specifically to Italy, it is related to the international literature that indicates how institutional quality matters for firms' location decisions, and consequently for economic performances (Bénassy-Quéré et al. 2007). Our analysis is also related to the literature on the social costs of crime, in particular with those works that analyze the effects of crime on the legal economy and the enterprise sectors (Krkoska and Robeck 2006; Bonaccorsi di Patti 2009).

Policy implications are consequential. In the case of Italy, better security conditions (and the improvement of local socioeconomic contexts) would increase regional attractiveness to FDI, and probably the effectiveness of policies aimed at promoting regional development.

Appendix

Table A9.1
Description of variables and sources

Variables	Description	Sources
FDI	Average FDI inflow in the provinces in the period 2004 to 2006 (in logarithms). Data refer to the investment flows and do not include commercial credits and banking sector transactions.	Italian Exchange Office (UIC)
Population	Resident population in each Italian province (in logarithms). Proxy of the size of the local market.	Elaborated from ISTAT Census data.
GDPpc	GDP per capita (in logarithms). Proxy of the level of development.	Elaborated from ISTAT data.
Size	Provincial GDP on the GDP of Italy. Proxy of the size of the local market.	Elaborated from ISTAT data.
Incentives	Variable of proxy of the financial incentives granted to firms, given to the investment projects granted under the Law 488/92. Data refer to the projects for creating new production plants in the industrial sector (excluding "special industry" calls for proposals)	Ministry for Economic Development—Ipi-Print databank
Firms	Number of firms in nonagricultural sectors, per 1,000 inhabitants	Elaborated from ISTAT data.
Export	Total export on GDP	Elaborated from ISTAT data.
Patents	Number of European patents presented to the European Patent Office (EPO)	European Patent Office—Unioncamere
Big firm	Share of firms with more than 50 employees out of the total number of firms	Elaborated from ISTAT data.
Infrastructures	Synthetic index of infrastructure endowment (excluding ports) in percentage terms compared nationwide.	G. Tagliacarne Institute

Table A9.1
(continued)

Variables	Description	Sources
Extortion	Number of crimes of extortion denounced per 10,000 inhabitants.	Elaborated from ISTAT data, "Territorial Informative System on Justice" (online databank).
Association	Number of crimes of criminal association denounced, including "Mafia" association, per 10,000 inhabitants.	Idem
Attacks	Number of (bomb) attacks, per 10,000 inhabitants.	Idem
Arson	Number of cases of arson, per 10,000 inhabitants.	Idem
Theft	Number of thefts, per 10,000 inhabitants	Idem
Robberies	Number of robberies, per 10,000 inhabitants	
Organized crime	Sum of extortion, attacks, arson, association (as defined above), per 10,000 inhabitants.	Idem
Property crime	Total number of crime against property (with the exception of that included in the "organized crime index")	Idem

Acknowledgments

We thank Cláudia Costa Storti, Paul De Grauwe, and the participants at the CESifo Venice Summer Institute 2008 on "Illicit Trade and Globalization" for their comments to a previous version of this work. We also thank three anonymous referees for their invaluable comments and suggestions.

Notes

1. The term "Mafia" comprises different criminal organization: *camorra* is the name of Campania-based organized crime, *Cosa nostra* of Sicilian-based crime families, '*Ndrangheta* of Calabria-based crime families, and *Sacra Corona Unita* of the Apulia-based crime families.

2. For the French case, see Mayer (2004); for Spain, see Hermosilla and Ortega (2003); for Britain, see Devereux et al. (2007); and for Greece, see Kokkinou and Psycharis (2004).

3. According to the data contained within the Annual Report of the Parliamentary Commission of Inquest on criminal organizations (2008), in the area of the judicial district of

Catanzaro, in Calabria, companies that resist the pressures from organized crime are practically nonexistent; furthermore the report carries the denouncements made by the representative of a large tour operator, Parmatour, who declared that tourist resort villages in Calabria were systematically subject to extortion.

4. The issue of security and its importance for internal and external investments in the Mezzogiorno has long been part of the political and economic debate in Italy. Recently a series of events has made this issue one of the most urgent for development in southern Italy. The Federation of Anti-racket and Anti-usury Associations (FAI) has proposed the establishment of a "security tutor" for foreign firms interested in investing in the Mezzogiorno (FAI, *Anti-racket tutoring, Experimental three-year project*, Naples, December 12, 2007). One of the motivations behind the project was a declaration made by the president of the Italian Council of Ministers, on November 17, 2006: in effect, that organized crime represents a significant deterrent for foreign firms interested in investing in southern Italian regions. The governor of the Bank of Italy, Mario Draghi (Draghi 2011), also highlighted the social and economic effects of criminal infiltration in many economic sectors.

5. By definition, a direct investment enterprise is an incorporated enterprise in which a foreign investor owns 10 percent or more of the ordinary shares or voting power for an incorporated enterprise, or an unincorporated enterprise in which a foreign investor has equivalent ownership (IMF 2000).

References

Alegría, R. 2006. Countries, Regions and Multinational Firms: Location Determinants in the European Union. ERSA conference papers. European Regional Science Association.

Arlacchi, P. 2007. *La Mafia Imprenditrice. Dalla Calabria al centro dell'inferno*. Milano: Il Saggiatore.

Artige, L., and R. Nicolini. 2005. Evidence on the determinants of foreign direct investment: The Case of three European regions. UFAE and IAE working papers, available at http://www.ideas.repec.org/p/rpp/wpaper/0607.html.

Asmundo, A., and M. Lisciandra. 2008. Un tentativo di stima del costo delle estorsioni sulle imprese a livello regionale: Il caso Sicilia. In A. La Spina, ed., *I costi dell'illegalità. Mafia ed estorsioni in Sicilia*. Bologna: il Mulino.

Baltagi, B. H. 2008. *Econometric Analysis of Panel Data*. Chichester, UK: Wiley.

Barba Navaretti, G., and A. J. Venables. 2004. *Multinational Firms in the World Economy*. Princeton: Princeton University Press.

Barba Navaretti, G. R., B. L. Benfratello, and D. Castellani. 2009. Il Mezzogiorno e gli investimenti diretti esteri. Centro Studi Luca d'Agliano, Milano.

Barrios, S., H. Görg, and E. Strobl. 2003. Multinationals' location choice, agglomeration economies and public incentives. Discussion paper 17. CORE.

Basile, R. 2001. The locational determinants of foreign-owned manufacturing plants in Italy: The role of the south. Working paper 14/01. ISAE.

Basile, R. 2004. Acquisition versus greenfield investment: The location of foreign manufacturers in Italy. *Regional Science and Urban Economics* 1: 3–25.

Basile, R., D. Castellani, and A. Zanfei. 2008. Location choices of multinational firms in Europe: The role of EU cohesion policy. *Journal of International Economics* 2: 328–40.

Basile, R., D. Castellani, and A. Zanfei. 2009. National boundaries and the location of multinational firms in Europe. *Papers in Regional Science* 4: 733–48.

Bonaccorsi di Patti, E. 2009. Weak Institutions and Credit Availability: The Impact of Crime on Banks Loans. Questioni di Economia e Finanza 52. Roma: Banca d'Italia.

Bénassy-Quéré, A., M. Coupet M., and T. Mayer. 2007. Institutional determinants of foreign direct investment. *The World Economy* 30: 764-782 CEPII.

Brand, S., and R. Price. 2000. The economic and social costs of crime. Home Office Research Study 217. London.

Broadman, H., and F. Recanatini. 2000. Seeds of corruption: Do market institutions matter? Policy Research working paper 2368. World Bank.

Broadman, H., and F. Recanatini. 2001. Where has all the foreign investment gone in Russia? Policy Research working paper 2640. World Bank.

Bronzini, R. 2004. Distretti industriali, economie di agglomerazione e investimenti esteri in Italia. In Banca d'Italia, *Economie locali, modelli di agglomerazione e apertura internazionale.* Conference proceedings. Roma: Banca d'Italia: 355–88.

Buonanno, P. 2006. The socioeconomic determinants of crime: A review of the literature. Working paper 63. Economics Department, Università di Milano-Bicocca.

Catanzaro, R. 1991. *Il delitto come impresa. Storia sociale della Mafia.* Milano: Rizzoli.

Centorrino, M., and F. Ofria. 2008. Criminalità organizzata e produttività del lavoro nel Mezzogiorno: un'applicazione del modello 'Kaldor-Verdoorn.' *Rivista Economica del Mezzogiorno* 1: 163–89.

Centorrino, M., and G. Signorino. 1993. Criminalità e modelli di economia locale. In S. Zamagni, ed., *Mercati illegali e mafie. L'economia del crimine organizzato.* Bologna: il Mulino: 75–91.

Committeri, M. 2004. *Investire in Italia? Risultati di una recente indagine empirica.* Temi di discussione del Servizio Studi 491. Roma: Banca d'Italia.

Confesercenti. 2007. SOS Impresa. 10° Rapporto, Confersercenti, Roma.

CPI—Commissione parlamentare d'inchiesta sul fenomeno della criminalità mafiosa o similare. 2008. Relazione annuale sulla 'ndrangheta. Roma.

Cracolici, M. F., and T. E. Uberti. 2009. Geographical distribution of crime in Italian provinces: A spatial econometric analysis. *Jahrbuch für Regionalwissenschaft.* 29: 1–28.

Crozet, M., T. Mayer, and J. L. Mucchielli. 2004. How do firms agglomerate? A study for FDI in France. *Regional Science and Urban Economics* 1: 27–54.

Czabanski, J. 2008. *Estimates of Cost of Crime: History, Methodologies, and Implications.* Berlin: Springer.

Daniele, V. 2005. Perché le imprese estere non investono al Sud? *Rivista Economica del Mezzogiorno* 4: 795–818.

Daniele, V. 2009. Organized crime and regional development. A review of the Italian case. *Trends in Organized Crime* 12: 211–34.

Devereux, M. P., and R. Griffith. 2003. The impact of corporate taxation on the location of capital: A review. *Economic Analysis and Policy* 33: 275–92.

Devereux, M., R. Griffith, and H. Simpson. 2007. Firm location decisions, regional grants and agglomeration externalities. *Journal of Public Economics* 91: 413–35.

Draghi, M. 2011. Le mafie a Milano e nel Nord. Aspetti sociali ed economici, Intervento del Governatore della Banca d'Italia. Università di Milano. Speech notes available at http://www.bancaditalia.it/interventi/integov/2011/mafie-al-nord/draghi-110311 .pdf.

European Commission. 2006. *Study on FDI and Regional Development.* Final Report by Copenhagen Economics. Brussels: European Commission.

Gambetta, D. 1996. *The Sicilian Mafia: The Business of Private Protection.* Cambridge: Harvard University Press.

Globerman, S., and D. Shapiro. 2002. Global foreign direct investment flows: The role of governance infrastructure. *World Development* 30: 1899–1919.

GPF-ISPO. 2005. L'immagine del Mezzogiorno d'Italia in 11 Paesi del mondo. Market research conducted by GPF-ISPO for the Italian Ministry of Economics and Finance, Rome.

Habib, M., and L. Zurawicki. 2001. Country-level investment and the effect of corruption: Some empirical evidence. *International Business Review* 10: 687–700.

Hermosilla, A., and N. Ortega. 2003. Factores determinantes de las decisiones de inversión de las multinacionales industriales implantadas en Cataluña. Document d'Economia Industrial 13. Centre d'Economia Industrial.

IMF. 2000. Report on the survey of implementation of methodological standards for direct investment, Washington, DC.

IPI—Istituto per la Promozione Industriale. 2005. *Aree dei Consorzi Industriali censite dall'IPI nelle regioni dell'Obiettivo 1 e relativa disponibilità di terreni,* IPI—Dipartimento di economia applicata, Rome, 2005 (http://www.sifli.info).

Konings, J. 2004. The employment effects of foreign direct investment. *EIB Papers*, European Investment Bank, 9: 87–108.

Kokkinou, A., and I. Psycharis. 2004. Foreign direct investments, regional incentives and regional attractiveness in Greece. Discussion paper 10. Department of Planning and Regional Development, University of Thessaly.

Krkoska, L., and K. Robeck. 2006. The impact of crime on the enterprise sector: Transition versus non-transition countries. Working paper 97. European Bank for Reconstruction and Development.

La Spina, A., ed. 2008. *I costi dell'illegalità: Mafia ed estorsioni in Sicilia.* Bologna: Il Mulino.

La Spina A., and G. Lo Forte. 2006. I costi dell'illegalità. *Rivista economica del Mezzogiorno* (3–4): 509–70.

Lampe von. K. 2004. Measuring organized crime: A critique of current approach. In P. C. Van Duyne, M. Jager, K. von Lampe, and J. L. Newell eds., *Threats and Phantoms of Organized Crime, Corruption and Terrorism.* Nijmegen: Wolf Legal, pp. 85–116.

Mayer, T. 2004. Where do foreign firms locate in France and why. *EIB Papers*. European Investment Bank 9: 38–61.

Mariotti, S., and M. Mutinelli. 2005. *Italia multinazionale 2005. Le partecipazioni italiane all'estero ed estere in Italia.* Rome: ICE—Istituto Nazionale per il Commercio Estero.

Marini, D., and F. Turato. 2002. Nord-Est e Mezzogiorno: Nuove relazioni, vecchi stereotipi. Rapporti Formez-Fondazione Nord-Est.

Marselli R., and M. Vannini. 2003. What is the impact of unemployment on crime rates? In M. Baldassarri and B. Chiarini, eds., *Studies in Labour Markets and Industrial Relations.* Basingstoke: Palgrave Macmillan, pp. 207–30.

Olson, M. 1984. *Einaudi Notizie.* Circolare ai soci della Fondazione Einaudi. Rome.

Paoli, L. 2004. Italian organised crime: Mafia associations and criminal enterprises. *Global Crime* 1: 19–31.

Pelegrìn, A., and C. Bolancé. 2008. Regional foreign direct investment in manufacturing. Do agglomeration economies matter?" *Regional Studies* 4: 505–22.

Peri, G. 2004. Socio-cultural variables and economic success: Evidence from Italian provinces 1951–1991. *Berkeley Electronic Journal, Topics in Macroeconomics* 1, art. 12.

Sylos Labini, P. 1985. L'evoluzione economica del Mezzogiorno negli ultimi trent'anni. Discussion paper 46. Banca d'Italia, Roma.

United Nations. 2007. *Crime and Development in Central America: Caught in the Crossfire.* United Nations Office on Drugs and Crime. New York: United Nations.

Wei, S. J. 2000. Local corruption and global capital flows. *Brookings Papers on Economic Activity* 2000: 303–54.

Wooldridge, J. M. 2002. *Econometric Analysis of Cross Section and Panel Data.* Cambridge: MIT Press.

World Bank. 2002. *Building Institutions for Markets: World Development Report 2002.* Oxford: Oxford University Press.

Zamagni, S., ed. 1993. Mercati illegali e mafie. *L'economia del crimine organizzato.* Bologna: Il Mulino.

10 The War on Illegal Drugs in Producer and Consumer Countries: A Simple Analytical Framework

Daniel Mejía and Pascual Restrepo

10.1 Introduction

During the last decade there has been a drastic intensification of the war against cocaine production and trafficking, not only in Latin American producer countries but also in some main consumer countries, such as the United States. For instance, in Colombia, where roughly 70 percent of the cocaine consumed in the world is produced, over the last eight years, the United States and the Colombia have allocated huge amounts of resources to combat production and trafficking under the so-called Plan Colombia.[1] According to the Colombian National Planning Department (DNP 2006), between 2000 and 2005, the US government spent roughly 3.8 billion USD in subsidies to the Colombian government for its war against illegal drug producers and traffickers. Colombia for its part spent about 6.9 billion USD during the same period. About half of the Colombian expenses (amounting to about 3.4 billion USD) and about three-quarters of the US subsidies (about 2.8 billion USD) have gone directly to financing the military component of the war against drug production, trafficking, and targeting the organized criminal organizations associated with these activities (DNP 2006, tab. 2). Nevertheless, most available measures show that the availability of cocaine in consumer countries has not gone down significantly, nor has the price of cocaine shown any tendency to increase, as one might expect given the intensification of the war on drugs (see Mejía and Posada 2010). While the number of hectares of coca crops cultivated in Colombia has decreased from about 163.000 in 2000 to about 80.000 in 2006—as a result of intense aerial eradication campaigns—potential cocaine production in Colombia has only decreased from 695,000 kilograms per year in 2000 (right before the initiation of Plan Colombia) to roughly 610,000 kilograms per year in 2006 (see

UNODC 2007).[2] Consistent with the observed data just described on potential cocaine production and the relatively stable figures for consumption trends, the price of cocaine at the wholesale and retail levels in consumer countries has remained relatively stable since 2000.[3]

In the United States, where about half of the cocaine produced in the world is consumed, the federal government currently spends close to 12.5 billion USD each year on different components of the war on drugs. Approximately 7.7 billion USD (about 60 percent) is spent on policies aimed at reducing the supply of illegal drugs, among them domestic law enforcement, interdiction and the provision of subsidies to drug producer countries. The other 4.8 billion USD (about 40 percent) is spent on policies aimed at reducing the demand for drugs, among them, prevention campaigns and the treatment of drug addicts (see ONDCP 2007, tab. 1).

This chapter develops a simple model of the war against illegal drugs in producer and consumer countries that accounts for strategic interaction among the actors involved in this war. These actors include an illegal drug producer and trafficker, the government of the drug producer country, the government of the drug consumer country, and a wholesale drug dealer located along the border of the consumer country. We explicitly model the (wholesale) illegal drug market, which allows us to account for the feedback effects between anti-drug policies and market outcomes (quantities and prices) likely to arise as a consequence of such large-scale policy interventions as Plan Colombia.

In the producer country the government comes into conflict with the drug producer and trafficker over the fraction of illegal drugs successfully produced and exported to the consumer country. In modeling the conflict between the government and the drug producer and trafficker, we abstract from explicitly modeling the conflict over the control of arable land necessary for the cultivation of illicit crops.[4]

Following the analysis of Grossman and Mejía (2008), we assume that the drug consumer country's government uses both sticks and carrots to strengthen the resolve of the drug producer country's government in its war against illegal drugs. Additionally the drug consumer country's government uses prevention policies and provides subsidies to the drug producer country's government in an attempt to minimize the amount of illegal drugs transacted in the market. While the former are aimed at reducing the demand for drugs through educational campaigns and by providing treatment to drug addicts, the latter aim at reducing the supply of illegal drugs coming from the drug producer country.

Importantly, we study how anti-drug policies implemented in consumer and producer countries interact and affect one another's effectiveness. Our analysis shows how the equilibrium allocation of resources between these two alternative policies crucially depends on the price elasticity of the demand for illegal drugs in the consumer country; on the effectiveness of prevention and treatment policies in reducing the demand for illegal drugs; and on the effectiveness of anti-drug policies in the producer country. In particular, we show how the relative allocation of resources to subsidies for the war on drugs in producer countries should be smaller when the following conditions exist: the demand for illegal drugs is relatively inelastic; prevention and treatment policies are relatively more effective; and the anti-drug policies being implemented in producer countries are relatively less effective.

We calibrate the model using the available data on the cocaine markets as well as data on the war against cocaine production, trafficking and consumption in Colombia and the United States This calibration exercise allows us to recover some important unobservable parameters, such as the relative effectiveness of interdiction efforts, the effectiveness of prevention policies in reducing the demand for cocaine, and the cost facing Colombia from illegal drug production and trafficking activities.

One of this chapter's main contributions is that it provides a formal analytical framework for understanding the interaction between anti-drug policies implemented in producer and consumer countries. Importantly, by explicitly modeling the illegal drug market, we are able to account for the feedback effects between policies and market outcomes likely to arise as a result of large-scale policy interventions, such as those implemented under the war on drugs in producer and consumer countries. While there have been some important attempts at developing models of the war on drugs in producer countries (Grossman and Mejía 2008; Mejía and Restrepo 2008) and consumer countries (e.g., Becker, Grossman and Murphy 2006; Rydell et al. 1996; Caulkins 1993), there is no model in the literature that studies the interaction between anti-drug policies implemented in both consumer and producer countries. An important exception is the recent contribution by Chumacero (2006), who develops a dynamic general equilibrium model of the war against illegal crops cultivation, on the one hand, and that against illegal drug production, trafficking and consumption, on the other.[5] His main contribution relies on the calibration of some of the key parameters of the model, that are then used to assess the effects of three alternative policies—making illegal activities riskier, increasing the penalties for illegal activities, and legalization.

The rest of the chapter consists of four sections. Section 10.2 constitutes the core of the chapter, develops the model, and explains the motivations and choices of the actors involved in the war on drugs. This section also derives the equilibrium of the model. Section 10.3 presents the results of the calibration of the model using the available data on the cocaine market, some key figures reflective of the war against cocaine production and trafficking in Colombia, and data on the allocation of resources for prevention and treatment policies in the United States. Section 10.4 concludes.

10.2 The Model

We model the war against illegal drugs as a sequential game. In the first stage of the game, the drug consumer country's government chooses the optimal allocation of resources between prevention and treatment policies, on the one hand, and enforcement policies, on the other. The enforcement policies take the form of a subsidy the drug producer country's government in order to strengthen its resolve in the war against illegal drug production and trafficking. Both sets of policies have the same objective, namely to reduce the amount of illegal drugs transacted in the consumer country at the wholesale level. While prevention and treatment policies target a reduction in demand, enforcement policies (subsidies to the producer country's government) aim at thwarting the availability of drugs in the consumer country—that is, at reducing the supply of illegal drugs. In the second stage of the game, the drug producer country's government comes into conflict with drug producers and traffickers over the fraction of illegal drugs successfully exported.

We start with the second stage of the game—that is, with the conflict between the drug producer country's government and the illegal drug producer and trafficker over the fraction of illegal drugs successfully produced and exported.

10.2.1 The Drug-Trafficking Game

The Interdiction Technology Let q be the fraction of drugs that survive the government's interdiction efforts. The interdiction technology is such that q is determined endogenously by a standard contest success function,[6]:

$$q = \frac{s}{s + \varphi r}, \tag{10.1}$$

where r is the amount of resources the government invests in the interdiction of drug shipments (radars, airplanes, speed boats, etc.), s is the amount of resources that the drug trafficker invests in trying to avoid the interdiction of drug shipments (submarines, speed boats, airplanes, etc.), and $\varphi > 0$ is a parameter capturing the relative effectiveness of the resources invested by the government in trying to interdict illegal drug shipments. Note that the fraction q of illegal drugs that the drug trafficker successfully exports (equation 10.1) is an increasing and concave function of the ratio

$$\frac{s}{\varphi r}.$$

The Drug Trafficker The problem of the drug trafficker is to choose the amount of resources to invest in trying to avoid the interdiction of drug shipments so as to maximize his profits, π_T. More precisely, the drug trafficker's problem is given by

$$\max_{\{s\}} \pi_T = p_c q \lambda L - s. \tag{10.2}$$

The first term in equation (10.2) is the price of drugs at the border of the consumer country, p_c, times the fraction of drugs that survives interdiction efforts, q, times the amount of drugs produced in the consumer country, λL. This last term is the product of the productivity per hectare of land per year, λ (e.g., the number of kilograms of illegal drugs that can be produced through the cultivation of the illegal crop on one hectare of land in one year[7]), times the number of hectares of land under the drug producer's control, L.[8] The last term, s, denotes the amount of resources invested by the drug trafficker in trying to avoid the interdiction of illegal drug shipments.[9]

The first-order condition of the drug trafficker's problem in equation (10.2) is

$$\frac{\partial \pi_T}{\partial s} = 0 \Leftrightarrow \frac{\varphi r}{(s + \varphi r)^2} p_c \lambda L = 1. \tag{10.3}$$

Equation (10.3) describes the best reaction function of the drug trafficker to every possible choice of resources employed by the government in its interdiction efforts, r.

The Drug Producer Country's Government Following Grossman and Mejía (2008), we assume that the drug consumer country's government uses both sticks and carrots in attempting to strengthen the resolve of the drug producer country's government in its war against illegal drugs. The stick is the threat that the interested outsider will label the country a narco-state, resulting in its being ostracized by the international community.

Let us assume that from the perspective of the drug producer country's government, the drug consumer country's decision to apply the label narco-state includes a stochastic element.[10] To allow for this stochastic element, we assume that the drug producer country's government perceives the probability of its being labeled a narco-state to be equal to the ratio $D/\lambda L$, where λL is the amount of drugs that could potentially be produced and exported annually, and $D = q\lambda L$ is the actual production and exportation of illegal drugs. Let c denote the annual cost in dollars that the drug producer country's government anticipates would result from being labeled a narco-state. Thus the expected annual cost associated with the possibility of being labeled a narco-state equals the product of c and q $(D/\lambda L = q)$.

The carrot employed by the drug consumer country is the subsidizing of the drug producer country's armed forces. This subsidy is a fraction, $1 - \omega$, of the resources that the drug producer country allocates to interdicting drug shipments, r.

The objective of the drug producer country's government is to minimize the sum of the costs associated with illegal drug production and trafficking. These costs are given by the sum of the expected cost of being labeled a narco-state and the cost of fighting the war against drug production and trafficking. They equal the amount of resources invested by the government in interdiction efforts, r, times the fraction actually paid by the government, ω. The problem for the drug producer country's government is

$$\min_{\{r\}} C_T = cq + \omega r, \tag{10.4}$$

where q is determined by equation (10.1).

The first-order condition for the government's problem is given by

$$\frac{\partial C_T}{\partial r} = 0 \Leftrightarrow \frac{-\varphi s}{(s + \varphi r)^2} c + \omega = 0. \tag{10.5}$$

Equation (10.5) is the government's best reaction function to every possible choice of resources employed by the drug trafficker in avoiding the interdiction of illegal drug shipments, s.

10.2.2   The Drug-Trafficking Equilibrium

Using equations (10.3) and (10.5), we can find a locus of points in the space $(r/s, p_c)$ for which the drug-trafficking game is in equilibrium[11].

Definition 1 (GE Locus)   All pairs $(r/s, p_c)$ that satisfy the following expression represent possible equilibria for the drug-trafficking game:

$$\frac{r}{s} = \frac{c}{p_c \lambda L \omega}.$$ (10.6)

According to the expression for the GE locus, a higher price for the illegal drug in the consumer country will lead to lower relative spending by the drug producer country's government on the war on drugs. This is so because a larger p_c increases the marginal returns for the drug trafficker of allocating resources to avoiding interdiction; this naturally induces the trafficker to fight relatively harder than the government.[12]

Using the expression (10.6), and inserting it into the drug trafficker's reaction function (equation 10.3), we are able to derive an explicit expression for the government's and the drug trafficker's level of expenses in the war on drugs (both as functions of the parameters of the model and the price of drugs in the consumer country, yet to be determined). These two allocations are given respectively by

$$r = \frac{\varphi c^2 (\lambda L \omega p_c)^2}{\lambda L \omega^2 p_c (\lambda L \omega p_c + \varphi c)^2}$$ (10.7)

and

$$s = \frac{\varphi c (\lambda L \omega p_c)^2}{\omega (\lambda L \omega p_c + \varphi c)^2}.$$ (10.8)

In turn, if we insert r and s from equations (10.7) and (10.8) into equation (10.1), the fraction of illegal drugs that survives the government's interdiction efforts in equilibrium (i.e., the fraction of drugs exported successfully) is given by

$$q = \frac{\lambda L \omega p_c}{\lambda L \omega p_c + \varphi c}.$$ (10.9)

The fraction of drugs that survives the government's interdiction efforts is an increasing and concave function of the price of drugs; of the fraction of the drug producer's government's expenses paid for interdiction efforts, ω; and of potential cocaine production, λL. A higher relative efficiency in the government's interdiction efforts, φ, or a larger cost for being labeled a narco-state, c, decreases the fraction of drugs successfully exported.

We now turn to a description of the drug market equilibrium.

10.2.3   The Drug Market Equilibrium

First, let us assume that the demand for drugs along the border of the consumer country is given by a general demand function of the form:

$$Q_c^d = \frac{a(l)}{p_c^b}, \tag{10.10}$$

where Q_c^d denotes the demand for drugs by drug dealers along the border of the consumer country, and $a(l) \geq 0$, with l denoting the allocation of resources to prevention policies (educational campaigns, treatment programs for drug addicts, etc.) aimed at reducing the demand for illegal drugs in the consumer country. Naturally we assume that $a'(l) < 0$—that is, as more resources are allocated to prevention and treatment policies, the demand for illegal drugs decreases (i.e., the demand for drugs shifts to the left). Here p_c is the price of illegal drugs along the border of the consumer country, and b is the price elasticity of demand for illegal drugs at the wholesale level along the border of the consumer country.

Second, the supply of drugs in the consumer country is given by

$$Q_c^s = \frac{s}{s + \varphi r} \lambda L. \tag{10.11}$$

According to equation (10.11), the supply of drugs in the consumer country is equal to potential drug production, λL, multiplied by the fraction of the production not interdicted, q (see equation 10.1). Note that equation (10.11) expresses the supply of drugs in the consumer country as a function of the ratio of the expenses for the war on drugs in the producer country, r/s.

In the drug market equilibrium, we must have $Q_c^d = Q_c^s$. Equating expressions (10.10) and (10.11) and rearranging them, we are now able to define a locus of points in the space $(r/s, p_c)$ for which the illegal drug market along the border of the consumer country is in equilibrium.

Definition 2 (ME Locus)   All pairs $(r/s, p_c)$ satisfying the following expression represent possible equilibria of the drug market along the border of the consumer country:

$$\frac{r}{s} = \frac{\lambda L p_c^b}{\varphi a(l)} - \frac{1}{\varphi}. \tag{10.12}$$

In contrast with the GE locus, under the ME locus, a higher price for illegal drugs along the border of the consumer country will lead to greater relative spending by the drug producer country's government on the war on drugs. This positive relationship between the ratio of spending on the war on drugs and the price of illegal drugs in the consumer country arises because a higher ratio, r/s, means a smaller supply of drugs; given the demand, the price of illegal drugs, p_c, has to increase in order for the drug market to remain in equilibrium.

We can now use both loci described above to graphically represent the equilibrium of the second stage of the game. Recall that the GE locus describes all pairs of points $(r/s, p_c)$ for which the drug-trafficking game is in equilibrium, while the ME locus describes all pairs of points $(r/s, p_c)$ for which the drug market is in equilibrium. The two loci are represented in figure 10.1.

We can now study how changes in the structural parameters of the model shift each of the two loci, and how these changes in turn change the relative allocation of resources for the war on drugs and the price of illegal drugs. At this point we focus on changes in the allocation of resources with respect to prevention and treatment policies, as well as enforcement policies in the form of subsidies to the drug producer country's government (which will be the focus of our analysis once we turn to the analysis of the first stage of the game). Figure 10.2 shows how the price of illegal drugs and the relative spending on the war on drugs change as l increases. Figure 10.3 shows the effect of a decrease in ω (an increase in the subsidy to the drug producer country's armed forces in its war against illegal drug production and trafficking). While an increase in spending in the consumer country on prevention policies aimed at reducing consumption reduces the equilibrium price of drugs and increases the government's relative spending on the war on drugs (thereby reducing the equilibrium fraction of drugs successfully

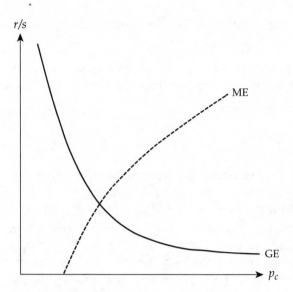

Figure 10.1
Drug trafficking and drug market equilibrium loci

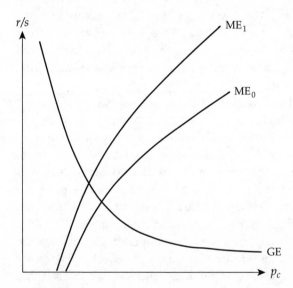

Figure 10.2
Effect of an increase in treatment and prevention policies on the ME locus

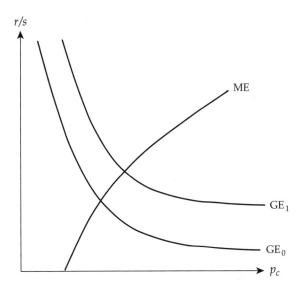

Figure 10.3
Effect of an increase in the subsidy on the GE locus

exported), an increase in the subsidy increases the equilibrium price of drugs at the consumer country's border and the producer county's government's relative spending on the war on drugs. Note that an increase in the subsidy generates two opposing forces on the ratio, r/s —it increases the price of illegal drugs and thus increases the drug trafficker's incentives to invest resources in evading interdiction (as the price of drugs increases); it also increases the drug producer country's incentives to invest resources on the war on drugs, as the marginal cost of doing so goes down. The net effect is an increase in the ratio, r/s (as shown in figure 10.3). Importantly, an increase in the subsidy provides by the drug consumer country induces an increase in the total resources invested on the war on drugs, $r + s$—that is, an increase in the subsidy to the drug producer country increases the intensity of the conflict as measured by the sum of resources invested by the two actors involved in this war.

A representation of the equilibrium of the model in terms of the two loci described above is helpful for understanding how changes in the parameters of the model affect the relative allocation of resources to the war on drugs and, correspondingly, the fraction of drugs successfully exported. However, the equilibrium of the model can also be represented using a standard supply and demand framework. From

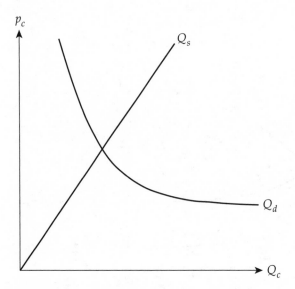

Figure 10.4
Drug market equilibrium (supply and demand)

equation (10.9) the supply of drugs along the consumer country's
border (i.e., the supply of drugs net of interdiction) is given by

$$Q_c^s = \frac{(\lambda L)^2 \omega p_c}{\lambda L \omega p_c + \varphi c}. \tag{10.13}$$

In turn the demand for drugs is given by equation (10.10). The graphical representation of the equilibrium at this stage of the game, represented in a simple supply and demand framework, is depicted in
figure 10.4.

Solving for p_c in both expressions and making $Q_c^s = Q_c^d$, the equilibrium quantity of drugs is determined by the following implicit equation, which depends on the parameters of the model as well as on the
two choice variables for the drug consumer country's government,
l and ω (yet to be determined in the next subsection):

$$F(Q_c, l, \omega) = Q_c^{(1+b)/b} \varphi c + a(l)^{1/b} \lambda L \omega (Q_c - \lambda L) = 0. \tag{10.14}$$

Using the expression for the equilibrium quantity of drugs in the
second stage of the game, we are now able to determine the sign of the
effect of changes in the parameters of the model on the equilibrium
quantity of drugs. The following are the main comparative statics
results at this stage:

$$\frac{\partial Q_c}{\partial l} = \frac{-\partial F/\partial l}{\partial F/\partial Q_c} \leq 0.$$

An increase in prevention policies aimed at reducing the demand for drugs in the drug consumer country decreases the amount of illegal drugs transacted in equilibrium. On the one hand, $\partial F/\partial Q_c > 0$; on the other, $\partial F/\partial l > 0$. This is because $Q_c - \lambda L < 0$. Recall that λL is potential drug production whereas Q_c is the amount of drugs transacted in equilibrium. With at least some interdiction (i.e., where $q < 1$, as is in fact the case in equilibrium; see equation 10.9), the amount of drugs transacted in equilibrium is always less than potential drug production. Conversely, a decrease in l (i.e., an increase in a) increases the amount of illegal drugs transacted. We elaborate more on this point in the next section of the chapter, when we consider the optimal allocation of resources to prevention policies in the drug consumer country:

$$\frac{\partial Q_c}{\partial \omega} = \frac{-\partial F/\partial \omega}{\partial F/\partial Q_c} \geq 0.$$

A decrease in subsidies to the drug producer country in its war against illegal drugs (i.e., a lower $1 - \omega$) increases the quantity of illegal drugs transacted in equilibrium. Again, this result follows from the fact that $Q_c - \lambda L < 0$. Intuitively, a larger marginal cost for the drug producer country's interdiction efforts will induce its government to spend less resource on the interdiction of drug shipments. As a result the supply of drugs to the consumer country (net of interdiction) will increase. Again, this point will be elaborated in more detail in the next section of the chapter.

$$\frac{\partial Q_c}{\partial \varphi} = \frac{-\partial F/\partial \varphi}{\partial F/\partial Q_c} \leq 0$$

and

$$\frac{\partial Q_c}{\partial c} = \frac{-\partial F/\partial c}{\partial F/\partial Q_c} \leq 0.$$

An increase either in the relative efficiency of the drug producer country's government in its war on drugs or in the cost to the drug producer country of being labeled a narco-state will lead to a negative shift in the supply of drugs. This is because the drug producer country's government will allocate relatively more resources to its interdiction efforts.

As a result the equilibrium fraction of drugs successfully exported (equation 10.9) will decrease:

$$\frac{\partial Q_c}{\partial \lambda} = \frac{-\partial F/\partial \lambda}{\partial F/\partial Q_c} \geq 0$$

and

$$\frac{\partial Q_c}{\partial L} = \frac{-\partial F/\partial L}{\partial F/\partial Q_c} \geq 0.$$

An increase in λ, the productivity per hectare of land used in the cultivation of illegal crops, or an increase in L, the land under the control of drug producers, will increase the amount of drugs produced and exported in equilibrium. An increase in productivity or in the amount of land controlled by drug producers shifts the supply curve outward. As a result the price of drugs goes down and the quantity of drugs in equilibrium goes up.

    We now turn to an analysis of the first stage of the game—that is, the stage at which a choice is made between prevention policies and policies aimed at curtailing the supply of drugs by increasing subsidies for the drug producer country's interdiction efforts.

10.2.4   Anti-drug Policies in the Consumer Country: Prevention and Treatment versus a Supply Reduction in Producer Countries

In the first stage of the game, the objective of the drug consumer country's government is to minimize the amount of illegal drugs transacted along its border. To achieve its objective, the drug consumer country carries out prevention and treatment policies aimed at reducing the demand for illegal drugs, together with enforcement policies, in the form of subsidies to the armed forces of the drug producer country in its war against illegal drug production and trafficking.

    More formally, the objective of the drug consumer country's government is

$$\min_{\{l,d\}} Q_c \quad \text{subject to} \quad l + d = M \quad \text{and} \quad d = (1 - \omega)r^-, \tag{10.15}$$

where Q_c is the quantity of illegal drugs transacted along the border of the consumer country in equilibrium; M is the consumer country's total budget for treatment and prevention and supply reduction policies; l is the allocation of resources to prevention policies (i.e., to the reduction of demand); and d is the total amount of resources that the drug consumer country grants to the drug producer country in the form of subsidies to finance its expenses in the war against illegal drug trafficking. The total amount of subsidies, d, is equal to the marginal subsidy, $1 - \omega$, times the resources spent by the drug producer country on its war against drug production and trafficking, r^-—that is, d is the total amount of resources allocated by the drug consumer country's government to reducing the supply of illegal drugs coming from the drug producer country.

Using equations (10.7) and (10.13), and the fact that $d = (1 - \omega)r^-$, we can solve for ω in terms of the model's parameters, the total amount of subsidies provided by the drug consumer country's government, d, and the quantity of illegal drugs transacted, Q_c:

$$\omega = \frac{cQ_c[1-(Q_c/\lambda L)]/\lambda L}{d+\{cQ_c[1-(Q_c/\lambda L)]/\lambda L\}}. \tag{10.16}$$

Inserting the expression for ω obtained in equation (10.16) into equation (10.14) allows us to express the quantity of drugs transacted in equilibrium (i.e., the equilibrium level Q_c) as a function of the model's parameters and the two instruments of the drug consumer country's government, l and d, through the following implicit function:

$$S(Q_c,1,d) = Q_c^{(1+b)/b}\varphi c + a(l)^{1/b}\lambda L \frac{cQ_c[1-(Q_c/\lambda L)]/\lambda L}{d+\{cQ_c[1-(Q_c/\lambda L)]/\lambda L\}} = 0. \tag{10.17}$$

Using the implicit function in equation (10.17)—which defines the equilibrium quantity of illegal drugs as a function of the two instruments of the drug consumer country's government—we have that the optimal allocation of resources between prevention and enforcement policies is determined by the optimality condition[13]

$$\frac{\partial Q_c}{\partial l} = \frac{\partial Q_c}{\partial d} \rightarrow \frac{\partial S(Q_c,l,d)}{\partial l} = \frac{\partial S(Q_c,l,d)}{\partial d} \tag{10.18}$$

Intuitively, the optimally condition in equation (10.18) states that the drug consumer country's government will adjust the allocation of resources between prevention and deterrence policies until the two are equally effective at the margin in reducing Q_c, or equivalently, until the marginal cost of reducing Q_c by one kilo through subsidizing deterrence policies is exactly equal to the marginal cost of reducing Q_c by one kilo through an investment in treatment and prevention.

We derive the expressions for

$$\frac{\partial S(.)}{\partial l}$$

and

$$\frac{\partial S(.)}{\partial d}$$

from equation (10.17), and the optimality condition in equation (10.18) becomes (after some algebraic manipulations)

$$\frac{1}{b}\frac{a'(l)}{a(l)} = -\frac{1}{d+cq(1-q)}. \tag{10.19}$$

In order to find a close form solution to the problem of the drug consumer country's problem, let us assume that

$$a(l) = \frac{A}{l^\theta}, \tag{10.20}$$

where $A > 0$, and $\theta > 0$ is a parameter capturing the efficiency of prevention and treatment policies in reducing the demand for drugs. More precisely, the parameter θ captures the percentage reduction in the demand for drugs as a result of a 1 percent increase in treatment and prevention policies.

We use the functional form for $a(l)$ from equation (10.20) so that the optimality condition in equation (10.19) becomes

$$\frac{\theta}{b} = \frac{l}{d+cq(1-q)}. \tag{10.21}$$

This equation implies that if θ is big and b small—such that prevention policies are very effective at reducing demand and demand is very inelastic—then prevention policies become more effective at the margin in reducing Q_c. However, if θ is low and b is large—such that prevention policies are not very effective at reducing demand and demand is more elastic—then deterrence policies become more effective at the margin in reducing Q_c. The point that b reduces the effectiveness of supply reduction policies relative to prevention policies is consistent with the previous findings by Becker et al. (2006). We refer to the right-hand side expression of equation (10.21) as the critical value for θ/b.

Values of θ/b larger than this threshold imply a reallocation of resources from supply reduction to treatment and prevention policies; values below this threshold imply a reallocation of resources from treatment and prevention to supply reduction policies.

10.3   Calibration Strategy and Results

In this section we use data from the cocaine market at the wholesale level, as well as available data on the outcomes of Plan Colombia, in order to calibrate the unobservable parameters of the model.

Table 10.1 briefly describes some of the data used in calibrating the model's parameters.[14] We use the average for all outcomes of the war on drugs in Colombia and the United States, as well as the outcomes from the wholesale cocaine market between 2005 and 2008, in order to calibrate the parameters of the model. Although we don't have a direct estimate for the US allocation of resources to prevention and treatment policies aimed at reducing the demand for cocaine, we do know the total amount of resources spent by the US government on policies aimed at reducing the demand for illegal drugs—about 3.8 billion USD in 2006 (see ONDCP 2007). We assume that roughly 7 percent of these resources (or about 250 million USD) were spent in the reduction of cocaine consumption.[15]

Table 10.1
Data used in the calibration exercise

Definition	Variable	Observed	Source
Drug seizures[a] (kgs)	$(1-q)\lambda L$	127,000	UNODC
Cocaine price/kg at the US border (USD/kg)	p_c	32,400	UNODC
Colombian cocaine in the wholesale market	Q_c	445,000	UNODC
US budget for prevention (USD)	l	250 million	ONDCP 2007
US budget for Plan Colombia[b] (USD)	d	593 million	GAO 2008
Hectares of land with coca crops (has)	L	86,000	UNODC
Kilos of cocaine/hectare/year (kg)	λ	6.66	UNODC
Colombian expenditures on the war on drugs	ωr	561.6 million	DNP

Note: All numbers are averages for the year 2005, 2006, 2007, and 2008.
a. Seizures adjusted by assuming 70 percent purity.
b. See Mejía and Restrepo (2008) for an explanation of how this number was constructed.

Using the equilibrium value for the observations in our data, we are able to jointly calibrate θ, φ, ω, A, and c (see the appendix for details of the calibration procedure). We assume that the price elasticity of the demand for drugs at the wholesale level, b, is 0.65.[16] However, θ is estimated on the assumption that the United States allocates resources optimally between treatment and prevention, on the one hand, and supply reduction policies in Colombia, on the other—that is, assuming that θ/b equals the critical ratio defined by equation (10.21). We also present the estimated value for this threshold as a useful policy measure, in the event that the United States has not allocated subsidies optimally. In such cases and given an empirical estimation of θ, one would only have to compare θ/b to the actual ratio in order to determine if more resources should be allocated to treatment and prevention, or to policies aimed at reducing the supply in producer countries. Table 10.2 presents the results from the calibration exercise, together with the confidence intervals for each point estimate.

According to the results presented in table 10.2, θ, the parameter capturing the efficiency of prevention policies in reducing the demand for cocaine in the United States, is estimated to be about 0.14. This parameter can be interpreted as the percentage of reduction in the demand for cocaine at the wholesale level that results following a 1

Table 10.2
Calibration results

Parameter	Value
b	0.65
θ	0.14
	(0.11–0.18)
Critical ratio, θ/b	0.22
	(0.18–0.26)
φ	0.79
	(0.50–1.23)
ω	0.49
	(0.43–0.54)
c	3.3 billion USD
	(2.5–4.2 m)
A	5.8×10^9
	($1.1 \times 10^9 - 33.0 \times 10^9$)

Note: 90 percent confidence intervals constructed from 10.000 Monte Carlo simulations are shown below each estimate in square brackets.

percent increase in the resources devoted to prevention and treatment policies. In other words, we estimate that a 1 percent increase in the funding of prevention and treatment policies would decrease the demand for illegal drugs at the wholesale level by about 0.14 percent. The critical ratio for θ/b for current expenditure levels is estimated to be 0.22. This estimate implies that if (contrary to our assumption about the optimal allocation of resources) $\theta \geq 0.22b$, then the United States should reallocate resources away from supply reduction efforts and toward prevention policies; conversely, if the opposite holds, then the US government should reallocate resources from prevention to supply reduction policies in producer countries in order to reduce Q_c.[17]

The parameter φ, which captures the relative efficiency of the drug producer country's government's efforts on the war on drugs, is calibrated at about 0.79. Conversely, the resources spent by drug producers and traffickers on the war on drugs are 1.27 times more efficient $(1/0.79)$ than those invested by the drug producer country's government.

Our estimate for ω implies that the United States has funded about 51 percent $(1 - \omega)$ of Colombian (military) expenses on the war on drugs.

We calibrate the cost to the Colombian government of being labeled a narco-state, c, to be about 3.3 billion USD, about 2 percent of current Colombian GDP. This number lies within the range of the variable assumed in Grossman and Mejía (2008) and is in line with the total cost perceived by the Colombian government due to drug production and trafficking activities (see Mejía and Restrepo 2008).

Finally, in order to check the robustness of the results just described, we conduct 10,000 Monte Carlo simulations by adding random perturbations to the data used in the baseline calibration exercise. Using these simulations, we create a 90 percent confidence interval for each of the estimated parameters. Figure 10.5 presents the distribution of point estimates for all the calibrated parameters, along with the 90 percent confidence intervals (the areas in dark gray).

10.4   The Costs of the War on Drugs and the Interaction between Supply and Demand Reduction Policies

Assuming that resources are optimally allocated, the marginal cost to the United States of reducing Q_c by one kilogram by subsidizing supply reduction policies in Colombia should be the same as the marginal cost

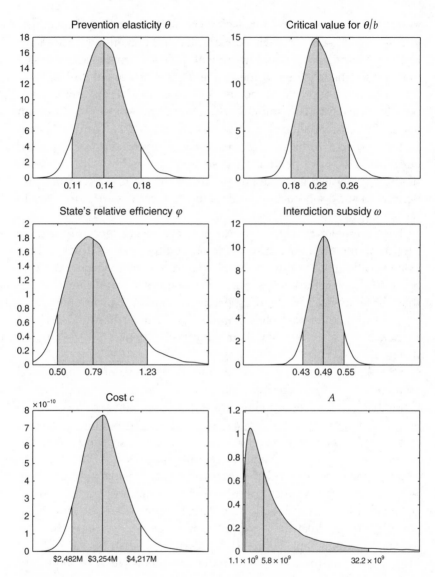

Figure 10.5
Calibration results

of reducing Q_c by one kilogram by investing in treatment and prevention policies. These numbers can also be calculated using the inverse of the Lagrange multiplier of the budget restriction for the drug consumer country's problem (see equation 10.15). Using the calibrated parameters, we obtain a figure for the marginal cost of about 19,000 USD. In other words, we estimate that the marginal cost of reducing the wholesale transaction of cocaine by one kilogram is about 19,000 USD, either by spending on prevention and treatment policies or by subsidizing Colombia in its war against illegal drug production and trafficking.[18]

To compare the marginal cost of supply-side interventions in reducing the amount of cocaine transacted in international wholesale markets with the marginal cost of reducing the amount of cocaine transacted in retail markets in consumer countries, we need to multiply the above-mentioned marginal costs by a factor of about 12.5. This conversion factor has to do with the fact that the price of cocaine transacted in wholesale markets in producer countries (Colombia in this case)—about 12,000 USD per kilogram—is about 8 percent of the price of cocaine in retail markets in consumer countries—about 150,000 USD per kilogram, where $12.5 = 1/0.08$ (see Mejía and Restrepo 2008 for details).

Moreover this result is robust to small perturbations in the data used to calibrate the model, as shown in figure 10.6, whereby we plot the

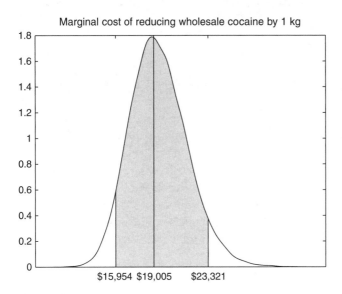

Figure 10.6
Marginal cost

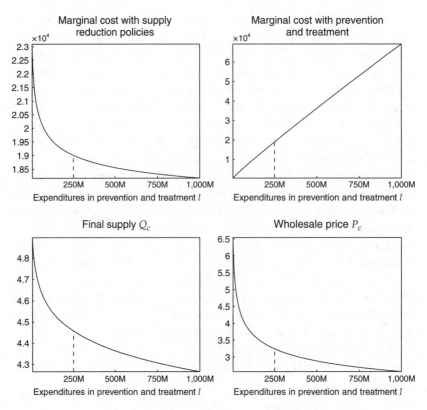

Figure 10.7
Simulations of an exogenous change in l

empirical distribution of these marginal costs using the 10,000 Monte Carlo simulations.

To address the interplay between supply reduction policies and prevention and treatment policies, we explore the effects of prevention on drug markets by exogenously changing the value of l while leaving the value of d constant. That is, using the calibrated parameters, we estimate the equilibrium value for all variables in the model for different values of l and a fixed value of d (d = 561 million). Figure 10.7 shows the results of this exercise, with l plotted along the x axis, ranging from 0 to 1 billion, and the variables of interest plotted along the y axis.

Finally, we explore the effects of supply reduction policies on drug markets by exogenously changing the value of d while leaving constant the value of l. That is, using the calibrated parameters, we estimate the

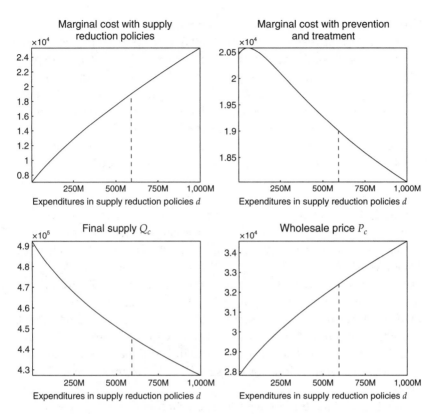

Figure 10.8
Simulations of an exogenous change in d

equilibrium value of all the variables in the model for different values of d and a fixed value of l ($l = 250$ million). Figure 10.8 shows the results of this exercise with l plotted in the x axis, ranging from 0 to 1 billion and the variables of interest in the y axis.

10.5   Concluding Remarks

The model developed in this chapter is a first step toward understanding the interrelationship between respective anti-drug policies in consumer and producer countries. Modeling the motivations and choices of the actors involved in the war on drugs using economic tools (more precisely, game theory tools) is an important step toward understanding the outcomes of this war. This chapter develops a simple model of the war on drugs in producer and consumer countries in order to explain how resources are allocated by the different actors involved in it, the equilibrium outcomes, and outcome responses to exogenous changes in some of the model's key parameters. Importantly, we explicitly model illegal drug markets, which allow us to account for the feedback effects between policy changes, prices, and the strategic responses of the different actors involved likely to arise as a result of large-scale policy interventions such as Plan Colombia.

We use the available data on the cocaine market at the wholesale level in consumer countries, as well as outcomes from the war on drugs under Plan Colombia, to calibrate the unobservable parameters of the model. More specifically, we estimate that a 1 percent increase in the resources invested in prevention and treatment policies in the United States would decrease the demand for cocaine at the wholesale level by about 0.14 percent. We estimate that the relative efficiency of resources spent by Colombia on the war on drugs relative to the resources spent by drug traffickers in this war is about 0.79. According to the results of the calibration exercise, the cost perceived by Colombia of being labeled as a narco-state is of about 3.3 billion USD (about 2 percent of Colombia's GDP in 2008). Also we estimate that the marginal cost to the United States of reducing the amount of cocaine transacted in wholesale drug markets by 1 kilogram is about 19,000 USD.

Finally, the chapter studies the interaction between treatment and prevention policies in consumer countries, on the one hand, and policies aimed at reducing the supply of drugs in producer countries, on the other. The results show that the marginal cost of supply reduction policies in producer countries decreases with the scale of treatment and prevention policies implemented in consumer countries, and vice versa.

Appendix: Model Calibration

In order to calibrate the subsidy granted by the United States for supply reduction policies, we use the following equation:

$$\omega = \frac{M_{COL}}{M_{US} + M_{COL}} = 0.49$$

in which $M_{COL} = \omega r^-$ and $M_{US} = (1 - \omega)r^-$ are Colombian and US expenditures, respectively on supply reduction policies in producer countries.

We calculate q using the reported number of seizures by Colombian authorities, which gives

$$q = \frac{\text{seizures}}{\lambda L} = 0.78$$

Using the equilibrium value for $\omega r^- = M_{COL}$, we can rewrite it as

$$M_{COL} = cq(1 - q),$$

and we obtain

$$c = \frac{M_{COL}}{q(1-q)} = 3.3 \text{ billion.}$$

Using the equilibrium expression for q, we can isolate φ and obtain

$$\varphi = \frac{p_c \lambda L \omega (1-q)}{qc} = 0.79.$$

In order to obtain the elasticity of treatment and prevention parameter θ, we assume that the United States allocates resources optimally. This implies that the ratio θ/b must be equal to the right-hand side in equation (10.21), and assuming that $b = 0.65$, we obtain

$$\theta = \frac{lb}{d + cq(1-q)} = 0.14.$$

Finally, the scale parameter is adjusted in order to reproduce the correct market size by using the equation

$$A = Q_c l^\theta p_c^b = 5.8 \times 10^9.$$

The equations above show how to obtain all the parameters from the observed data. In order to analyze how sensible is this calibration to the data fed into the model, we conduct 10,000 Monte Carlo simulations in which we add perturbations to each of the observations used to calibrate the model. These perturbations are centered at zero and have a standard deviation equal to 10 percent the value of the observation. Moreover these perturbations are independently drawn from a truncated normal distribution, so that the value of the observations for all the simulations is between half and twice the original value.

Notes

1. Plan Colombia is the official name of a program that, among other things, provides the institutional framework for a strategic alliance between the Colombia and United

States to combat the production and trafficking of illegal drugs (mainly cocaine), and likewise the organized criminal organizations associated with these activities.

2. During the same period, coca cultivation and cocaine production increased slightly in the other two major producer countries, Bolivia and Peru. As a result the total figures for potential cocaine production have remained relatively constant for the last 6 to 7 years (see UNODC 2007; Mejía and Posada 2010).

3. The wholesale and retail prices of cocaine decreased rapidly between 1990 and 2000, but since then have remained relatively stable. See Costa-Storti and De Grauwe (2007) for an explanation of this phenomenon based on the increased globalization of illegal drug markets.

4. See Grossman and Mejía (2008) and Mejía and Restrepo (2010) for models in which this particular front on the war on drugs is explicitly studied.

5. The title of his paper, "Evo, Pablo, Tony, Diego, and Sonny" is quite suggestive of the fact that, in it, he studies the war on drugs at almost every stage: illegal crop cultivation (Evo), drug production (Pablo), drug trafficking (Tony), and drug consumption (Diego).

6. A contest success function (CSF) represents "a technology whereby some or all contenders for resources incur costs in an attempt to weaken or disable competitors" (Hirshleifer 1991). In this case the CSF determines the fraction of illegal drugs successfully exported to the consumer country as a function of the government's interdiction efforts and the drug trafficker's efforts to avoid such efforts. See Skaperdas (1996) and Hirshleifer (2001) for a detailed explanation of the different functional forms of CSF.

7. In the case of Colombian cocaine, the yield/hectare/year ratio was, for 2006, about 7.4 kilograms of cocaine per hectare.

8. See Grossman and Mejía (2008) and Mejía and Restrepo (2008) for models that include conflicts between the government and drug producers over the control of arable land suitable for cultivating illegal crops.

9. In equation (10.2) we assume that the cost of producing illegal drugs is zero. In reality, the main costs of illegal drug production and trafficking are those associated with avoiding the eradication of illegal crops and the interdiction of drug shipments; the cost of actually producing illegal drugs is negligible. This assumption is made for analytical simplicity, and does not modify the main results obtained below.

10. What we have in mind is the Drug Certification Process, established in 1986, whereby each year the US government evaluates the level of cooperation and measures taken by all illegal drug producer and transit countries against illegal drug production and trafficking. Those countries not certified face a number of consequences with direct and indirect costs. For instance, noncertification "requires the US to deny sales or financing under the Arms Export Control Act; to deny non-food assistance under Public Law 480; to deny financing by the Export-Import Bank, and to withhold most assistance under the FAA with the exception of specified humanitarian and counternarcotics assistance. The US must also vote against proposed loans from six multilateral development banks." See http://www.usembassy-mexico.gov/bbf/bfdossier_certDrogas.htm.

11. Recall that r, s, and p_c are endogenous variables of the model.

12. This result arises from the assumption that the cost from illegal drug trafficking to the drug producer country's government does not depend on the price of the drugs, but rather on the amount of drugs successfully produced and exported relative to potential production.

13. This optimality condition is obtained using the implicit function theorem to find the expressions for $\partial Q_c / \partial l$ and $\partial Q_c / \partial d$.

14. For a thorough description of the data on the cocaine markets, the war on drugs, and so forth, see Mejía and Posada (2008). The data used in this calibration are the same data used by Mejía and Restrepo (2008).

15. As the reader will see below, the results are robust to changes in this assumption.

16. Given our limited data, we cannot estimate this parameter. However, the assumption that $b = 0.65$ is in line with the results obtained in Mejía and Restrepo (2008).

17. The reported value for θ is in accord with our assumption of an optimal allocation of resources that satisfies $\theta = 0.17b$.

18. This estimate of this marginal cost is relatively close to those obtained in Mejía and Restrepo (2008).

References

Becker, G., K. Murphy, and M. Grossman. 2006. The market for illegal goods: The case of drugs. *Journal of Political Economy* 114 (1): 38–60.

Caulkins, J. 1993. Local drug markets' response to focused police enforcement. *Operations Research* 41 (5): 848–63.

Chumacero, R. 2006. *Evo, Pablo, Tony, Diego, and Sonny*. Mimeo. Universidad de Chile.

Costa Storti, C., and De Grauwe, P., 2007. Globalization and the price decline of illicit drugs. Working paper 1990. CESifo.

Departamento Nacional de Planeación (DNP). 2006. Balance Plan Colombia: 1999–2005. Bogotá.

Government Accountability Office (GAO). 2008. Plan Colombia drug reduction goals were not fully met, but security has improved; U.S. agencies need more detailed plans for reducing assistance. GAO 00-71, October.

Grossman, H., and D. Mejía. 2008. The war against drug producers. *Economics of Governance* 9 (1): 5–23.

Hirshleifer, J. 1991. The technology of conflict as an economic activity. *American Economic Review Papers and Proceedings* 81 (2): 130–34.

Hirshleifer, J. 2001. Conflict and rent-seeking success functions: Ratio vs. difference models of relative success. In J. Hirshleifer, *The Dark Side of Force: Economic Foundations of Conflict Theory*. Cambridge: Cambridge University Press, pp. 89–101.

McDermott, J. 2004. New super strain of coca plant stuns anti-drug officials. *The Scotsman*, August 27.

Mejía, D., and C. E. Posada. 2010. Cocaine production and trafficking: What do we know? In P. Keefer and N. Loayza, eds., *Innocent Bystander: Developing Countries and the War in Drugs*. Washington, DC: World Bank, ch. 7.

Mejía D. and Restrepo, P., 2008. The war on illegal drug production and trafficking: An economic evaluation of Plan Colombia. Documento CEDE 19, Universidad de los Andes.

Office of National Drug Control Policy (ONDCP). 2007. National Drug Control Strategy, FY 2007 Budget Summary. Washington, DC.

Rydell, P., J. Caulkins, and S. Everingham. 1996. Enforcement or treatment: Modelling the relative efficacy of alternatives for controlling cocaine. *Operations Research* 44 (5): 687–95.

Skaperdas, S. 1996. Contest success functions. *Economic Theory* 7: 283–90.

United Nations Office for Drug Control (UNODC). 2007. *World Drug Report*. Available at.http://www.unodc.org/unodc/en/data-and-analysis/WDR.html.

Index